Empress amazin' keep s! the World. Peace .ful, ·ing Love B

And Along Came a Lion...

A Compilation of Politically Charged
Essays, Conversations and Motivational
Perspectives

Revised Edition

2017

Davis J. Williams

Enjoy your Earthday

The right of Davis J. Williams to be identified as Author of this work has been asserted in accordance with sections 77 and 78 of the Copyright, Designs and Patents Act, 1988.

First published in Great Britain with 2014, TamaRe House

Second edition, 2017, TamaRe House
25 Brixton Station Road, London, SW9 8PB, United Kingdom
+44 (0)844 357 2592, info@tamarehouse.com, www.tamarehouse.com
Copyright © Davis J. Williams, 2017

A CIP catalogue record for this book is available from the British Library.

This publication employs archival quality paper.

ISBN: 978-1-908552-57-0

TamaRe
House

And Along Came a Lion...

Davis J. Williams

Davis Williams

WARNING!

You are recommended to read this book...

If you are scared to speak up and challenge those in authority, this book will provide you with excellent reasons why you need to STAND up and show some guts - **Be afraid no longer!**

If you are tired of listening to lies from politicians and MPs, read this book. It will expose their hidden agendas and how you fit into their plans - **Know your enemy!**

If you are tired of all the injustices, police brutality, racism and discrimination and feel powerless to stop it, read this book. You will realise that you are not the only person who feels this way. Some have taken some great steps to challenge those abusing their so-called power. **Embrace their ideas and release your inner lion!**

If you want to get a general idea of how people who are oppressed, disenfranchised (excluded) and disrespected feel about their current political and economic position, read this book. It will give you a little insight into their journey. **Each one, teach one, reach one, become one - One love!**

If you have a number of questions, always curious and need answers, this book will definitely touch on some of the topics that are causing you sleepless nights -**The truth will set you free!**

If you want to know what eating healthy is and what to avoid, this book will point you in the right direction-**Health is wealth!**

If you are tired of waiting for someone to come and help you, read this book! You will discover that no one is coming to save you.

Why? Because you are the one you have been waiting for - **You have the power, you are Neo!**

If you are at a place in your life where you feel there is more to life than this, reading this book will open your eyes to another perspective - **Don't be afraid!**

If you want to have a better life for the ones you love, but need a little direction, motivation and reason, read this book. One of the essays may spark something great inside - **Tell the youth the truth!**

If you want to read a series of bite-sized essays, stories and ideas that introduce you to different controversial and historical topics then this book is definitely for you.

Disclaimer

We are not responsible for the opinions of those who have contributed to this book.

And Along Came a Lion is a book that contains various stories, truths, expressions, ideas and thoughts.

And Along Came a Lion to ROAR in the face of LIES, DECEPTION and PROPAGANDA

And Along Came a Lion, can't you hear the lion's ROAR? This Lion is now awake and ready to take control of his/her life

Where can you find this lion we speak of?

This Lion Resides Within You

"You can discover what your enemy fears the most by watching the methods he uses to control you."

Words from a wise person

Davis Williams

<u>Someone asked me what type of book I am writing,</u>

<u>this is what I said</u>

"This book is a survival tool kit."

It is being presented to the world as a collection of conversations, ideas, stories, definitions and analytical breakdowns of different people who have different worldviews.

Once you understand the contents of this book,

you will be better equipped to navigate safely through this dangerous but fantastically confusing; simplistic yet contradictory, commonsensical and cryptic, obvious but deceptive environment that we call SOCIETY.

Share this information widely with others,

but be careful; there are a lot of controversial topics raised within these pages.

You may or may not agree with some of the stories, concepts or testimonies which is fine, as everyone starts their journey to self-empowerment from different places.

Book Cover Created By Tokio Aoyama

A few years ago I hosted an event in London where I met a humble man sitting on the panel of experts. When I was introduced to him I was amazed at the array of artwork he had produced. Tokio Aoyama has worked with many musicians such as Georgia Anne Muldrow, Dead Prez, Dudley Perkins, Snoop Dogg, Janis Gaye (Marvin Gaye's ex wife), Omar, Akala, Ras G, and many others. After a few conversations Tokio was able to capture my vision and created this masterpiece that I called "DNA"

Deoxyribonucleic Acid (DNA) is the blueprint of who we are. Our DNA, the double helix (kundalini rising or the rising snake) is so complex that it could stretch from the earth to the sun and back 600 times. If unwound and linked together, the strands of DNA in each of your cells would be 6 feet long. With 100 trillion cells in your body, that means if all your DNA were put end-to-end, it would stretch over 110 billion miles. That's hundreds of round trips to the sun! Your DNA tells you that we are 99.9% alike and that ALL OF YOUR ANCESTORS resides within your DNA,

Kendrick Lamar says it the best "I got, I got, I got, I got Loyalty, got royalty inside my DNA"

Greatness can only be achieved once we learn how to unlock the magic that is stored within one's DNA. We all have royalty within our DNA, greatness and this painting represents that moment when I felt my DNA explode and left me exposed to the greatness that dwelled within it, yes that's right, the painting is of me, without the facial hair.

Realising that I had GOD within my DNA had me feeling like a lion, the mighty warrior, the self-proclaimed King of the jungle. I felt powerful and unstoppable. Notice though, in the background there is a shady character, waiting in the shadows. He represents doubt and fear. He represents the media, music, adverts, propaganda and FAKE NEWS. Tapping into your DNA and its magic is something he fears, because once you do that HIS WORLD will end. This character, and his family have created a whole world structure designed to keep you submissive, self-destructive and powerless.

Reprints of this masterpiece will be available for sale at my book launch in October.

And Along Came A Lion - Your Personal Guide To Clarity In A Chaotic World

Poem

And Along Came a Lion...

From the concrete jungle,

the first thing you will hear is this Lion's roar,

Loud and fierce from his hardened core.

Being oppressed by the hunters and those wanting his throne,

this glorious Lion doesn't care anymore.

This Lion is magnificent, with a mane that's golden brown,

regardless of what others say, he is a King but wears no crown.

Deafening was this Lion's roar,

in strength and pride this Lion stands.

Truth and honesty was the way he ruled,

as king throughout the concrete, urban lands.

For miles around his roar could be heard,

letting others know that he had a voice.

Roaring out his challenge to those who tried to silence him,

this Lion had been oppressed for so long, running away was not a choice.

Davis Williams

Regal was his stature.

Fearless was his stance.

This Lion had had enough

of those wicked men killing his chance.

Wicked men in suit and ties,

their shiny shoes, smug look, dirty plans, dirty hands.

Supplanting themselves in his homeland.

Leaving him the hell alone is his only damn demand.

Africa: that was the ancestral land of his forefathers,

stolen by those wicked thieves and robbers.

They tried to steal the gold, diamonds, blood, sweat and their rights.

Their names, language and culture: when are, the other Lion's going to fight.

They stole their jewels: Nobody can stand them jerks.

Today they have even taken the Lion's dance and called it 'twerk''!

They want to be a Lion,

but their own interest is flattening Lions with an iron.

A well-known Lion by the name of Mutulu Olugbala (stage name M1 from Dead Prez)

said it best:

You rule the land.

You rule on the sea.

You claim you're the man,

But you don't rule me.

You poison the air

With fear everywhere,

But you don't fight fair.

I know you're scared

Ask Libya or Palestine,

Africa or Cuba

Iraq or Pakistan.

Many of us don't even understand.

WAKE UP!

STOP BEING SCARED!

The Lion's roar has been silent for way too long.

There is a Lion within us all.

Davis Williams

What will it take for your Lion to roar?

And Along Came a Lion

MESSAGE TO THE LIONS READING THIS

"You are NEO"

N.E.O

Rearrange the letters and you get

O.N.E

You are the One

You are the ONE that you have been waiting for all your life. You are the chosen one. If you watch the film THE MATRIX, you will notice that NEO didn't just become NEO. He was called Mr. Anderson first, his government name. Mr. Anderson was an employee and agent of the system, a human battery and just like all batteries, their sole function was to fuel something or someone receiving nothing in return, just like a slave.

Mr. Anderson transformed into NEO through a process of **experience**, **experiment** and **exploration**.

Mr. Anderson worked in a dead-end job and lived in horrible surroundings; he was always late for work and had issues with authority.

<u>Does this sound familiar?</u>

Mr. Anderson knew something was not right about his life, but he had to live the life he was familiar with, until someone told him different. That someone was his mentor, Morpheus.

To help you understand this, all you need to do is remember the 3 E's.

The three E's or 555 (E is the 5th letter of the alphabet, more on this later).

The First E – Experience

For Mr. Anderson to become NEO he had to go through various Experiences for him to understand the situation he was in. Some experiences can be good and others, bad. Mr. Anderson was confused, not knowing the answer to his questions until Morpheus, his guide and mentor gave him access to another paradigm. When Mr. Anderson was first exposed to the truth, he doubted it. The only way he could believe was for him to Experience the truth. Experience is the greatest teacher. That is what role models are there for, or that archetypal father figure. It is said that, 'a mother's role is to PROTECT the child, whilst the father's role is to PREPARE the child'.

Morpheus prepared Mr. Anderson to become 'The ONE'.

The Second E – Experiment

Once Mr. Anderson (Thomas Anderson/Doubting Thomas) was unplugged from The Matrix, he was encouraged by Morpheus to Experiment. Experiment with what? Experiment with his mind. He was told that he had never used his mind before because he was a slave to The Matrix. He had never been taught how to think, but groomed to follow instructions and to obey authority, just like a robot. I am sure you have seen films: The Bourne Identity (Matt Damon), SALT (Angelina Jolie) and The Manchurian Candidate (Denzel Washington). If you have, then you should understand how humans have been groomed and conditioned to act a certain way. Morpheus encouraged Mr. Anderson to free his mind, break all barriers and NEVER BE AFRAID. Fear is just a thought and once you change your thoughts, fear disappears. However, this is easier said than done especially when you have been CONDITIONED NOT TO believe in your ability.

The Third E – Explore

Once all barriers have been dropped, fear is no longer the issue and you have an undeniable belief in your ability. Only then can you begin to explore.

For Mr. Anderson to become NEO his beliefs, values and habits had to die. Everything that was stopping him from becoming great, had to go. Once Mr. Anderson died, NEO was born. NEO believed in himself. NEO took his mind to places that had once scared him. NEO did things that nobody else could accomplish.

NEO was the ONE.

How to read this book

And Along Came a Lion is a compilation of essays written by Davis J Williams. Politics has played a massive part of my life, at first I was angry at the world for different reasons but didn't actually realise that the reason why I was angry was because of politics.

I was angry because I blamed politics and MP's, Prime Ministers for the state of the world, and by blaming them I forgot about myself and the role I played in my life. I relinquished my power and gave it to others begging them to change my social condition.

Many times I confronted MP's and those in 'alleged' power and noticed that, even though I would articulate my social condition as CLEAR AS DAY, they didn't hear me, they did not care and they did not care that they did not care. Privilege.

So I decided to write this book, a variety of politically charged essays and conversations sharing the experiences and observations of those who have been silenced by society. In order to continue a certain perspective, a certain narrative, in order for them to continue the lie they must silence those who are carrying the truth.

Each essay is given a date. The dates are symbolic dates, once you have read this book it should make sense if you were paying attention. The essays and motivational perspectives are not related to each other, they are all independent so you can read essay 20 today and essay 2 the following day.

Every essay however is intricately linked, there is a golden thread that connects each and every word, sentence and essay.

PLAY TO WIN

KNOW THE RULES

KNOW YOUR OPPONENT

KNOW YOUR SELF

Essay One

May 14th 1922

The not so famous speech of

Takurnekof Gloc written by Davis J Williams

Before I begin with my speech I would like to thank Mr. Ivan Jacobson and his dedicated team for inviting me to this fantastic annual event and giving me the opportunity to share my experiences with you all in attendance today.

Greetings fellow brothers and sisters, associates and the likes, please allow me to introduce myself to you.

My name is Takurnekof Gloc and I am a travelling man hailing from a city called Coberg, Germany. I am from a royal bloodline of seasoned hunters renowned for travelling the world hunting and capturing various animals. We have been in this game for ten generations and hope with your help, we hope to be around for another ten.

Please allow me to share these words with you as we have a lot in common, despite you guys looking elegant and regal in your attire and me wearing combat clothing, a funny hat and uncut hair.

(The audience laughs)

As a mere hunter, I feel privileged to be in the company of some of the world's most influential minds who have socially engineered a lifestyle and culture that runs deep into every facet of today's society.

Just so you know, my family has been instrumental in creating a catalogue that boasts over two million animals being transported to various zoos around the world where they are used for people's entertainment and amusement. The animals we catch vary from the exotic to the dangerous; you name it, and we have interacted with it.

Regardless of the variety of animals we catch, the animal that is always in greatest demand is the lion and the lion is the only animal that we, the Glocs focus on these days, simply because no one can catch a lion like us. Many hunters are afraid of lions in their natural habitat, but the Glocs and the lions have an understanding.

Catching animals used to be our main and only focus but over the years, catching animals has become a conduit for other achievements.

Allow me to explain... (sips water)

Hunting and capturing lions is a gruesome business and because of the methods used, not all the lions make it to the zoo as some die during the hunt, but that's ok because we simply sell their body parts for substantial amounts of money.

It's business, never personal!

As you can imagine, capturing lions involves travelling around the world. It is a strenuous task but rewarding nonetheless.

Before we capture any animals we first survey the territory, making friends and building relationships. This is central to our work.

We often meet generous and welcoming village chiefs who teach us about their culture, customs and traditions, something that they take seriously and something that is of the utmost importance to us. One custom that seems mandatory across the Third World is the offering of gifts. I have lost count of the number of women I have been offered by Chiefs as gifts, in the hopes that we share our gifts with them; gifts that they know will enhance their way of life.

These primitive and backward people have never come across a mighty people like the Glocs, so in the nature of goodwill and cultural development, we always share whatever we have at our disposal, with these people. Being  the uncivilised and GOD-less people that they are, it is in our best interest to help wherever possible. Money and technology are of no use at all, for their needs are simple and primitive. What is of great importance, are the stories about my highly skilled and successful family, our legacy, our contribution and our wisdom. These people need to understand that we, the Glocs, are mighty, and they can be like us, only if they listen to us and adopt our values, principles and worldview.

They already worship and admire us for our contributions, but to ensure that their families, friends, associates and generations to come recognise us as such, we had to become more creative with our methods, methods that enable us to influence every facet of their existence. This is where we are now, and what we are about to share with you all.

Listen carefully.

When I sit with these fools I do not share stories about economics, warfare, education or how to become independent. That will be foolish because we do not want them to rise up and take control of their affairs. We aim to become the caretakers of their existence.

The best way to achieve our goal is to take something that they hold in high esteem and to destroy it, only to rebuild it with something we endorse. These people respect and fear the lion, so that is what we focus on.

The best way to solidify our might in the pages of history is to use the lion as our conduit.

When these puny people gaze upon my physical appearance, my collection of captured Lions and my amazing views, it suddenly becomes obvious to them that I am mightier than a stupid lion and mightier than them!

To demonstrate our might, we would invite the indigenous adults to accompany us on a hunt. They are not allowed to enter into the capture zone because I do not want to be blamed for any accidental deaths. Whilst observing from outside the capture zone, the villagers would hear me battle with the lion until there's silence.

Then I would appear from the smoke as victor. The villagers would then dance, beat drums and celebrate, as my feat was a sign of courage they have never seen. Without any weapons or traps, I would capture scores of lions with my bare hands. I am the master of entering the lion's domain, a place where their so-called local African hunters cannot even comprehend, and through my skill, strength and superior intelligence, the lion is utterly dominated.

　Davis Williams

When I return from the hunt, the villager's most respected hunters have to bow down and hail me as a master of their world. My knowledge of the jungle is far superior to that of the so-called "king of the jungle."

Lions are known for their fearlessness and bravery, the Wizard of Oz told you that, but this is not a Disney tale. Any preconceptions that these villagers had about the Lion and the jungle within which they dwell have been corrected through our intervention.

The truth is subjective and we have to present them with our version of the truth.

We teach them how to do as we do.

We share our customs, culture and our vision with these villagers.

We travel throughout these under-developed lands and visit schools, their rotting communities, places of congregation, everywhere, to ensure that they know about our contributions, stories and achievements.

My family has received the highest honours, our stories and testimonies are divine, every word we say is true, whatever they have been taught needs to be discarded. Their customs, their ways, their worldview has not served them well at all.

Look at them.

Wait, don't look at them.

Don't listen to them.

Look at us.

Listen to us.

Our story is the dominant story!

My truth is the single account (HIS-STORY).

People often try and QUESTION my dominance over the lion, the so-called "King of the Jungle." They say that the lion is held in high esteem due to its courageous prowess and magnificence. They spread lies about how the lion is able to describe the unknown realities of the jungle in which it dwells, realities that I am unaware of!

What a load of poppycock!

Those who try to undo our great humanitarian works will be punished openly for everyone to see and when we do, we will strike fear into the souls of those who dare to rebel against our authority.

I have looked the lion in the eye and trust me, they're afraid of me! Why do these idiotic people say the lion is great, why? I don't understand? That is why they need our intervention, at all costs. The lion cannot communicate, so how do these peasants even know?

(The audience laughs)

So with our version of events, it is imperative that we leave our legacy behind so we can improve their lives.

Brothers and sisters, it is impossible to control someone if their values and beliefs do not reflect ours.

Brothers and sisters, you need to learn how to make your story the single story.

Brothers and sisters, you need to mute those who bicker and use whatever medium you have at your disposal to ensure that your

Davis Williams

message travels wide and far. I have had to terminate those who disbelieve on many occasions. We had to burn historical records simply because they spread lies.

Sometimes you have to exert your force. If done correctly, you will need only minimal force, as your battle is not a physical one but mental. Control their mind and their body will follow. Brothers and sisters, we are all joined here in one accord simply because we share a common vision and a common story. We need to ensure that our story remains the only story and protect our privileges from those beneath us.

Thank you.

The audience of 59,000 people stood up and gave a ROARING ovation.

You can tell a lot about your enemy by the methods he or she uses to hold you down.

Remember that point.

What was the point of that speech?

The tools to control people are varied but trust me, when someone feeds you misinformation, they do so for a reason; they have their motives and more often than not, the root of their motivation is **fear.**

Fellas, remember the time you were cheating on the love of your life? Yes! That dark-skinned beauty with the luscious lips, hips and all that good stuff. Even though things were great between you, you got greedy and yearned for more. Even though you invested heavily into your future, married her, had children, and a house with a massive garden. You were happy, generally speaking.

However, a few moments of weakness, a drink too many, a buff honey dipped lady and negative peer pressure led to you doing the **unthinkable**.

You went in on her, literally, but as soon as the deed was over, you lost interest.

Embarrassed, ashamed and regretful you pushed that dangerous memory all the way back into the depths of your mind.

"Honey...how was your night out?" The wifey asks innocently.

You couldn't lose her over a foolish fling, it was just a fuck...you didn't make love, you just *fuccckkkeeeddd* right?

You had no choice but to feed your wife misinformation, in your attempt to contain the situation. The control is totally **necessary**, because if she ever found out you cheated on her, your life would be turned upside down. So, this control is based on fear, but from your point of view, completely justified.

When understanding the speech of Takurnekof Gloc, you need to consider one fundamental thing: the hunter was fearful of being forgotten, and irrelevant so he does WHAT HE HAS TO DO to establish and maintain his undeserved privileges. It's about survival, it's about maintenance and it's about fear.

So, what did Takurnekof do?

He created a myth.

He created ONE MASSIVE LIE.

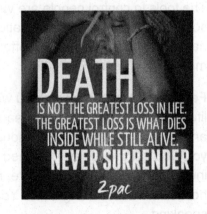

DEATH
IS NOT THE GREATEST LOSS IN LIFE.
THE GREATEST LOSS IS WHAT DIES
INSIDE WHILE STILL ALIVE.
NEVER SURRENDER
2pac

And he repeated this LIE, this MYTH, OVER and OVER and OVER AND OVER AND OVER AND OVER again until people began to BELIEVE THE LIE.

Over time, the lie became THE TRUTH.

Rule NUMBER ONE.

Mind control is based on repetition. For those who have pets, are coaches, parents or someone who merely wants to change a habit, understand this point:

The Hunter, **Takurnekof Gloc,** boasts and celebrates his alleged accomplishments by repeating his mantra to those who have no choice but to listen. At first, they resist but after a while they conform because it is the only message they hear.

"I conquered the lion ... the lion is stupid! I navigated through the dark jungle, outsmarted and ultimately overpowered him."

For all we know the lion might have been shot with a gun, poisoned by a dart, or caught in a trap. Maybe there was no lion in the first place.

The point is this, it does not even matter how the lion was caught.

The only thing that's important is the lion is dead and the hunter will always celebrate and exaggerate the hunt simply because the lion cannot speak.

No one heard the lion's story.

No one cares because no one cares about a loser.

History is the truth agreed upon.

Today the lion's story is being suppressed and the hunter celebrated.

Tomorrow your story and truth could be suppressed whilst the Prime Minister and his crooks can hide the truth and spread lies through the media.

Last week the wife tried to tell her story, but her husband beat her up after a few beers. She won't be trying that again in a hurry.

Years ago, President George Bush refused to release important footage relating to 9/11, whilst those in mourning cannot get closure for their loss, and their squeaky voices of truth fall on deaf ears.

More recently, the London riots started because the police continue to lie about the death of Mark Duggan, Smiley Culture and Stephen Lawrence. Need I say more?

It is in these circumstances when one voice, one story, one truth dominates the other, and a dangerous spiral of events occur.

Dominant stories and single truths are so damn powerful they can rewrite history. When you habitually hear biased, single truths from dominant sources (media) about a group (i.e. young people), stating that they are thugs, feral, hopeless, gangsters, corrupt, and Godless how will they be viewed by the public?

What is even more disturbing is how young people view themselves, as they reflect on what they are told. I now have a different understanding of the saying 'sticks and stones will break my bones but names can never hurt me.'

Each one of us has a story to tell, a story that is indicative of the fact that the lion exists within each and every one of us.

All we need to do is listen to the story of the lion.

Be fearless.

The lion that is brave, courageous and born free is you.

Oh yes, **Takurnekof Gloc is not a real person but his essence lives on in many racists today!**

In politics, an organized
minority is a political majority.

Jesse Jackson

Essay Two

23rd July 2011

Enter the mind of the author
Written by Davis J. Williams

"History is not everything, but it is a starting point. History is a clock that people use to tell their political and cultural time of day. It is a compass they use to find themselves on the map of human geography. It tells them where they are but, more importantly, what they must be."
John Henrik Clarke

This book is a product of over ten years of intensive qualitative observations made by myself and others I associate with. During my short, but intense journey searching for understanding, justice, spiritual and professional growth I have come across many people who I have grown to love dearly. These people have fought night and day to address: High crime levels, people living in fear, injustices (refer to Stephen Lawrence, Mark Duggan or Trayvon Martin) and prejudices towards different social groups, taxes, globalisation, traumatic experiences, violent crime, drug abuse, ill-health, anger and disorder, all of which are high on the agenda for these freedom fighters.

"It is not what you know, it has always been about who. Who you know determines what you will become."

Regardless of what the television shows you - the drama and bad news, the stereotypes and propaganda - there are some remarkable individuals, inspirational organisations and social movements trying their hardest to bring social order, hope and sustainability to their own lives and the lives of others. The battle between good and evil, some may call it. You may see them in action but trust me, there are great forces at work; positive forces that are on your side!

Diamonds, precious jewels and metals are formed only by tremendous amounts of stress and pressure. I have witnessed families break up and the health of good people deteriorate because of their endless work ethic, as they refuse to accept the social condition they find themselves and their loved ones in. I have listened to them speak and what they say is tear-jerking. Their eloquent rhapsodic commentary always captivates the most agitated listener, both young and old.

Whilst some people promptly 'clock-out' of work at five o'clock on the dot, these outstanding individuals make no distinction between their paid job and their divine purpose because to them, it is one and the same.

> *'Your career is what you are paid for. Your calling is what you are made for.'*

These marvellous warriors are always in conflict with people trying to control them. The police, racist managers, government officials deem their actions threatening, dangerous and potentially damaging to their privileges and status, so shutting them down becomes their priority.

IT'S TIME TO STAND UP!

IT'S TIME TO LET YOUR INNER LION ROAR!

So, there I was, living my life, busy busy, work work, bills bills and *EastEnders* or *Match of The Day* on the side. Life was gooooood. Well most of the time anyway. I say most of the time, because when I had finished working, there was nothing on the television and all other distractions were unavailable, I had time to myself to reflect and this always caused me stress. Deep thinkers know what I am talking about.

Feet up, music in the background and off came that mask.

This was not a *Phantom of the Opera* type of mask; it was a mask that was invisible, a psychological and magical mask; one that had the ability to change my character and my attitude whilst protecting my feelings and my inner child. It helped me cope with the madness in my life. When I first received this mask, it was plain, it lacked character and flamboyance, but over the years I have personalised it and now it fits just fine. My mask, my wonderful pacifier, made me ignorant ('to ignore') and it allowed me to conduct myself in a manner that fell in line with what the system expected of me.

The system loves when people stand in line, does not question authority and accept their single and dominant story. The system loves when you are not a threat to them. The system invests BILLIONS of pounds to ensure you stay in line.

I was able to absorb insult after insult, stay silent about injustices and discrimination, whilst the government passed laws that violated my human rights. This mask allowed me to do nothing, but complain regularly on *Facebook* or my Blackberry Messenger. Wearing this mask in public was as necessary as it was for me to wear a belt, socks or my baseball cap. This mask made me blind to the dramas of road life, allowing me to look at other black boys as enemies, not caring who the real enemy was; it made me numb and cold-hearted. I recall days when I gazed in the mirror for hours experimenting with different facial expressions, hand gestures and walks, all to hide the real me.

Yes, that mask. Can you relate?

When you are all alone and all distractions are removed, do you feel that splinter in your mind? That splinter, that itch, the sense that something is just, not right?

I am from London, known for its diverse, rich culture, a culture that consists of an amalgam of religions, traditions, values and customs. Some think the best way to survive in a city like ours is to integrate, listen to authority and embrace, rather than disrupt the rat race.

From a young age, I was told to work hard, get a good education and then get a job working for someone else. I was told to keep my head down and stay in line, but I found it increasingly difficult to strive in a system that saw me as a human battery. It felt like I was living a massive contradiction, living a life that was counterproductive and directionless. I would always blame someone or something for my lack of success. The mask that once kept me comfortable, now brought out acne on my 'T-Zone', so I decided to leave it in my bag occasionally. Every time I removed this mask, I found myself questioning my motives, my future and my destiny. I would always observe my friends and wonder if I should be doing the same thing or if I should be following the script that was written by 'the hunter'. A script impotent, predictable and unable to fly in the sky like eagles, but forever pecking from the floor like chickens. It was tough for me and caused a lot of internal conflict and disputes with friends, because we found it hard to conform to what everyone else was doing or thinking. We had many debates and it was during these thought-provoking reasoning sessions that certain things were revealed to me. Questioning and probing made me realise that there were blatant cracks in our current path and understanding in relation to life itself.

Becoming increasingly agitated with that damn splinter in my mind, I would ask my friends simple, deep questions, in my search for understanding, but they refused to entertain the conversation. They seemed captivated, but scared at the same time. I don't know what they experienced. A few weeks later, I received a text from one of my spars. It said, "Big man, you can't be asking the man dem questions like that in public, in front of the honies G. Them questions are too deep G. When you asked all these questions about who I am- about life and the system - I felt like I had nowhere left to hide. You can't be putting me on the spot like that. My reputation is on the line, family."

He continued, "The truth is, I have these deep thoughts all the time my brother, trust me and it drives me crazy! I tried to smoke it away, I tried to bury it, forget it, drown it with vodka and coke, but that question never dies, it was like it's alive, trying to breathe, trying to free itself, telling me to stand up and make that all-important decision. You're right, deep down I know that something is not right. I know I need to set myself free and deep down I am absolutely petrified. But fam, this is the road fam, you can't be showing people all that emotional sh*t out here G. That sh*t will get you killed."

Sadly, for many of us, we are so used to acting and pretending to be someone else, we have forgotten who we really are.

Never forget your truth and don't let anyone lie to you when telling you about you!

When my daughter was four, she and all children of that age accept their truth. They relish it. Their truth makes them remarkably outstanding and distinct. Their truth makes them fearless and outspoken; somewhere along the line adults, fake friends or even enemies start to define their authentic truths and their perception of themselves; truths and perceptions which in turn limit their potential, resulting in these young bright stars becoming more and more dim, introverted, shy and ordinary.

"Ahhhhhhhhhhh!"

A mother screams uncontrollably as she sees Incy Wincy Spider climbing along the wall. She runs out the house begging her neighbour to remove it. The mother's three-year-old daughter closely observes mummy's strange, irrational behaviour. This was not the first-time mummy ran away from a spider. The last time she was so afraid, that she contemplated climbing out of the window.

Before seeing this behaviour from her mum, the little girl played with spiders all the time as she found them quite interesting. Removing each of the spider's legs from its body always amused her. But one day, a few weeks and several screams later, the little girl saw a spider and she started screaming and running around as if her hair was on fire. She was uncontrollable.

"Hold on... I thought she liked spiders?" I thought, "She was not scared the other day!"

It is so easy to forget your truth, the truth that made you brave and free but somehow, some way, directly or indirectly you became infected by someone else's truth. We are living in a society where your truth is suppressed which is why my intention here, is to share with the world some of the Lion's truths, stories, experiences and strategies.

My name is Davis J Williams, aka 'The 5ive Star General' and this is my very long introduction.

5

Take a Break, Breathe, Inhale, Exhale, then come again.

Forget DEADications

This is our LIVication

I would like to dedicate this book to those who have come before me. I am simply saying this because they were, are and always will be, exerting their energies on everyone. They are known by many names around the world. Some call them God, Jesus, Allah, guardian angels and the Spirit of God whilst others call them Orisha's, Ancestors (global), Spirits from the other side, The All, Eloheem, The Gods, Mother Nature or simply various expressions of yourself.

I wish to dedicate the contents of this book to all the above.

ÀSE

àṣẹ (ah-Shay):
A YORUBA WORD MEANING POWER, COMMAND, AND AUTHORITY. ITS THE ABILITY TO MAKE WHAT YOU SAY HAPPEN. "SO IT IS" OR "SO IT WILL CERTAINLY BE."

Breaking Bread and Pouring Liquor

(Acknowledgements)

Before I begin, I would like to thank a few people. There are some people that I can sit down and break bread with, whilst with others, all I can do is pour some liquor (Ashe) as they have made the transition from physical to spiritual.

Firstly, I would like to thank my Mother for being my rock, my anchor and my guide. I love you mum, and without you nothing would be possible. Dad, also known as (aka) Spiking (Ashe), I would like to thank you for providing the way and for complementing mum's work to produce the man I am today. Thank you for the lessons, for being there and for the many happy memories. And thanks for the number FIVE... I am still trying to work it out.

I would like to thank my brother Desmond for helping me be the coolest guy in school and for being my advice centre and road map. You taught me all the tricks of the trade and I Am, because You Are.

To Diane, my sister for always being a positive source of reference and someone I can always rely on. You're always happy and smiling, I love you guys. Widombum, lol (laugh out loud).

I would like to shout out my baby girls: Makaylah, my first-born beauty. I love you; when you get older this book will be one of your manuals to greatness. Makeda and Micah (Ashe) I love you. Thanks for the advice and guidance, and thanks for helping me win the iPad; it was awesome.

You are my legacy and what I do is for you. When I see, you I see me, an enhanced and improved version. Do daddy proud.

Greetings Makai, the new addition to the tribe. You've been with us only a short time, yet you already have your own juice company. That's ma boy!

My nephew Zack, you have grown so much. Remember though, you will never be taller than King Uncle Davis.

I would also like to thank my Michelle aka Mango for being my rock, soul-mate and best friend. What you have brought to my table has fed me and will sustain my appetite for years to come. I love you and I love gravity. I have never met a girl who had so much game and only you can hang with a guy who has game like me.

Thanks to my close friends, my dawgs, Mervyn, William, Springer, Jacko, Julian, Erick and Elick, Jesse, Peter, Sickers, John, Tim, Embley, Jigga, Scrubba, Lizzie, Marlon, Suzella, Obaign, Dan, Ken and Ivan, Clem, Conrad. To the football massive: Forest Hawks, East Side FC, Flamengo, Hamzah Aymer my uncle from another ummmmm yer. Big up old school, Kings Academy, big up Manners, Carlito and Mark for holding the fort, Eternal Flame, to the Stewart family, mum (ashe) and dad, to the Oscars, to the Williams, Cousin Malcolm, Sharon, Aunty Sonia. To the St Villes from Dominica, Roy my bigger cousin, Zachariah my best nephew, I am so proud of the way you have grown; keep on doing the thing, this book is for you Zackster. I could literally write a book on all of the characters above, you might be introduced to them later on.

Big up Strength in Numbers, Undiluted Expressionz, Love is Just a Verb, Wayne, Illz, JV, Skitz, Gliddy, 1T, Wise, 7, Change, Life, Rosh and the rest.

Very special thanks to the scholars, too many to mention, those who are here now, and those whose shoulder I now stand on (ashe).

Big Up Manhood Academy, The Naked Truth and DetoxHD family

Ashe.

5

Take a Break, Breathe, Inhale, Exhale, then come again.

The Lion's Roar

"Are you a warrior or a coward? A warrior fights for people whilst a coward fights against his people. A warrior protects his people whilst a coward's only concern is protecting himself. A warrior takes care of his woman and children, whilst a coward runs away from his children and disrespects his woman. A warrior, like a true solder, plans for tomorrow, the coward is afraid of success and lives for today - YOLO. A coward is a threat to the community whist the warrior removes threats to the community. A warrior stands up and defends his rights whilst the coward doesn't have any rights to defend because he sold them all. So I ask you again, are you a warrior or a coward?"

Davis Williams

Essay Three

14th May 2006

Am I an agent of the system?

Written by the alter ego known as 5ive (Davis J Williams)

"While showing you the brilliantly bright light with his left hand the magician has an opportunity to pick your pocket with his right. Sometimes it's better to focus on what someone is not telling you instead of listening to what they are."

~ 5ive

I was in Brixton the other day, where I met up with a respected community member who accepted my invitation to be interviewed for a youth project I was coordinating. This elder had a wealth of experience working with the community, especially with young people, helping them to become better citizens. He has over 37 years of experience and not surprisingly, had a lot to say.

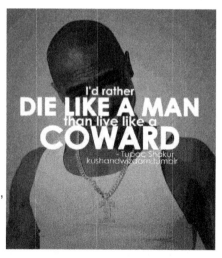

We sat.

I asked a few questions and patiently listened and absorbed the knowledge being presented to me for two hours; I realised he wasn't going to stop unless I intervened.

But he wouldn't stop!

Don't you just hate it when people talk non-stop without realising that the person they're talking to is not even listening? For almost an hour, he barked on about things that had no relevance to the interview. I had already briefed him about the topic of conversation, so listening to him veer off course frustrated me.

There I was, listening reluctantly, waiting for him to take a breath, so I could quickly intervene with another fundamental question before he started talking again.

So...

"Why did the older generation not leave a legacy for the young ones of today? Many young people I come in contact with don't respect the older generation, claiming they didn't do anything for them."

His left eye nearly popped out of his head and he stood up. This must have struck a nerve.

"We failed miserably", he said in a deep and contemplative voice.

"We failed so badly, that many of my peers cannot even see it. Let me explain."

He continued,

"The youth now and the youth when I was growing up are very, very different my friend. The youth now squabble over foolishness and are quick to buss shot after people who look just like them. They look at each other and see an enemy."

He spoke with such passion. He continued,

"The youth of today are not interested in their culture and heritage and to be honest, I don't blame them one bit. When you look at other communities like the Indians, or the Chinese, or even white people, they never forget their history or ancestors. They worship and acknowledge them. They name streets after them, their gods look like them, and their music, teaching methods and diet reflect their culture."

He stood up as he continued and a few passers-by started to gather around him.

"You know why black youths show no interest in their history and culture? It's simple. Their culture has not done anything for them. The elders always refer to history and historical situations, but we never lived by the lessons we were taught. We make the same mistakes and look where that has put us. We haven't got our act together and passed our wealth on to our children. Instead, our children have inherited our poverty and social status. The black youth of today are in an awful state, mentally, socially, economically and politically and we're to blame because when we came to Britain, many of us chose not to create better for the future."

"We harp on about Egypt, how great a people we were and how we educated other cultures, but the truth of the matter is this: that knowledge is not paying bills for those in poverty, nor is it giving justice to those who have lost family members at the hands of the police. This knowledge holds no political power. A lot has changed over the years and we are to blame, it's that simple. When we were growing up and looked at each other, we saw brothers and sisters; we were clear about who the enemy was, and trust me my friend, the enemy wasn't someone who looked like me!"

He continued,

"In the 60's, the racism was blatant. Skinheads would chase us constantly simply for being black. We were hated and deprived of all the opportunities that young people today take for granted. Racism was blatant at all levels, from shopkeepers, bus drivers, employers and those in authority, like the police. My local shop had a notice saying 'NO DOGS' and 'NO BLACKS'. Just think about that for a second... It wasn't that long ago."

"We used to get buss up and then dropped off in areas where the skinheads hung out with racist police officers. Obviously, the skinheads would finish the job."

"The police would arrest us for no reason at all, it was horrible. The police were the biggest gang and we were their number one target."

He continued,

"The harassment, the unprovoked attacks on innocent, law-abiding people brought the community closer together. We were new to this country, so it took us a little while to truly understand what was happening, but once we got our bearings and sense of awareness, we began to rebel and ask for justice. I say ask, because we weren't quite ready to take it just yet."

"Years went by and people became increasingly tired of asking for change and justice. We were given empty promises from the government, MPs and high-ranking officials. The injustice had to stop! Those who sought justice had done everything they thought they could; they attended meetings, signed petitions, went on marches and demonstrations; you name it, they did it, but nothing ever changed. Dying in police custody, or getting attacked by racist skinheads was still fucking people up. We still had shit jobs and we were being treated like dogs!"

"More years went by and during this long and arduous journey people became more educated and aware of how the system worked. This awareness brought about a change in us, a change that was potent but extremely subtle and invisible."

There is a saying -
When the axe entered the woods
The trees said LOOK,
The handle is one of us.

"Me and my people came here as skilled workers who were focused on building a community for generations to come. We were unified, had close family connections and we were clear who our enemy was. As a unified body, we openly rebelled against those who influenced and controlled our lives. There were marches and demonstrations organised by people who loved to make noise but generally speaking everyone had real contempt for anything political. We just wanted jobs, better housing and equal opportunities. Most importantly we wanted the police to get off our backs."

We were tired of fighting and resisting, so key community figures decided to try a different approach, by taking off their revolutionary clothes and replacing it with a suit."

He continued,

"They thought it might be an idea to fight the battle from within, so they applied for jobs in the local councils, the police and other public bodies in order to heal the fracture in the community using the political route. These revolutionary leaders signed employment contracts with the council and charities, funded by grants from the government, the very same government blamed for creating the problem in the first place.

Initially things looked promising. They fought from the inside and tried their hardest to improve our social conditions.

They attended strategic council meetings, sat on various committees, board meetings and taskforces. For once we, as a community, were able to communicate with people we previously deemed untouchable, powerful and elusive. We were finally able to look the devil in the eye on his own playing field.

Every week there was a meeting about something. Meetings, meetings and more meetings! Every time we wanted to change something we were always met with some kind of opposition or

The Lion's Roar
Do you know how powerful words are? Let's take a look at the word **BLACK.** Many people refer to themselves as black but the reality is this. They are **not black,** but varying hues of **brown.** According to the dictionary, everything attached to the word Black is negative, whilst **white** represents what is pure and good. Check it out for yourself, *black* sheep, *black* heart, *black* listed, *black* cat, *black* magic, *black* plague, *black*mail. All negative. No wonder we are so aggressive to each other, we've been taught to hate the colour of our skin. Calling yourself black could have a subconscious effect on your attitude towards people who look like you.

Davis Williams

complicated procedures. To cut a long-ass story short, after a while, it seemed as if our efforts were yet again in vain. We became impotent, weak and pathetic as the system easily deflected our complaints of our new community leaders and their and attempts to improve our social condition.

It was not all negative as the government, on occasion, did adopt or alter a policy here and a procedure there, but ultimately, things remained the same. Some would actually argue that it had gotten worse, more subtle and more covert. The game had changed massively. They didn't openly call us coons as much as they did in the past, but they became sneakier, to the point that our enemies could even smile in our face.

Still, many of us remained employed by the system, pledging to fight from within. Others found it impossible to adjust to the council's linear operational model. Instead many started their own groups and charities that directly reflected their interests and worked in partnership with the council when necessary. This led to a rise in the number of charities and voluntary sector organisations whose primary focus was and still is to create a better community by empowering local people, both young and old. This became the ideal outlet for passionate social change-makers."

And the battle continued.

So here we are today, talking about the same issues we were talking about in the 1960s. Complaining about racism, lack of opportunities, and lack of unity among the African-Caribbean communities. Police target our children and make sure they either fail in school, or end up in prison. If that fails, we will make sure they remain neutral and encourage them to never try changing society in any positive way. We keep looking for someone else to do something when in fact, we are the ones we have been waiting for."

"You see my friend, we keep getting lost in translation. You are sent from pillar to post, given the run-a-round, lied to, deceived coerced and distracted until you give up the fight. All we need to do is stand up, invest in our children, teach them the truth and take the education of our children into our own hands. We keep on making the same mistakes, we keep having the same discussions, and we keep on betraying our own people by not supporting our pregnant women and selling drugs in our own community destroying it from within. We need to learn lessons from the Jews and Asians who make sure their children are aware and proud of their culture and heritage but prepared for the future. We on the other hand are trapped in the past, talking about how great we were, how the pyramids were built, great inventors and ancient worlds. Then we allow our kids to go to a school that teaches them nothing about who they are. We allow our children to produce songs that are negative. We fail to be great examples for them to follow. We allow TV, radio, films, music and newspapers to misrepresent our image, history and most importantly lie about who we are. We sit there and let them do it. Then blame them when they do! We don't trust each other and we certainly don't support each other. The Polish have twelve people in one room, so do the Asians and other cultures in order to raise enough capital to purchase one building, two shops, and three businesses and so on. Do we do this? No way, we hate each other way too much! We just don't admit it."

He went silent, as he wiped the sweat from his brow.

This man's story touched my soul. I could see the pain in his eyes when I was speaking to him. He was so passionate, pushing his lips all over the microphone as if he wanted to make sure every word was heard. The mouthpiece was left moist from the heat of his breath, his words leaving a lasting tone.

His story made so much sense to me. I understood why things failed back then, in the 1960's and 1970's, with regards to the older generation not creating an infrastructure that today's young people can inherit.

Today we are still having the same conversation.

This is deep; we can learn a lot from the elder's explanation about why certain things did not happen in his day. He stated clearly that people went to work for the system, a system that they had issues with, because they wanted to create the change from within.

Let me link this all up now.

I have worked within some of London's toughest urban communities, sitting at the feet of those elders who fought in the Brixton riots and working with young people labelled unreachable and even feral. It has always frustrated me how these young people have been let down by adults who basically just don't care enough.

Why do I say that? With the resources in place and a skilled, committed workforce delivering a variety of apparently life changing projects, it has always bothered me how these groups and ideas have failed to bring about the change they say is their 'mission statement'.

It's true that the odd child or group of youngsters have showed some improvements, but not as a whole, or as a community. If you speak to grassroots workers and to young people themselves, they would tell you that things have in fact gotten worse.

Crime and disorder is on the increase, health is on the decline, cultures are being diluted and politicians are becoming more blatant and ruthless with their agendas. CCTV is everywhere, social media sites like Facebook and Twitter have reduced people's right to privacy. The police are legally allowed to collect young people's DNA regardless of whether a crime has been committed. Meanwhile, celebration of gangs, knives and gun crime has reached astronomical levels. Young people are killing their peers over respect or lack thereof. This is indicative of a generation who are prepared to do whatever it takes to see change.

Many call them gangs, thugs, trouble-makers or ignorant animals with no future, whilst many community champions believe that these same young people are actually the chosen ones who possess that fight, energy and will-power to bring about the change we all dream of.

All they need is some guidance.

As a professional, man, parent, uncle and human being I often reflect and ask myself why? Why are things getting worse? Millions of pounds are being pumped into new laws and superficial strategies focused on addressing anti-social and deviant behaviour by the younger generation. Is the money being spent by the wrong people? Those who need it don't get it and those who have it, squander it.

What you see depends on what you are looking for.

If all you talk about is problems, problems will show up. If you focus on solutions, then you will find them. I can pay witness to the fact that if you focus on the positive and seek opportunities in all your daily encounters, in time you will be rewarded.

There I was drowning in questions; over-worked, under-valued and under-paid, but open to solutions. I was looking for inner peace, because what I saw around me, as a passionate observer, baffled me. I needed to find answers. Why are things not getting better even though there are a million organisations aimed at changing the world?

What is going on?

What happened next changed the way I worked with young people, forever.

5

Take a Break, Breathe, Inhale, Exhale, then come again.

One day, I decided to take my little girl to the park as the weather was nice. I took her to a park where my friends and I used to play football when we were young. I had fond memories of this park for various reasons so decided to take a trip down memory lane and share some of these stories with my child.

It was Saturday 23rd May 2009, West Ham Park, London where me and my daughter KeKe (what I affectionately call her), decided to watch some football sitting on the grass and eating some cornmeal porridge that I'd bought from Calabash, a West Indian restaurant situated around the corner from the park. The sun was beating hard on my head and my phone wasn't ringing for once - I was loving it! The football match we were watching was between two local sides with players who were around 14 years old. The game was fast and furious and I found my leg twitching every time someone took a shot at the goal; I am a football player myself, so was itching to get involved.

Suddenly the game paused as two black boys who were on the same team started fighting; they were on the losing side and just frustrated with each other's performance. It was an awful scene with kicks and punches flying from all directions.

It was so violent that it took several teammates to restrain one of the boys.

"Daddy, are they playing? Can we play?" my daughter asked innocently as she tried to understand what was going on.

Watching them roll on the ground trying to restrain him was really sad to see.

Amongst all the commotion one of the players had enough so he left the affray, went to his bag took out his phone and made a call, seemingly calling for backup.

That was the word.

Within seconds of the call being made rumours of a local gang coming down to deal with the matter began to circulate. The atmosphere was tense and everyone involved was frantic.

Parents and supporters who watched from the side-line did so with disgust. Being used to scenes like this, I sat there watching, eating my Cornmeal Porridge and entertaining my child. Normally I would have gotten involved and intervened, but the player's managers were there and my priority was my daughter. Nevertheless, I stayed close just in case, as this was my manor and I had to be responsible.

To my left was a middle-aged African woman who I thought was a parent but I later found out wasn't. We both remained where we were, watching the story unfold. Being a sociable guy I turned to the lady and asked if her son was involved. She said no, but did comment on the players' behaviour and the behaviour of young men in general; she was clearly not pleased. We engaged in small talk, sharing thoughts on what we had both observed; she seemed quite honest and sincere as we bounced off each other's energy. As the conversation progressed, my mood and focus changed and I wondered who she really was, and what she was doing there. Was she a police officer?

She looked in her mid-forties, wore a nice suit and had neat, beautifully styled sister locks. It is always good to network, to reason and find out who's who in this big beautiful world; as the Bible says, *people standing next to you could be angels in disguise.* I thought perhaps she could open up some doors for me; I introduced myself with my business card: *'Davis J Williams, CEO, The Sun's Cycle* (my life coaching company at the time).

"Mmmmmmm, thank you", she said and asked,

"What is the nature of your business?"

I happily responded,

"I am a trouble shooter, community activist, youth consultant, project manager, life coach and social entrepreneur."

I explained why I do what I do and shared my views about the government, the police, so-called 'black on black' crime, identity and how incidents like what we had just witnessed on the football pitch was by social design, mind control and poor leadership. I explained that I had worked for many recognised

charities and youth groups sharing my experience and knowledge, but was currently trying to build my own enterprise based on my vision.

"I am always happy to work with those who share similar views to mine. As the saying goes, *one hand can't clap.* Who do you work for? You look like someone important."

She listened intently to my articulate and passionate reply and gave me a warm and sincere smile. Her reply was totally unexpected.

"My dear, I work for the *National Lottery.*"

The Lion's Roar

"The word police and policy is the same word. A policy is a course or principle of action adopted or proposed by a government, party, business, or individual: the administrations.

ORIGIN late Middle English: from Old French policie 'civil administration,' via Latin from Greek politeia 'citizenship,' from politēs 'citizen,' from polis 'city.' **Realise PLEASE** that **politics** is the key to our freedom. If you hate the Police, you hate Politics, but most cats don't even know what politics is. Everything is politics. Got housing issues? That's politics. Need work? That's politics. Living in an area of high crime? That's politics.

Everything is politics!

Despite me being open about who I was and what I stood for, she was vague about what she actually did; usually, when people choose not to go into great detail about something, I always find it best to avoid asking direct questions, take the hint and try a different approach. Being aware that the National Lottery gives millions to charities and good causes and being the trouble-maker I am, I decided to push her a bit.

Based on our initial conversation, I could tell that she was honest and open; her hairstyle suggested that just maybe, she was down with the struggle, so I felt comfortable enough to continue probing.

"The National Lottery? That's really interesting. I hope that you don't take offence but why is it that so much money is given to local groups to fix up the community, but nothing seems to get better? I have received a few grants in the past and frankly I think the lifeline of projects are unrealistic; funding should last for at least five years, not twelve weeks. Something just doesn't seem right."

But her reply both moved and shocked me. As a matter of fact, what she said totally changed the way I looked at youth work, business and the world in general.

"Young man, let me be frank. I won't tell you my name for reasons, which will become clear after this conversation. Listen, when the government is involved in community development you must expect the unexpected. Nothing in politics happens by mistake; everything is planned and coordinated. I have worked in this field for twenty-three years now and I know first-hand that it is not always about helping the community. I am personally responsible for giving billions of pounds to groups for a good cause, but a major part of my role does not only include the distribution of funds, it also and most importantly, involves obtaining intelligence about certain social groups and sharing that information to central government and other agencies that focus on research or other studies. What people don't know is that the government uses information obtained from charities to create policies and laws that help MPs, investors and large corporations maintain the status quo; it's called counter intelligence. Crime reduction is not good business, but sustaining crime is. We have to be seen to actively address the issue, whilst, covertly maintaining it at the same time. I only learnt this by accident and it's not something I tell people."

"If the government really wanted to stop crime, they would, it's that simple." "Did you know that people who work for charities, youth groups or indeed anyone who receives public funding actually works indirectly for the system, helping them obtain information that they, the ruling class cannot get themselves? Everyone knows that the system is oppressive, but people refuse to connect the dots because they, like me, have bills to pay. I have been working in the industry for many years and it is only now that I am beginning to realise that things are not what they seem."

"Young man, would you ever work for the police?"

"No."

To be honest I was stunned; what she had just revealed was profound. I wanted to hear more so that reply had to do for now.

She smiled and continued to break it down to me.

"You have police, policy and politician; three words which derive from the same source. Politicians sell the idea; once the idea has been brought a policy is created and the police enforce the policy. So, if someone really hates the police you would think they would also hate those who instruct the police, that being MPs, local government and parliament. It's pretty clear to me that some people have had the wool pulled over their eyes. So, to be honest, you ought to have as much distaste for the government and politicians as you do for the police."

"As a matter of fact, you shouldn't even be working for the council, charities or youth organisations as they are a part of the problem."

I didn't believe her initially so I took out my phone and did a search on the internet.

Ding ding ding ding! That was a first round knockout!

I was stunned, shocked and confused, I was like... what the hell?!

"So, let me get this right - if you work for a charity or community group for example, you're really an informer and government agent, getting personal information and passing it to those who have wicked intentions. So even though I may be doing good work, it's counterproductive?"

"You're on the money, Money!" The woman ended the lesson by adding,

"When you submit a funding application to The National Lottery, you have to tell them everything; what your plan is, what young people are disclosing, the demographics of the group and so on. When you evaluate your project, you tell them what worked, what didn't, what was said, how they reacted. Your data is used as evidence that is used to give decision makers information that will help them to remain in power - we call that counterintelligence."

I felt cheated, sick and disillusioned, yet liberated with what was being revealed to me. Like any game, knowing the rules is vital if you want to win; everyone has their part to play in the game of life. It is equally an advantage to know the rules of the game from both the player and judge's perspective. I learned that in order to understand the community's issues, I had to look at it from another point of view.

In life, it's really important to speak to different people about their take on certain situations, some call this diversity. The person on the ground has a totally different view from the person in the trees.

What did I learn?

The rules change according to who you speak to.

I am so thankful that the bigger picture was revealed to me that day. All I need to do now is plan and act accordingly.

The battle has just begun, let the fight begin. I am not afraid.

CREST OF COBURG (GERMANY)

Is this Sambo? A Gollywog? Or a KING?

This is actually the Crest of Coburg - Coburg is a city in Germany. We were taught that this image was negative, racist and represents a stain in the history of African. However, let's look at this from another **_perspective_**.

Firstly, what is a crest, or coat of arms?

A coat of arms or family crest has long been a symbol of a family's identity and values. Originally used to identify warriors dressed in armour, each knight chose symbols and colours to represent his family or clan. These family crests or coats of arms have been passed down through generations.

So, what is this AFRICAN MAN doing on a GERMAN coat of arms? I thought Germany was a country founded and ruled by white Europeans?

What role did African families play with the development of Europe?

Read on and find out...

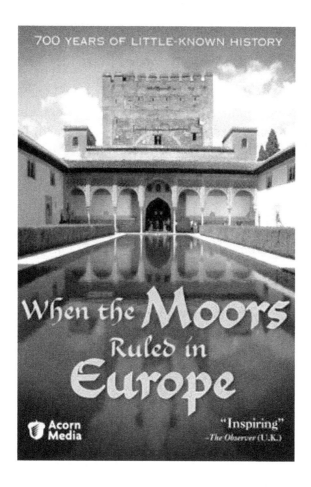

Essay Four

5th December 2012

The Illuminated Ones

Written by the alter ego known as 5ive (Davis J Williams)

They say I'm getting money. Must be Illuminati. Talking to the Holy Ghost. In my Bugatti."
William Leonard Roberts II (aka Rick Ross)

What do Elton John, Jay Z, Hulk Hogan, 50 Cent, Lady Gaga, Drake, Michael Jackson, Elvis Presley, Will Smith, Tom Cruise, Beyoncé and Madonna all have in common?

They are all stars.

In fact, they are all superstars.

Wait, they are actually megastars. Stars, Stars, Stars.

When I was, younger I wanted to be a star, serious, I did.

Why are we calling them stars though?

Why not super-moons, super-wind, super-sun? Or simply super performers?

Why *stars*?

One thing is for sure, stars are everywhere, maybe not in London, New York, Tokyo or other big polluted cities, but if you were to visit the countryside, and looked up at the sky, you will see stars, thousands of them decorating the midnight heavens.

They are seen and heard in the media, on commercial radio stations, television, *MTV*, Hollywood, newspapers, politics, sport and absolutely everywhere. If you ever want to be entertained or stimulated there will be a STAR waiting to guide you, a star to show you the way.

Remember the story of the Three Kings in the Bible who were guided by a star, leading them to Jesus' birthplace?

Stars produce light, as well as being used to lead and guide, light can be used to blind and confuse.

Remember a time when you were sleeping, you were tired because you went raving the night before; you were knocked out cold, thoroughly enjoying your snooze. The curtains are closed tight, the room in total darkness. Then dad (or mum) entered your room and turned the light on and you had a rude awakening? The horrors!

Or perhaps the time you were in a rave it was dark, the music was pumping melodic tones. You were dancing and talking to some Goddess the connection was there you were laughing and energies were flowing. Everything was NICE!

THEN some idiot turns on the light. Your pupils contract as your eyes adjust to the brightness. You looked at the person you were talking to, the person who made you laugh, who could dance well and was stimulating your mind with decent conversation.

Now you spot her big, busted toes poking out of her high heels; you cringe as you slide your Blackberry phone back into your pocket. You were about to ask for her number, before the light rudely introduced you to her features. But to be honest you weren't looking too hot yourself! The girl noticed that you had razor bumps on your forehead and your shirt was not a brand name. Once the lights came on you began to judge and discriminate, your perception totally changed. One minute you were loving the dark corner of the rave, now you couldn't wait to escape. You were pissed off!

Why do people these days love the light and are afraid of the dark? The dark, ohhhhhhh that is where monsters dwell, where the unknown lives.

Light is the product of a reaction. Light occurs because a combination of energies merge; Hydrogen and helium interchange with one another in an eternal dance.

Bright, famous *superstars* have produced books, guides, essays and publicity materials to try and entice people into the light, encouraging them to conform to a certain lifestyle- like a moth is attracted to the light bulb. There's nothing wrong with this; they are entitled to do as they please, but I want you to be aware of the dark stars.

Every star is a sun, and every sun has a solar system, a number of planets revolving around it.

Let's take a look at our Sun, which is in fact a star. All the planets, including Earth revolve around this Sun. The Sun is at the centre of our solar system and controls everything that sits within its orbit. It is said that if The Sun moves one inch, life on earth would vanish.

When you see a bright star in the sky what you are actually seeing is a chemical reaction, resulting in a burst of energy you perceive as light. Imagine your gas cooker; you see the flame but know that the flame cannot exist if there's no gas to feed that flame. The flame is the end product.

The real essence, core and soul of the star, the unrecognised and unmentioned catalyst is the darkness, the hidden and rarely acknowledged centre.

Light is born out of the darkness; darkness is not born out of light.

Let me introduce you to the legend of the dark star.

Several years ago, my manager asked me to manage and deliver a project for a local agency. The project's lifeline was six weeks. I was young, optimistic, single and committed; even though the pressure was immense I refused to let my manager down. I suffered many sleepless nights, living on endless coffees and Red Bulls, with my lazy manager breathing down my neck. After five weeks, I completed the project and had a week spare to double-check that everything was watertight.

The project was a massive success. It received media attention, celebrity endorsement and won numerous awards that propelled my manager to great heights; in fact, she received a promotion and some other privileges – she even got an MBE, shining like a star; all off the back of my hard work. The project however, became my employer's intellectual property because I signed a contract waiving my rights. I didn't mind though because I was getting paid even though it was peanuts, given the results. The project became a pilot for many similar projects of its kind, generating tens of thousands of pounds from central government, sponsors and investors.

My contract expired on completion of the project and I was left unemployed; the funding had expired so they could no longer pay me so I had to go to the jobcentre and search for another job. I was still living at home with my mum and my street credentials remained pretty much the same. There was nothing to celebrate, apart from an updated CV and improved confidence. I felt conned, cheated and used. In my opinion, I was a Dark Star, the unrecognised, unmentioned catalyst that made it all happen. Dark Stars are the catalyst behind social movements; they create social trends that influence governmental policies. You never hear about them because their views, stories and concepts go against the views and stories of the bright, popular, wealthy and bright stars.

Until the lion has its storyteller, the hunter will always glorify the hunt.
African Saying

5

Take a Break, Breathe, Inhale, Exhale, then come again.

There are some social structures, agencies, organisations, media campaigns and powerful, organised people who are passionate about preventing you from learning the truth about who you are. It is business to them and in order to become successful, they need you to remain ignorant, allowing them to establish and maintain global empires. For example, it costs on average £140,000 per year to lock up one young offender in prison. ONE.

Research shows that after locking someone up, the chances of them reoffending, being homeless and/or living in poverty is extremely high. So £140,000 is what it costs for one young person to go prison for a year all paid for by the taxpayer. If £140,000 was invested in that young person's education for that year instead, what would be the outcome? Who is this? A potential pilot, doctor or even prime minister? Who knows? But that would be bad for business. If I owned a prison secretly, I would be happy to see my prisons full. It's called good business. If only young people knew the truth about how the prison system really works and what a vital part of the plan they are.

The media bombards us with subliminal images, high technology and trivial gossip. They create a society that places high value on material things; like iPhones. Apple products render even the most diligent student powerless to the constant tweets, texts, updates and news feeds. Its major feature gives you the ability to communicate with your friends, family or social networks in an instant. You are just connected to everything, what a buzz. Why wait? Why be patient? "Get it now" is the mentality I see, hear and experience on a daily basis.

"Get rich or die trying" is a path many choose as they strive to get instant gratification and damn the consequences. Young people today are under intense pressure to have the latest car, device, expensive jeans or handbag, believing these items will bring them closer to power and success. After years of being told that they're worthless and will never amount to much, it's not surprising that they seek comfort in such things and everything is moving so fast!

Instant meals, catch-up television, Sky+, microwaves, takeaway food, full-time jobs, parties, constant traffic, instant messaging and 24-hour supermarkets all accelerate our lifestyle, giving us little time to ask ourselves Socratic questions.

Stop and breathe.

An impala sits at a local water hole in the jungle, quenching its thirst as he sees a massive, hungry athletic lion approach. The lion is confident in capturing a great meal for his family. The impala panics; its escape paths running through its head all at once; not being able to process all that information, it goes into a state of hyperarousal. The over stimulation puts the impala into a state of shock.

The lion pounces, and the impala is caught. The impala is no match and doesn't even put up a fight. Its blood pressure drops. It gets colder and rigid to play dead.

The impala freezes, it does not move a muscle, its heart beat and temperature drops. The lion, noticing these changes, thinks that the impala is dead, so the impala is stored somewhere secure for future consumption. The lion leaves the impala thinking it's dead, but of course it's not. Once the lion disappears, the impala's heart rate increases, body temperature rises and it escapes.

Human beings have a similar response to this. We call it procrastination, or the freeze-response where you have several things to do, and you end up doing none of it due to your frozen state.

Can you relate? Being constantly distracted and stimulated prevents you from doing what you really want to do. You may think you are, but maybe, just maybe, you are doing what these corporations want you to do and being who they want you to be.

"Who are you?" is the most basic question one can ask another. According to Life Coach Noreen Makoswe, many of us struggle to give a good answer because we end up defining our status (married, single, divorced, etc.), what we have, where we live, what we own or we describe our character or profession.

This is all well and good, but the aforementioned do not define you; they simply describe what you do or what you have and not who you are 'being'.

To successfully answer the question, you must first strip yourself of all these labels and truly embrace who or what is left.

Knowing who we are means that irrespective of what people think about us or what happens around us or to us, our core remains unchanged. We remain focused and sure of ourselves; confident and unperturbed. Self-belief is an important virtue when it comes to being true to oneself, because how you see yourself may be totally different to how others see you. I might see myself as a king - a smart, courageous, ambitious person, but not everyone would agree with me.

Who am I? Am I my name?

A name is just a series of words written on a piece of paper. Am I John, Claire, Nana, Babatunde, Shaniqua or Bobby? Who are you really?

When I ask people, this question they usually tell me their name or what they do for a living. Let's start with your name. How do you know that your name is actually your name? Yes, you were there at the time of birth, but can you remember that far back? Did you choose that name or was it given to you? What was your name before you were born? I named my child when he was 2 weeks old, before that he had no name, but he existed. The point being, a name is given to you, it is not who you are. Some people don't like their name so they choose to change their name. You are not your name.

Some people get married and change their name. Having a name is like a label or an attachment. As for you, you are a human being, a living entity that had a name attached to your human self by way of a birth certificate, which is a legal agreement issued by the government.

I am a SUN!

Have you ever thought about why young males are referred to as 'son' by their parents?

'That's my son over there. Isn't he lovely?' 'My dad had two sons', or is it two 'suns'?

We all breathe in oxygen, and breathe out carbon dioxide.

This chemical reaction is known only when something is burning. Fire needs oxygen to survive and it releases carbon dioxide as a bi-product of this reaction.

We all have a region between our breasts (or just below) called the solar plexus. Please make note of the word 'solar', which means sun. The car is solar powered. Have you heard that term before? Solar powered, meaning powered by the sun.

If you drink Firewater (aka Rum) from Dominica, that internal solar/sun ignites, just like a real fire. Everyone knows that if you throw alcohol or liquid ether on a flame it will become highly flammable.

Naturally you are a warm-blooded creature maintaining a natural body temperature of 98.6 degrees Fahrenheit or 37.0 degrees Celsius. The only time your body loses heat is when you're ill and the only time you have no heat in your body is when you are dead, because that flame has been snuffed out. This is also evidenced in how we label small children who are very intelligent; we call them 'bright'.

"Ahhh, Johnny is so bright!" Is the sun bright? You better believe it.

A child or person who is slow is often called dull or dim. Again, this relates to one's ability to radiate like the sun. For those living in London, I know you understand what is meant by a dull, grey day. So, what are they all referring to?

The only thing I can imagine is the sun and its ability to shine. In relation to the solar plexus, the English language offers a small clue to help connect the dots. A child who is dim, and lacking confidence is labelled as having low what? Did you choose the same word as me? Yes, you did! They have low self-esteem. Look closely at these words, self-esteem, self-esteem, self is steam, self is **steam**.

I am steam.

We are 70% water so just like a hot cup of ginger tea we emit steam.

Therefore, someone who has low self-esteem is someone whose inner light or inner flame is weak, which results in low levels of steam.

Low steam can be related to fog, whereas high steam can be related to the skies, the clouds in the heavens. I could go on.

As I've already explained, every star you see in the heavens is actually a sun and every sun has a solar system. I believe we are all stars, in human form and your solar system is the environment around us.

If you stand still and look around you will notice that everyone and everything revolves around you. We are all the centre of our universe and you are the sun that everything revolves around. Some stars shine bright, other beams cannot be seen with the naked eye because of all the pollution, or perhaps you are short-sighted. Stars come in many different shapes and sizes and are totally unique. Over time some stars explode, whilst others implode. This is the same as human death, it affects the future of others. When a star dies the orbit of other stars is affected and the ripples that continue create cause and effect; the law of Karma.

They say when our Sun explodes; this universe will cease to exist in the form it is now.

And finally, in the Bible, in the book of Psalms 84:11 it says *"For the Lord God is a Sun and our Shield."*

It says **Sun**, not son.

We go to church on 'SUN-day', Malachi 4:2 refers to the Sun of Righteousness when referring to God.

In the Koran it says *'Allah is the Light of the world'.* My common sense tells me that there is only one light of the world. The Sun at sunrise.

Every star has its own unique shape and its own patterns, orbits and cycles. However, we tend to find it difficult to understand our own orbit or cycle. We are often more influenced by other people's orbits, patterns and cycles.

Time is a cycle, not a line and everything occurs in patterns, so be present and aware of your own personal patterns.

The Sun in your chest is not a physical sun, because if it were physical you would be able to see it; just because you cannot see it does not mean it doesn't exist. The examples given are some that I am aware of and there may well be many more. You can't hear a dog whistle but dogs can, we are surrounded by radio waves, telephone conversations, satellite communications, wireless interactions, microwaves and other particles vibrating at different frequencies.

Social Constructs

Things do not exist until society speak them into existence.

Jack is facing Jill, toe to toe. Jill tells Jack to lift his right hand and indicate which direction right is. Jack follows the instruction. He is pointing at a betting office.

Jack then tells Jill to lift her right hand and indicate which direction right is. Jill follows the instruction. She is pointing to the nail shop.

Who is pointing in the right direction?

They are both right simply because social law empowers your opinion, an opinion that is fed and nourished by your perception or world-view. However, according to universal law, there is no right or wrong, left or right, up or down. Universal law strips you of your world-view and adopts a more holistic approach.

A universal law that helped me understand this subject was an ancient law called 'The Law of Vibration'.

This law states that everything vibrates or moves; nothing sits idle. Everything is in a constant state of motion. You could look at anything under a microscope and you'd see the particles vibrating, even if they appear solid and still. From the gaseous gas, to the densest matter, everything is in a constant state of vibration.

As everything vibrates, we discover there are literally a billion degrees of vibration; from the electron to the biggest thing you can imagine. Everything is in motion and energy is emitted at every level.

Are you a physical being or are you a non-physical being?

Who are we?

What have you been tricked into accepting as the truth?

Are you intrigued to find out more? Are you afraid? Don't be, that is what they want.

They want to regain control, disempower you and plunge you into darkness where the inner light cannot be found.

In fact, who are 'they'?

The Lion's Roar

Do you know how powerful words are? Let's take a look at the word **BLACK.** Many people refer to themselves as black but the reality is this. They are **not black,** but varying hues of **brown.** According to the dictionary, everything attached to the word Black is negative, whilst **white** represents what is pure and good. Check it out for yourself, *black* sheep, *black* heart, *black* listed, *black* cat, *black* magic, *black* plague, *black*mail. All negative. **No wonder we are so aggressive to each other, we've been taught to hate the colour of our skin.** Calling yourself black could have a subconscious effect on your attitude towards people who look like you.

Essay Five

5ᵗʰ January 2012

Program "Me"

Written by Davis J Williams

"This is your last chance. After this, there is no turning back. You take the blue pill - the story ends, you wake up in your bed and believe whatever you want to believe. You take the red pill - you stay in Wonderland and I show you how deep the rabbit-hole goes."
Morpheus

To experience, is to be in touch with the moment and embrace the different emotions one feels in that moment. Many believe that emotions are feminine expressions and that displaying them is a sign of weakness.

When you focus your energy on your past, it keeps you in a place that no longer actually exists. To remain in the past is to be stuck! If you are blocking yourself from manifesting in the present moment what can then become your future reality?

Human beings are a remarkable species; we are creators of our own reality. It begins with the mind, the processing of one's thoughts, then these thoughts become things.

What do you spend most of your time thinking about?

What do you talk to your friends and family about?

You are like a computer, which has been downloaded with a

program which in return will manifest on the screen as and when you command it. Your thoughts are the programme which you select for download; the energy which you apply to that thought is your command to manifest it. To be in control of your thoughts is to be selective of the programme you choose to download to reality.

Check out the movie, *The Matrix*.

In this film, they use a term 'plugged-in'. I take it this means that when one is plugged in you have no control over the programs which are downloaded to your reality. To be in control of your thoughts is a way to filter your mind from the thoughts or programs that serve any purpose. Once you have your mind functioning with only thoughts of your desires and is of a positive vibration, you become NEO, you become 'The One'.

To fill the mind with worries of bills, fear and the lack of money, is exactly what you will create as your reality. Rather, see yourself paying those bills, challenge yourself and face that fear, or picture yourself having the money and see what happens. You conscientiously and subconsciously create your reality by visualising and focusing energy on what you want, where you want to be and how you want to live, by changing the way you think and what talk about.

That may sound silly, but it's true.

This process is not just something you practice when you want something, but rather an everyday way of behaviour that enables you to have what you desire, always.

Take some time now to review your current environment and the circumstances you find yourself in.

Is this a reflection of your current thought process? Or is it a reflection of what others around you are thinking? Remember, ideas are bullet-proof. You cannot stop someone from planting an idea into your mind; positive or not is irrelevant as anyone at any time can implant a foreign thought into your mind.

These are questions we should ask ourselves instead of continuing to create what we don't want or necessarily need.

Focus on the things you want in life...

not on the things you are not interested in, or worse still, fear.

Our thoughts are like energy waves, which vibrate through the universe sending out messages of command.

Let's see how this affects you.

If you and your friends spend a lot of time together, you will begin to co-create together subconsciously. Your thoughts become entwined with theirs and you may even know what the person is thinking at times. The results of this are amazing. Whilst you are thinking about something your comrade can read your mind, subconsciously.

Peter: I am craving a cheeseburger.

Johnson: Hey, I was just thinking about that! Stop reading my mind! There are advantages and disadvantages to co-creating. If you and the other person's thoughts are of the same *wavelength* and both want to start a business for example, you will both have ideas and visions of how this business may work. This form of co-creating can be quite advantageous. However, using the same example, you may want to start a business to help others and the other party wants money and has no interest in assisting others, this may co-create different outcomes and a mixture of wanted and unwanted desires as your thoughts are not in sync.

The point here is to remember how sensitive you are as a human being and to remember that you hold the power and the key for what happens next in your life. Take the time to play with your thoughts and observe your mind's activity. Sensitivity stems from the senses, of which you have five physical ones, smell, taste, sight, touch and hearing. Being sensitive is being in tune with your senses.

Most of today's rappers such as Rick Ross, Common, Nicki Minaj, Drake, and Lil Wayne share their manifestation techniques with you daily. Listen to the things they regularly focus on and talk about; money, cars, clothes, big houses and living nice. The spoken word is one of the most powerful ways of sending your message to the universe. In many old traditions singing, drumming and dancing, were ways to communicate with the gods.

Start today by sending out the thoughts of your choice to receive and manifest your reality.

How can I change my reality?

Sometimes in life we may find ourselves in a place that seems inconsistent with our thoughts or the choices we make. People and choices are key factors in life. The people you choose to surround yourself with and the choices you make can affect the map of your life.

A map is used as a guide to your desired destination.

What would life be like if you could select your own signposts create roads for your own map?

Perfect picture, right?

By surrounding yourself with people who are aligned with your divine thought processes is to select the signposts relevant to your destiny. These are people who influence and inspire ways for your roads to be built with firm foundations as well as the necessary skills and wisdom needed to travel along the road.

At times, we find ourselves at a crossroad; meaning one's internal state versus what is taking place in the environment is not aligned, and is out of sync, this leads to confusion about what to do next.

I am sure you can relate.

What do you do? You have a choice. Listen to and be influenced by others? Or listen and honour yourself, your vision, your aspirations and your path?

What choice you make next will determine how and when you arrive at your destination. Sometimes we feel inexperienced in what we desire, or feel we don't have the capability to achieve them even sometimes we fear the unknown.

These feelings are to be embraced. This is how we learn. Don't be afraid to demonstrate **who you truly are**, despite what others may think. Now, I am not advising to avoid advice and guidance when necessary, but rather to be diligent and selective in terms of where and whom you are getting this guidance from.

Some of today's most successful entrepreneurs once had an idea which nobody at the time took notice of and yet they're now living their dream. Be open about what you possess within you, as people will always judge and stereotype you. You can't change that. Try not to spend your time and energy trying to please those around you before pleasing yourself, to please oneself is to please all.

Change your reality today by powerfully selecting the signposts you choose to guide you and making choices that will build roads for a pleasant ride to your desired destination.

Emotions are simply energy in motion.

Motion.

Where are you going?

Where are your emotions taking you?

Where are someone else's emotions taking you?

Davis Williams

Essay Six

7th February 2011

Break the cycle

Written by the alter ego known as Sebastian (Davis J Williams)

Love is what we were born with. Fear is what we learned here.
Marianne Williamson

According to Law 4, of The 48 Laws of Power by Robert Greene, it says "Always say less than necessary. When you are trying to impress people with words, the more you say, the more common you appear, and appear to have less control. Even if you are saying something banal, it will seem original if you make it vague, open-ended, and sphinx like. Powerful people impress and intimidate by saying less. The more you say, the more likely you are to say something foolish."

Keeping that in mind, I will keep this essay very short.

Psychologists says takes 28 days for a person to lose or break an old habit, or to start a new habit. Whilst some scientists or psychologists argue that it is more like 21 days or 30 days, the fact of the matter is this: for you to create a new pattern of behaviour takes approximately one month.

Obviously, some habits are easier to break than others, like smoking for example; but with a little planning, focus and patience, it is possible to break any habit. Many of my closest friends have awful habits that they need to break, it's so annoying!

Janet – She is constantly trying to change the way she looks by hiding her strong African features. Her hair is always long, with half her face covered with it. Where did that habit come from?
Calvin – Always lying about his achievement, or what girl he met
Jamal – He is so damn negative, always putting himself down, saying he can't do anything, and that he doesn't deserve to be successful.
Darren – If he earns £100, he will spend £100 so he's always broke.
Timmy – Drinks and smokes way too much
Tyrone – Plays on his Xbox ALL day, and all night, all week
Elliot – He constantly fights with people over the smallest thing. He fights his teachers for asking him to remove his jacket, he fights strangers for looking at him,
Blessings – She refuses to leave her man, regardless of how many times he beats on her
Peter – His nails look like shit. He never cleans them. They are long and filthy, and he sucks him thumb like a baby as well, groooossseeee

I know these people very well, damn, we grew up together on the same streets. I often tell them about what I see, being an honest person, but for some reason they cannot admit it and are always making excuses.

I have come to realise that some people have habits they are totally blind to.

Keeping it moving.

It was my birthday recently and I decided to do something different. I thought about going to the same boring clubs, to listen to the same dry songs. However, I decided not to because these days, security demand that I present photo ID upon entry. Me going out with my passport or driver's license? ARE YOU CRAZY?! Do you think I want those crooked bouncers knowing who I am? And furthermore, where are my details going to be stored and by whom? Because of this, raving was out of the question, so I decided to do something a little different.

I decided to invite everyone to my crib, ordered some spare ribs, soda, and chilled, playing games and listening to some Breakbeats. It was small and intimate; my closest friends were there, people I had grown up with.

The banter was off the hook, I have not laughed so much in months.

Among those in attendance, was my mentor who is a personal performance coach; a motivational guru who is always smiling, always positive and always going on about how great everything is. Even though she was my mentor, she did not look like one, my mentor looked HOT!!! Her skin tone was smooth like caramel, her smile just lit up the room and her bodily curves were ultra-hypnotic. Oh, boy was I excited. A few weeks previously my mentor hinted that she would make my birthday memorable, she didn't specify how, but when a beautiful empress like Mary Jane tells you that on your birthday she has a special gift, one can only make one conclusion.

Mary Jane, my mentor, was the only person who was not known to everyone else because she was my mentor, my advisor and I kept her away from my cock-blocking brother. I only saw Mary Jane when I needed clarity on certain business decisions or when I found it difficult to overcome my personal barriers. You see, as a young child, I was always told by my mum that I would not amount to anything or that I would end up dead or in jail. Whenever my mum had something to say, it was negative and non-productive. My mum would freak out over the smallest of things. When you are young you don't really notice it because it is all you know, but after years of socialising, observing the way other parents spoke to my friends I noticed things were not normal. My four younger brothers were treated totally differently. They have a different father; he is still around, helping out here or there, but my dad, my old man, well, all I can say is, when it comes to Father's Day, my mother gets the card! He has never been there for me.

He put my mum through hell. He broke her heart and left me, a child who looks just like him. Mum always says that I take after him, that I am following in his footsteps, but I have never met him so how the hell am I supposed to know?

Growing up, my mum was extra tough on me and as a result, I had no love and I never showed any love. Years of insults and arguments, beats and punishments forced me to internalise all the negativity my mum pushed towards me. From that point, I became a person of rage. When I came out of prison for assault, the courts ordered me to attend a series of self-development sessions and that is where I met Mary-Jane.

After the spare ribs, had disappeared and the weed smoke had settled everyone started to wonder what was coming next; there were rumours of a stripper, a story created by me to ensure that people remained alert and sober. No-one wanted to be drunk around a stripper just in case they make a fool of themselves and it ends up on Facebook. It wouldn't be the first time!

"Listen cats, it's that time family."

Mary Jane stood up, released her long, neatly organised locks and walked over to the DJ decks and turned the music down low. Everyone thought they were in for a treat until she said...

"Let's get down to business!
Everyone repeat after me"

"Goals provide seeds of change in everyone's life. Goals provide

seeds of change in everyone's life. Goals provide seeds of change in everyone's life. Goals provide seeds of change in everyone's life."

Mary Jane had everyone repeating the mantra in a way that resembled a gospel choir. Peter was so energised he started to beat box thinking MJ was about to perform a rap or a song.

"Goals provide seeds of change in everyone's life. Goals provide seeds of change in everyone's life"

Blessings stood up also and started to dance (Azonto, Azonto) whilst the others kept the cipher energised and unpredictable.

"Goals provide seeds of change in everyone's life. Goals provide seeds of change in everyone's life."

In a passionate and soul piercing tone, Mary Jane, the transformational orator continued,

"Goals provide seeds of change in everyone's life. They help clarify who we are, what we need, and what we want in our life. Once you become specific about your goals, the actions you need to take will be shown to you, and your goals will begin to manifest. Precise goals produce clear results. Writing your goals down is an ancient art. When you do this simple task, it stimulates the seemingly magical power of attraction, the universal law that governs this dimension. By writing down a goal you give it power, creative energy and purpose.
Writing it down will help you discover the true calling of your heart and clarify your convictions. By engaging with the power of trust and responding to the synchronicity of the universe, you will find that unexpected doors will open to reveal new alternatives and options."

Then she turned to me, the birthday boy, and said this: -

"Greetings everybody, my name is MJ, and I have been Sebastian's performance coach for the past two years. When I first met Seb he was down and out. He had no income, he was homeless and things didn't look good. You guys know him; you know that his anger was a huge problem for him. But since I started working with him, he now has a stable job, he is running his own £2 million business, he has clear goals and has his anger on lock! Tell me when was the last time you saw him angry?"

"Yeah, that's true you know" said Darren, an old-school friend of Sebastian.

Normally anyone talking like this would've been shut down, dismissed and insulted, but people always listened to Mary Jane. She was just so cool and sassy, she *was one of us, she looked like us, and spoke like us and her swag was just so captivating.*

MJ continued,

"Today we are gathered here to celebrate Sebastian's earth-day, and my present to Seb is the gift of foresight which is defined as the ability to predict or the action of predicting what will happen or be needed in the future. We are all aware that our greatest friends can become one's formidable enemy and one is only as strong as their weakest link. My gift to Seb is the gift I gave to Seb when I first met him, the gift that got him to where he is today. This gift I presented to him months after we first met, this gift empowered Seb to dream, think big and visualise what he wanted from his life.'

She presented us with a sheet like this:

Financial / Career / Academic – Date your goal
(Example – By the 20th May 2013 I would have saved £400 for my holiday. My goal was specific, I didn't just say savings, I gave an actual amount, and when I would have it by)

**Physical Health & Well Being Date your goal**
I currently weigh 15 stone and I wanted to drop down to 12 stone of pure muscle, no fat, toned and I want to quit eating the carcass (red meat)

Personal Growth Date your goal

Spiritual Date your goal

Relationships Date your goal (not always sexual)

Lifestyle, Travel & Play Date your goal

Attitude: Date your goal

There were fourteen people at my small birthday gathering, and by the time the forms were given out three people left claiming something had come up. The cowards! The others remained and filled it in with enthusiasm. After this, we sat, smoked some weed and discussed our goals until 8am the following morning.

That was the best birthday I have ever had. That was last year and everything that I had written down on that simple form has come true, well, my short-term goals have anyway. You see, achieving your goals is like running a marathon; you need stamina, determination and inner strength.

If you are a warrior, a fighter and you believe in yourself, I urge you continue to read and take ten minutes, or more to fill in the goals sheet above. Be as detailed as possible. Once you have completed it, look at it every single day. Remember, it takes 28 days to change a habit, so if you're negative, it will probably take you 28 days to even entertain this exercise.

Essay Seven

23rd May 2010

Mind Games

Written by the alter ego known as 5ive (Davis J Williams)

"During war, conflict or beef, The Truth is so precious that she is always guarded by a bodyguard of lies."
Sobek Trismegistus

I am the baby of my family, literally! My brother is ten and my sister is nine years my senior respectively. Even though they were and still are great siblings, that age gap had a great effect on my childhood, leaving an impact that I am only realising now. It's not necessarily been a positive or negative impact, just an impact that deserves recognition. I was very spoiled (so I have been told) and was protected by my mother, something that I have no real complaint about, being the baby of the family.

My mother adopted the pink elephant approach. This approach can be seen in the following example: - try **not to** think of a pink elephant.

Go on, try your hardest. **Try again. Don't think** of a massive pink elephant. I am almost certain that you did picture a pink elephant, because the command 'think of a pink elephant' was inside the question.

You may have read or heard, your subconscious mind, the part of your brain responsible for all your natural functions like breathing, does not understand yes, no, good or bad, etc. It just pictures anything it detects through the five senses we have.

I am not saying that my mum is a certified psychologist, but she does understand the concept of not allowing certain words, images or ideas to enter my mind. Being spoilt meant I had a curfew when everyone else did not. I was not allowed to socialise with the scruffy looking people who were my friends; instead I was encouraged to remain innocent and just follow instructions. My mum was the policy maker (MP), and my dad was the enforcer (the police, Polic(e) and Polic(y).

I attended church every Sunday without fail and was involved in activities within the church. I was an altar boy, so I sang in the choir and helped the priest deliver an orderly mass. I went to a Roman Catholic Church and I also went to a Roman Catholic school. So did my brother, my sister, my cousin, my mum's friends and others who were connected to my family in one way or another. Being a Christian is something I just did without thought, after all, everyone else around me was doing the same thing.

Even though, I attended church on a weekly basis I did not really understand the religion. My understanding was not a requirement, my obedience was obligatory. You could have asked me any question about the Bible, my beliefs or about the church and my response would always be the same. "Why are you asking me that?" and my tone would have been deep and defensive. My faith was strong, so strong in fact that I could not quote one single bible verse, or defend myself against doubters. Following others can have that effect. Ask them young ones about the origin of their postcode violence and they haven't got a clue either. As far as I was concerned, my lack of knowledge was not an issue for me, I knew my way was right simply because my mother said so and my father enforced it. My mum wouldn't lie to me, would she?

Years went by and as I matured, I became more aware, not of the Bible and its teachings, but of my environment. I started to withdraw from the altar boy image because it was not getting me any girls or positive attention. I was seen as a nice, good mummy's boy who had good values and a solid home. Who wanted to be that? I wanted to be cool, hip and slick with the latest trainers, the best Click suit or Vikings footwear. I wanted the best Starter jacket and bleached jeans and designs shaved in my hair was an absolute must; all I wanted was for girls to see me. Having an 8.30pm curfew at 15 years old and not being allowed to travel away from my block meant that I could not accompany my friends to check Natalie and her friends who lived a few blocks away.

"Yo, you coming Leyton?"

"Where's Leyton?"

"Up the road man, how can you not know Leyton it's 5 minutes away on the bus? So what, you coming?"

"Sorry guys, I'm not allowed, I have to stay in, and it's too far anyway."

"But it is only 5pm and mate, why is your mum giving us that look from the window?"

I was around 14 or 15 years old at the time. After a while my friends stopped asking me out on their adventures because they knew what the answer would be. I was not bullied or teased because of it; having my older brother meant I was known and protected. Well, that was the perception anyway. The only downfall was that I missed out on a lot of gossip.

On the other hand, I did form a strong bond with some of my

neighbours who lived two streets away and together we played games like Blackjack, Run Outs and chilling in the area. Football was always a regular activity. My mum loved me playing close to home, because she could look out of her window and see where I was and if I couldn't be seen, she could always ask one of the other parents, as she knew them.

Or, she would send my dad out with the belt to find me.

'It takes a village to raise a child'

Everyone knows that

After a while, I got fed up of missing all the gossip. I felt left out of the loop, as the cool dudes at Sunday mass would boast about their adventures. Over time, my role within the church changed. It had to, because they were doing my head in. I started attending church late; I went from sitting at the front with mummy to sitting at the back or up on the balcony with the other young people. I basically changed who I associated myself with. This change gave me the opportunity to start afresh and this time do it right. I had already been labelled because of my former friends, but this slightly older crew didn't know me because they were from another part of town.

We gossiped and over time my character developed into another dimension. Even though I was not the finished article I was definitely cooler and charismatic, thanks to the lessons I learned from my failure. My brother, who lived in Boston USA at the time, would often bring back fashionable items that you could not get here in the UK. No one apart from me wore three **fingered gold rings, flash jackets, NBA basketball kit and real baseball hats**. Over the months my role within the group grew and my involvement within the church completely stopped as I decided to play Sunday league football instead.

Growing up, I was a very quiet person who was essentially a mummy's boy. Even though, deep down I was bursting to become someone else, I had to learn how to control and manage that urge that desire and that thirst for status. Due to my parents' intervention, I developed into an omega male rather than an aggressive, dominant alpha type.

The omega male is found in mythology, folklore and religions of virtually all world cultures. An omega male is someone who plays tricks or otherwise disobeys normal rules of behaviour. As the omega male, I loved to play tricks and games and in doing so I was also raising awareness and acting as an equaliser.

Some classical examples of omega males in world mythologies are Mercury in Roman mythology, Hermes and Loki in Greek mythology and Eshu in Yoruba mythology. As an omega male, I was always a clever and mischievous person, who tried to survive the dangers and challenges of the world using trickery and deceit as a defence. I am still like that now. Many children's fairy tales continue to use omega roles to highlight the extremes in the world. We are taught about the hero and the villain, why are they not teaching about the omega, trickster character?

Many authors and film makers do reveal the importance of the omega male and female to show people how it is possible to overcome a system of oppression from within.

A blatant example of omega and alpha dynamics can be seen in how the media and how films depict the character of the lion, and the monkey.

The monkey is often seen as the fool, the joker (watch Monkey

Magic for those born in the early 80's, if you're younger, visit YouTube) and his oppressor the lion (The Lion King).

The monkey is portrayed as the 'New World figuration', the rebel and rule breaker, whilst the lion is the authoritative figure. Even though the lion is King, and commands the monkey's movements, the monkey is still able to outwit the lion continually. The monkey can outsmart the lion because the lion does not understand the monkey's mannerisms or attitudes. The monkey acts figuratively, in a symbolic code; the lion interprets it to be literal and suffers the consequences of the monkey's ways. The monkey uses the same language as the lion, but he uses it on a level that the lion cannot comprehend. This is the same with the Illuminati, corporations, those versed in politics, lawyers and solicitors. Does this sound familiar to you? The result is that the lion loses his status as the King of the Jungle.

Omega males and females are the opposite of the alpha male. Omega males can have friends and close acquaintances, but prefer to do things on their own without the help of a group. Omega males generally don't belong to any cliques and have no desire to be the leader or most outstanding of said clique. Omega males have relationships with people from all groups and carry a resourcefulness and cunning (sometimes strength) to get a job done with their own skill. This being said, an omega male can have great pride without it manifesting as 'ego'. There are always exceptions. An alpha male MUST absolutely be perceived by his peers as the toughest, smartest and most popular. An omega male cares little for this recognition, but knows that he is all those things and more. Alpha males must have the support of his 'boys'. This can be the foundation for many shallow and superficial relationships. An omega male needs support from time to time, but has few true friends who know him intimately and generally shuns shallow acquaintances.

Two sides of the same coin, both being very effective in accomplishing goals.

The elders described omega males in this way:

> *"Two rams are butting heads while the female watches. The winner gets to mate the female, as he is the strongest and therefore the Alpha Male. But whilst the two rams are butting heads, competing for that Alpha Male status, it is the Omega male who creeps up and mates with the watching female whilst the others fight."*

I perceived my game to be so tight, I even got it tattooed on my arm, GAME-TIGHT. People always thought it had something to do with girls but they were wrong. It had to do with life, and my message was simple. In order to succeed in this game, we call life, only the best will be able to overcome barriers and trials. Your game needs to be tight. You need to know the rules of the game and win at all costs. I was an omega male, and people like me were rare. Game recognises game.

Moving on, I have always been an argumentative person, there is something about a healthy debate, argument or fuss that ignites the solar in my plexus (Refer to the essay 'The Illuminated Ones.)"

On occasion, to my disappointment there would be no sparks of a debate to awaken my senses, so the only thing I could do was to wind somebody up. I loved winding people up, creating pranks and observing people operate outside their comfort zone.

Life begins at the end of your comfort zone.

I loved going to local restaurants demanding discounts for the poor service. They would try and refuse and that would create a verbal joust, something that I craved. Bottom line, there would always be something to pick at, something small that I could exaggerate.

I would always pay close attention to detail; any slight discrepancy I would jump on, and create a story that would render the opponent useless. Pizza Hut was my favourite opponent - thanks for my free pizzas guys.

5
Take a Break, Breathe, Inhale, Exhale, then come again

On a warm, bright day in May 'the lads' decided to attend Luton Carnival. In the UK, Luton Carnival is nothing like the one in London, which is Europe's largest street festival. Luton's was more like a block party in comparison. During this period, I was a student, studying at the University of Luton (now University of Bedfordshire). For the first time ever, I was free to do whatever I wanted, because I lived away from home for my three years of study. I was surrounded by girls who were also away from home for three years, so every day was a bright day, if you catch my drift.

At the carnival, we loitered around the vibrant town centre

enjoying the music, each other's company and observing the eye candy. From time to time, we would take a stroll to check out the surrounding area, just to make sure that we tagged any new arrivals before the local playa-hating Lutonians interrupted our game. Those Luton boys hated us man. Luton was small, so everyone pretty much knew everyone. Being from London, our ways and mannerisms were foreign. We came with a fresh swagger - a swagger that the local girls loved.

Anyway, we with our suave, sophisticated swagger strolled through the carnival looking for some entertainment. During one of our rounds, we noticed that there was a bit of activity at the housing estate up the road. We saw people hustling and bustling on a small road that had been dead and lifeless before. We took a sharp left through an alley to see what was happening, expecting to see some fresh girls. We were six men strong and had intention and purpose. We strolled through, adopting the gangster stride, and that screw face, mean mug armour to ward off any drama. We thought we looked well sexy! I know I was anyway, can't speak for the others.

When we arrived at the hot spot we were shocked to see that there were no hood rats for us to manipulate, instead mature, respectable and cultured women setting up stalls and arranging their products in an enticing manner. They were vendors, selling their goods; be it whistles, jewellery and African crafts. There were guys there too but we were not watching them, we were interested in these Nubian sisters who greeted us with words we were unfamiliar with. I think they said "Greetings young king", or something deep like that, we looked at each other and said "Dude! These women are interrrresteddd!"

We stopped at the various stalls and looked at their merchandise. We had no intention of buying anything, but if we could hustle a free gift then cool, we would accept. Most of the vendors were of African descent and their dress code varied from casual urban wear to traditional African attire and everything in between. So, there we were, checking out the merchandise (and what they were selling) and out of the blue we heard someone call out,

"You brother, you know you're a **reptilian** right."

We gave him air, silence, no response because that statement deserved no recognition. It was random, foolish and couldn't be directed at us so we continued doing what we were doing.

"Yo! G, you! You know you're a reptilian right, what you saying?"

We heard him say it again, but this time there was more BASS in his voice. He had to be hollering at us, because there was no one else in the vicinity that he could have been shouting at.

I took the bait!!I responded to the worst insult ever, I was too curious to see why.

I looked up and saw a light skinned dude who looked like he could roll with us (i.e. he was black and had a close fade), the only thing that looked strange was that he was dressed in all black, looking sharp like they were going to a funeral; his pal to his left wore the same attire, but he wore a funny hat on his head, a funny round hat with a tassel dangling down, with strange symbols on it. This was known as a fez. When I looked up I was expecting a crack head, or someone drunk on some strong shit, so to see this oddly dressed dude surprised me.

You already know what was going through my head. Time to chief someone up, time to make someone bow down to my superior intellect. As I walked over to him I looked at him and said "what you say?"

"I said that you are a reptilian", he repeated.

I laughed out loud, shaking my head in disapproval at what he said.

"What the fuck you on about mate, are you drunk, what do you want?"

At this point, I really thought this guy could not mentally take me on, so I approached his stall ready to start dissin'.

To date, no one could test me because I was a master of my trade, arguing, tricking, dissing, insulting, twisting and evading. Just like a true politician (politics or politricks).

Let's go back 6 years for a moment.

At school, I used to walk around with a black book, with various insults, disses, and disrespectful jokes. Other guys had a black book with girl's numbers, but my book helped me to be sharp with my tongue and ready to take anyone on. If they ever tried to run joke on me that was my equalizer. I was the guy you did not want to verbally cross. Only a few of us possessed the 'black book' and trust me, once you memorised it, you became lethal. I am convinced Chris Rock, Eddie Murphy and other top comedians possessed such a book.

Back to reality, and there we were, at 'The Battle' that battered and flattered.

It was Mike Tyson verses Barry McGuigan and your boy Davis was like Tyson going for a first round knockout. My quick wit, sharper words and an analytical dissection of his dress code and unpleasing merchandise resembled vicious uppercuts and illegal head butts. It was on, people were laughing and yes, I could smell victory, a quick and easy one.

The guy was speechless, he had nothing to say, and rightly so, I was faster than him, smarter, better looking and slicker. Or was he just sizing up his next victim adopting Muhammad Ali's famous rope a dope approach? To this day, I cannot be certain, but if I was to guess, it sure feels that he sucked me in.

My verbal pillage lasted for about five minutes,

"Boy, I need a drink, my mouth is dry!"

Whilst looking left and right for a drink stall, the dude asked me to comment on his previous comment, and pointed out the fact that despite my five-minute spiel, I was yet to address his initial statement.

"Man, you still here?" I said in a cocky tone.

He quickly replied,

"Bro, you still ain't answered my question. Are you afraid of the truth? Why you still talking? Well you talk, but not once have you addressed the question. It's all good you entertaining your boys like a clown, but when all is said and done, a big man asked another big man a question and you're there running and avoiding it like a 'my youth'. I ain't here to entertain, I am here to change lives fam."

He was right.

I was hyping, gassing and saying a lot of things other than addressing his reptilian foolishness. At that point I decided to humble myself, just a little and address his point like an adult, after all, there is a time to run joke, and a time to be serious and he looked serious. But, I had my black book in my back pocket if he tried to run joke on me. I had no fear.

"Bro, you made the statement, so state your case."

To be honest I think you're talking some madness, but go on, I will give you your space", I retorted kissing my teeth at the same time.

By now, the crowd had dwindled down and only a few of my boys remained; the others thought I was being long so they decided to continue their search for girls.

"Go man, I will catch you up; let me just deal with this, keep your mobile on."

The dude instructed me to open my hands and spread out my fingers. I did so hesitantly with a puzzled look on my face.

The vendor asked, "What do you see?"

"I see my hand, fingers nails, what's your point?" I asked.

"That's what they want you to believe; if you look a little closer, in between your fingers, you will see fins, if you check your skin, you will notice you have scales, especially with your dry hands." He said laughing out loud because my hand was a bit dry that day.

He continued to explain,

"Bro, you are 70% water, 30% earth, you ejaculate semen, SEA MEN, and when you look closer you will notice that your sperm looks like tadpoles, sea creatures. Then as a child you are breathing in water for nine months, living in an egg, and when the water breaks, that is you breaking the egg. Once that egg is broken you are born."

I was silent because this is something that I had never heard before.

He continued.

"When God said let there be light who was there recording this event and where were they during the six days of God's creation? Remember, there was no land, earth, sun or anything, just the spirit of God moving across the face of the waters. Who was there with God, who wrote this? Whoever said it resided in water right?"

"Boyyyy, let me read that, I saw a Bible on the table, and wanted to check what he just said. This was the first time I had ever picked up the Bible to research, read or learn something related to a topic I claimed to know so much about.

Better late than never I guess.

When I picked up the bible, he asked me if I was a follower of Jesus. I said yes, and shared my experiences within the church. I told him that I was a believer and that the good book needs to be respected because of its authenticity.

He then asked me what I do for an occupation and told him that I was a science student at the local university.

He made a loud noise and started dancing on the spot, his fingers resembled a gun and his head was moving like a snake; it was like he was getting charged and ready for the knockout, or what I said excited him immensely, I am not sure which. Whatever it was, his attitude and demeanour changed and he now, mentally, had the upper hand.

I had never been in this position before, speechless and trapped. I could not find a way out of this corner, as he invited me into unchartered territory, on a subject I knew nothing about. The funny thing was that I should be familiar with this territory as I attended church for many years. I should have picked something up; I was a Christian, but I had never read or understood the word, the stories, I never challenged anything, I just accepted it, blindly.

Historically, when I was faced with an unfamiliar topic or an idea that did not tickle my fancy, I would ignore it, simple as that. I would ignore, then disengage or deflect, or simply change the subject. I tried to adopt this approach with the education system, with little success; my parents were pressuring me to get good grades, go to college, then university, before finding a good job. This meant I only adopted this approach outside of school, where my behaviour was not monitored and assessed.

"Aight, aight God, let me show you this." He took the bible and said to me, "Bro, you got common sense right?"

"Of course I do", I told him.

"Cool, cool, check this", he continued.

He opened the first page of the Bible, the book that I said I knew and took me on a journey, a journey that would change my life forever, one that I am still on today. A journey that has not only changed me, my perception, identity and mind-set. It created a ripple that has and still is affecting scores of close people around me.

"Just to make my point crystal clear, I will go to the first few sentences of this book, I will not even delve into the depths of this book. Are you ready bro?" asked Fez man.

"Go for it", I said.

Genesis 1, Verse 1

"Bro read it out loud", Fez man urged.

I did as he asked and started reading aloud.

[1]"In the beginning God created the heavens and the earth..."

"Question - beginning of what, G? The beginning of the world, the universe, the day, or hour? It doesn't specify. Don't answer that yet, just continue."

[2] Now the earth was formless and empty, darkness was over the surface of the deep, and the Spirit of God was hovering over the waters.

"Question - who was there recording all of this bro? Why was the earth void? Why didn't God just make the world perfect? Did God arrive and find the earth there? Don't answer yet."

I continued to read.

[3] And God said, "Let there be light," "Question - God can talk? Who heard him say let there be light? And there was light. Question - was this the sun bro? What came first science student, the sun or the waters? You can assume that the light he was referring to was the sun, right?"

Scratching my head, I continued to read.

[4] God saw that the light was good, Question - didn't God know that the light would be good? I thought God knew everything and he separated the light from the darkness.[5] God called the light "day" and the darkness "night." And there was evening and there was morning—the first day.

[16] God made two great lights—the greater light to govern the day and the lesser light to govern the night. He also made the stars. Question - was this the same light or a different light to the one in verse 3?

[26] Then God said, "Let us make mankind in our image, who is the

'us' being referred to here? In our likeness, who is 'our' exactly? And likeness meaning what? So that they may rule over the fish in the sea and the birds in the sky, over the livestock and all the wild animals, and over all the creatures that move along the ground."

[27] So God created mankind in his own image, in the image of God he created them; Question - He them? Male and female he created them. Question - is it a he or them? Did God make them or was it male and female? Who was recording this? Who was God talking to?"

And he went on and on and on. I won't go into the details of this conversation, but this gives you a little insight.

I was intrigued to know more and decided to buy some of his merchandise (Student loans rule baby!) and asked him one question,

"How come I have not heard this before? Why is this message not on the TV or radio?"

He started to freestyle about the system, about black history and how we are at war right now. He told me that my eyes were closed and if I am serious I need to open my eyes and realise what is really going on, as the saying goes "real eyes, realise, real eyes."

He continued,

"Have you noticed they call it 'black on black' crime? And why do they even call it black on black? You know you're not black right, you're brownish red? Tell me, why is black the common term used? Did you know the word black and nigger are the same word? RESEARCH IT! Have you noticed why they never teach you black history at school? Young black males are more likely to get stopped by police than anyone else. Every other race has a culture and history apart from us. All they want you to know is that you were once a slave and they freed you. Did you know that African people educated every culture on this planet? Did you know that Africans built the Pyramids, the only structures standing today that scientists cannot comprehend how they were built? Did you know that they want to keep you focusing on rubbish rather than encouraging you to be the best that you can? The biggest secret ever is that you are God, from a royal blood line."

He went on and on, talking about the invader's history, or HIS - Story, his distorted version of events and his attempt to rewrite history. Our story or MY-story, remains a mystery. They are hiding it from the world; they raped and pillaged the Motherland, stole our jewels, statues, secret books and scrolls, placing them in museums or locking them in the Vatican.

My brain was buzzing, my heart was beating heavily and my temperature rose. I went into deep thought; thoughts I never knew were within me. I was confused. My emotions were all over the place.

The guy said that there is something deeper happening here. It is not about breaking down the Bible and sounding smart and analytical. It's about freeing your mind and being in touch with your spiritual nature, your true nature.

It is truly amazing and humbling how an innocent exchange between two people can spiral into something life-changing, liberating and empowering.

Many of us are presented with ideas or beliefs that seem concrete, sincere and concise, which make us happy, secure and safe. However, have you ever analysed those ideas or beliefs? Scrutinised their origins? Collected factual evidence? Or ever listened to people who don't support your beliefs or ideas?

Sometimes his can reveal that the idea or belief that kept you safe and sound, the idea you held dear is 100% bullshit and that someone has been lying to you.

Knowingly, or unknowingly many of us are fed lies.

The truth is a lie agreed upon.

As Ice Cube said *"Check yo self before you wreck yo self."*

My ego was dented.

My pride was hurt.

The fighter spirit in me had a plan.

My ego wanted to prove that dude wrong and the only way to achieve that was to read up on the matter. Whilst reading books, watching videos on the internet and listening to educational DVDs, I discovered a lot of things that shocked me to my core and left me reflecting about the world and questioning myself.

During a period of several months, I read dozens of books, factual ones, not those baby father novels that entertain, but research books that investigated different topics; books that I never even knew existed. I read so many books that I started neglecting my assignments and my university studies began to suffer.

I remember having a massive debate with my physiology lecturer about the differences between the biology of a European compared to an African. You see, at that time I was reading a book by Carol Barnes which explained that there is a substance in all living matter called melanin, which is responsible for the colour of your skin and that of your eyes. In fact, melanin is the substance that protects everyone from the sun's damaging rays. The more of it you have, the more protection you get. The less melanin you have the less protection you have leaving you exposed to melanoma, which is a form of skin cancer.

Further reading on the subject, taught me that melanin gives black people superior physical, mental & spiritual ability because it refines the nervous system in such a way that messages from the brain reach other areas of the body more rapidly in those with dark skin.

Carol Barnes writes, "Your mental processes (brain power) are controlled by the same chemical that gives black humans their superior physical (athletics, rhythmic dancing) abilities. This chemical is melanin!"

As a science student, I was surrounded by scientists, so in order to validate what I read I had to ask someone who knew.

"Dr Peters, can I ask you a quick question?" I approached my lecturer after class. He was white, middle class and loved rugby. The degree course that I was studying was a very popular one. Every lecture we had was held in an auditorium that held at least two hundred students. However, out of these two hundred students I would say that no more than five students were of African, Asian or Caribbean descent. The other one hundred and ninety-five students were white.

Dr Peters always found the time to support me, even when I did not necessarily need it. Maybe he noticed that a young black man with tattoos all over his arms, with two gold teeth and an athletic appearance looked out of place in a predominately all white university faculty.

Nevertheless, I accepted his advice and guidance simply because he gave good advice.

"How can I help you young Davis?" he responded with his glasses hanging off his long nose.

"Yeah, I just wanted to know what melanin was and if having an abundance of it could improve my performance?"

Dr Peters raised one eyebrow and informed me that he did not know what I was talking about. After asking him again about melanin, what it was and its other influences, he accused me of confusing science with myth and that what I was talking about is pseudo-science (pseudo meaning fake or scam). He informed me that melanin did not exist and that whoever informed me of such things were uneducated.

Dr Peters was clearly not prepared to disclose anything sensitive and after a while he had to dash off. After that conversation, the support he once showed me disappeared and he started to adopt an aggressive, anti-social tone with me.

This was one of my many encounters as a confused boy trying to find answers to questions that made my heart heavy. Everyone I asked became defensive and unresponsive, claiming that what I was talking about was foolishness or that I was not making sense. My questions were not just related to melanin. It was related to everything from Islam, Christianity, food and entertainment to the English language, science, current affairs, identity, politics, economics and much more.

I began to question everything.

During my search for knowledge, truth and clarity, some of the things that I discovered rocked my world and shocked me to my core. I had many sleepless nights and at times what I discovered made me so fucking angry. Angry because I was lied to for all these years. Information revealed to me through DVDs, attending lectures, reading books and listening to elders, made me very scared and uncertain about the future. Everything that I trusted was now being scrutinised with a magnifying glass, as I began to investigate things for myself and my understanding of the things that I had been taught.

Every time I made a breakthrough, every time that I re-discovered something, information that went against what I thought I knew, I would always ask myself if it was real, or if it was just a coincidence?

Over time I noticed a dramatic change in myself. I became very aware and critical of everything. I wasn't paranoid, just hungry for knowledge and the more I wanted to learn, the more courageous, versatile and powerful I became. When debating a topic, Barack Obama for example, I noticed there were conversations that elevated to levels not everyone could have participated in.

I remember a time when I was having a debate about Barack with some friends; on one level, everyone could relate with what was said, that level of information entertained everyone at a low, mundane level. We were talking about Barack being a house Negro funded by Jews and being as crooked as all the other US Presidents. There were more positive discussions about having a black man in the White House being a positive image for children, and empowering them to learn more about politics. That debate was healthy one, but very general. However, when the conversation went to a deeper level that was researchable and factual people became negative and cynical, fearful and ignorant. As the conversation died down, I mentioned that Barack and Bush were related by blood, and that all the presidents were related. I stated that the bloodline runs through to the Queen of England, who is actually German – an awkward silence fell upon the group. I brought Illuminati, New World Order, secret societies and hidden agendas into the discussion and touched upon subjects that challenged people's beliefs.

Once again, I was talking to an empty room. I did not raise my voice, I did not adopt a defensive or aggressive stance, I ushered the next level in neatly, providing evidence and third person commentary.

So why was I talking to deaf ears all of a sudden? Why the sudden lack of interest?

You see, there is information - or "IN" FORMATION, common knowledge that keeps you 'in' formed, 'in line' and predictable, but there is something called OUT-FORMATION. This is knowledge that empowers you to break free of linear thinking; radical and outlandish knowledge that changes your perception. With 'Out 'formation you learn to be selective about what you say and to whom because you can seriously turn people crazy; or you can be judged for your extreme views, or unconventional and sometimes inconvenient truths.

Children operate from the 'Out 'formation perspective. They are creative, bold, honest dreamers. As they get older, however, this tends to disappear.

On your journey, you will come across many people who will test you; people so scared that they will want to you feel scared with them. Essentially the choice is yours.

Ideas are bulletproof. You **cannot stop** someone from implanting a foreign, weird thought into your mind because your mind is not yours. The mind is like the ocean that everyone has access to. Everyone has access to the ocean just like everyone has access to your mind. Once you hear an idea, your mind attaches to it, then processes it. Do you take the idea on-board the idea, or do you discard it? Do you investigate it, discuss it or run away from it?

You can continue living a lie, working for the government as an agent of negative and ignorant behaviour or you can know the truth and fulfil your true potential.

5
Take a Break, Breathe, Inhale, Exhale, then come again

Let's take another look at melanin.

Melanin gives people their skin pigmentation. The darker you are, the more MELANIN you have. Melanin is produced in the pineal gland which is a very interesting gland indeed. This gland is located deep in the brain and many great learned men and women in history say that this gland is of great, mystical importance. The Ancient Egyptians have described this gland as the 'Third-Eye' or the 'Eye of God', but I would suggest you Google 'pineal gland' because it is something we all have.

In parts of Africa, South America and India, the amount of melanin in the skin is heaviest because the people have been exposed to the most intense sunlight for generations. Northern Europeans by contrast have the least amount of melanin in their skin. The thickness of the outer layer of the skin is also a factor. People with darker complexions have thicker layers of skin and this is a factor that enhances the skin's filtering ability. The thinner the skin, the lower the melanin and the less protection it has from the sun. Sun tans are the result of both thickening and increasing of melanin in the skin. Keratin is the substance nails are made of. It also appears in the outer layer of the skin. Where keratin deposits are heavy, the skin has a yellowish, brown shade, as in the Mongolian populations.

Leading scientists are aware of what melanin is, but they will never disclose certain information in open forums including TV or in the newspapers. The reasons are obvious. They want to suppress who black people really are. We were once great rulers, kings and queens of the planet. Many say that MELANIN is in fact CARBON! WE ARE CARBON BASED... THE HUMAN BODY IS MADE UP OF 102 MINERALS STRAINED ALONGSIDE CARBON, HYDROGEN, & OXYGEN. The melanin composition is C-H-O-N [Carbon-Hydrogen-Oxygen-Nitrogen] where CARBON is the largest component of all.

Melanin: Black. 'A pigment that is ubiquitous in nature'.

Ubiquitous: 'Existing or being everywhere, especially at the same time; omnipresent'.

Omnipresent: 'The property of being present everywhere. According to Eastern theism, God is present everywhere.

The world's most popular superhero is Spider Man and his biggest nemesis Venom.

Venom; was the name given to the black, mysterious substance that attached itself to Peter Parker.

This substance is an extra-terrestrial (extra - terra - astral) symbiont, which is a Greek word meaning 'companion' or to live together, this becomes clearer when you notice the original colours of Spider Man, blue and red. These are also the colours of two notorious American street gangs, the Bloods and the Crips. There is a lot of division amongst these groups and Spider Man's colours reflect that, as well as his own internal conflict.

This black, carbonated substance enhanced every aspect of Peter Parker. It made him stronger and improved his speed, intelligence and confidence. Melanin is a superconductor, which means, the more you have, the more sensitive you are to everything.

An example of this was when Spider-Man went into the jazz bar in Spider-Man 3; Spidey is seen dancing in a jazz club, shaking what his mama gave him (a characteristic of melanin).

People of African descent are known for being able to dance, whilst white people are known for being the total opposite.

Studies have shown that those who are carbon dominant have improved cognitive skills, are more compassionate and spiritual. Have you ever been to a Roman Catholic/European church and compared it to a Pentecostal/African or Caribbean church?

In his book, 'The Developmental Psychology of the Black Child', Dr Amos Wilson uses test results taken from research of WHITE social scientists which show that regardless of racism black children show superior psychomotor development. When you understand melanin, and research the contributions of melanised people to our planet, it's clear that Africans and those from the African diaspora dominate.

Melanin can be kept clean by consuming Vitamin B, drinking lots of water and staying clear from certain drugs. Speaking of drugs, scientists always use white mice, or melanin recessive mice to conduct their tests. Why don't they use brown mice, mice with melanin? The founder of medicine was African. The founders of maths, science, language, art, mechanics, music, psychology, anatomy etc., were all carbonated beings. The pyramids, Black Wall Street, The Dogon Tribe, Ancient Egyptians, Eastern Islanders, The Moors in Europe, Black Jesus, Black Presidents, Real Royal Family, African Origins of Freemasonry, African Origins of Politics, The Olmec Civilisation, God is Black, Blacks in Asia are all key words for you to research in YouTube or Google. I would encourage you to research.

To summarise, melanin:

- Is not an element.

- Is the cause of pigmentation

- Provides many benefits to human beings.

- Protects us from the ultraviolet rays of the sun.

- Is also a mechanism for absorbing heat from the sun.

- Is the chemical key to life itself.

- Is the major organising molecule for living systems.

- Is found everywhere, in both animals and plants.

- Is essentially linked to DNA.

- Shows the potential to reproduce itself.

- Is a super conductor of high frequency radiation and neural transmissions.

- Is a semi-conductor of sound and heat energy.

- Is not only in the skin, it can be found in every organ and bodily cell.

What's interesting about carbon is that; it's made up of 6 protons, 6 electrons and 6 neurons, making carbon 666. We were told to hate this number and that this is the number of the beast, but carbon is made up of 666 and Africans are carbon beings. The tricks played on our minds are not straightforward which is why we must research everything. Just as with Spider Man or Super Man or any other superhero, having a great power can be a blessing or a curse. Remember, the magic ALWAYS begins at the end of your comfort zone. Don't be afraid to try something new or challenging because doing the same thing repeatedly and expecting different results is the definition of insanity.

Essay Eight

5th November 2007

Finding the Lion Within

Written by my mentor - Andrew Muhammad

"Your time is limited, so don't waste it living someone else's life. Don't be trapped by dogma - which is living with the results of other people's thinking. Don't let the noise of others' opinions drown out your own inner voice. And most importantly, have the courage to follow your heart and intuition."
Steve Jobs

The following is one of the greatest lessons I have ever learnt and can be summed up in ten magical, two letter words.

IF IT IS TO BE, IT IS UP TO ME.

Life is simply what you make it. I learned that if I wanted to be free it would be up to ME. How many of us spend our life looking outwards, scanning the horizon for some mystical leader or book that will take us to heaven? Or we find ourselves believing the lie that we are not worthy of true happiness and success. It's time to wake up like Neo in the movie Matrix - take the RED PILL.

You are magical. You are the best and you are awesome.

Take a moment now, stop reading, look in the mirror and say to your reflection,

"I AM AWESOME!"

Do that five times a day and see the difference in your life. Surround yourself with greatness and sooner or later that greatness will begin to rub off on you. What's the point of being a lion and not being aware of it? We must become aware of our own inner beauty, inner strength and royal self-esteem.

Many of you reading this may already know that I am contracted to work in schools all over the United Kingdom. The objective is to motivate pupils to achieve high grades in their exams, yet I know and appreciate that to achieve high grades in LIFE, exam results are only a fraction of what's needed. My life and my results changed based on my own level of self-awareness. In fact, I'd go further and say that all of our results are an expression of our own level of awareness.

The reason why I failed my school exams was that I wasn't aware that I could excel academically. The reason I worked in jobs that I hated was because I was unaware that I did not have to tolerate the crap I endured on a daily basis. The reason why many of us are doing what we are doing is because we're simply not aware that we can seek other ways.

I love sharing positivity with the young people I encounter. I tell them they are the captains of their own destinies and they control how their life turns out.

Therefore, true education is vital to increase that level of self-awareness. My true education didn't start in school, but through my brother sharing his books of self-knowledge with me. These books did more than just teach me about distant empires, dynasties and historical dates. They also broadened my awareness about the realms of infinite possibilities. They showed me that there were common laws of success, for both individuals and nations. I also learned that today's generation of young people are probably the BEST generation we have given birth to. I look at these young warriors and I can see true lions. Lions who are fearless and ready for action. There is nothing wrong with these young people; they clearly see that the world is full of hypocrisy and contradictions.

At school, they are rightly told not to bully others smaller than themselves and that love is the answer. They are rightly taught that revenge solves nothing in the long run and that they should respect and honour their peers. Yet when they turn on the TV, read the newspapers or go on the internet they see our governments and their agents do the exact the opposite. We see big, financially strong nations bully and attack weaker, less fortunate ones for their oil and mineral wealth. They see multinational corporations lining their pockets with wealth whilst people are starving. They see international bankers crash the economic system, yet still receive multi million pound bonuses whilst the everyday men and women lose their jobs and livelihoods.

Young people are lions that are not aware they are lions. My advice to them is to grow every day in self-awareness. Make it a duty to explore your values and test yourself every single day. Try to do something new at least once a week.

Brothers and sisters, I want my life to represent an IDEAL or a CONCEPT. I want to know that when people see me or my works, they see that nothing is impossible. They know they can achieve all their goals, ambitions and aspirations. So never be afraid to be a dreamer as all successful people are big dreamers. They imagine what their future could be, ideal in every aspect and then they work every day toward their vision, goal or purpose.

Never be afraid to be financially rich. It is truly a slave mentality to believe richness is equated to being evil and poorness equates to righteousness. Some of the best friends I have are financially rich and they are like saints. By contrast, some of the snakiest people I have ever had the displeasure to meet were ghetto poor. Money does not make the person, it is man that makes the money.

There are two basic uses for money:

Money can provide one with a comfortable life which will allow the freedom to develop our creative thinking.

It can provide a service to others without our physical presence. In other words, you could be asleep and yet your business is still performing a service; this is also known as a passive income.

None of us really own ANY money because when we depart from this earth not a penny of that money goes with us. It's not how much money we have that counts; it's what we do with that money whilst we have it.

Successful people understand that it takes another level of thinking to connect to the success zone. It' is not money but a way of thinking. For us to enter that zone, we must be ready to be mocked, maligned and misunderstood by those around us. Did you know that 95% of the wealth in this world is owned by just 1% of the population? That means 99% the population are fighting over the remaining 5% of the wealth. If you are living amongst the 99%, you will seem different if you try changing the pattern of your thoughts or the circumstances of your life. The 99% will ask why you are reading such books, why you are going to those meetings or why you're listening to certain things. You will be seen as different by your very nature of wanting to excel and grow. This is called thinking outside of the box. Schools don't generally encourage children and young people how to enter this zone so many of us spend our whole lives NOT thinking out of the box; and even sadder, most of us are not even AWARE that there is a box!

Growing up, I hated art classes in school because I felt I had no artistic value. I also remember a time when I was so financially poor I could not afford to buy a computer. Any basic help I needed I had to ask others for assistance. Sometimes the people I asked would make it seem like asking was an inconvenience so I would feel guilty for even asking. However, Alex, a good friend of mine offered me a free home computer and showed me some of the basics of using it. He also advised me to attend a very basic class on computer skills. I only attended two or three times, but my understanding of what one can do on a computer really developed.

As time went by I became more proficient, spending hours alone teaching myself through trial and error. Soon I was using parts of the computer others did not even know existed and created my own workshops that wowed people. The more I practiced, the more artistic I became. It was then I realized how much I loved art and how creative I really was. The point I am making is that we sometimes make the wrong evaluations of ourselves then live by those evaluations and imprison our true potential without even knowing it.

Since then I've had numerous individuals and organisations requesting me to teach others how to create artistic, professional presentations. I have trained IT technicians who tell me they have never seen someone use a computer the way I do. It also showed me that the same tasks I had been asking others to help me with I could do myself and probably better. If you pay attention, you'll see that you're surrounded with opportunities.

Many people believe that to be financially successful, they must be at the right place at the right time. Whilst this is correct, there is a small part missing. You must be AWARE that you are in the right place at the right time. There are many times I've been at the right place but didn't even know it. We need to be more aware of our opportunities in life.

It's said that life moves in cycles. If this is true, then studying history is the most valuable and rewarding of all subjects. History can prepare you for today and help you plan for tomorrow. I have been studying history seriously for the past thirty years and if there is one thing I've learnt from history, is that man does not learn from it. I would like to advise young people to learn from the past of their elders. They should not be doomed to make the same mistakes as those who went before them.

All religions and many scientists agree that everything we want or need in life is already here. The power and energy exists everywhere 100% of the time, but how does this apply to you and me? The mobile phone has always existed, but it took someone to discover the awareness of how to bring it out. The internet has always existed but it took someone to find the awareness of how to manifest it. Likewise, your GREATNESS exists right now but it is whether you will find the time, technique and awareness to allow it to emerge.

No scientist can say what you are capable of. That's down to you and me. You can create anything you want.

Now I can hear some of you saying *'Come on Brother Andrew, that's easy for you to say, but you don't know my story!'* I come from a one-parent family; I'm too dark, too short, or too tall; I'm too poor or I was born under the wrong star sign. My reply would be *'SHUT UP!!!!'* I'm not interested in your circumstances. Weak people blame circumstances for their failures. Successful people do not live bound by their circumstances. They create or change their circumstances to fit what they want in their lives. I'm sorry if this hurts, but life can be brutally straightforward at times. Life does not care about your personal circumstances. You and I have the ability because we were created to be supreme beings in this wonderful universe. Some of us are addicted to bad results, because we have chained ourselves to bad circumstances. We end up in jobs, organisations and relationships that we dislike yet we tolerate them, because we lack the awareness of change.

My advice to you all is to surround yourself with what you want to become. If you surround yourself with greatness it will affect you. You are worthy of true happiness and peace in your life otherwise you would not be here. I really don't care about what mistakes you have made in life. The Creator forgives you. How do I know that you are forgiven? If you were not forgiven you would not be reading these words. You and I can set things right. Let's take this opportunity with both hands.

You are such a unique individual. Just be yourself. That is something that you can be better than anyone else. Be yourself!

Listen to that small voice that speaks to you from within and follow it. In dark times that's your best friend and internal messenger. Try to obey it because it will lead, exhort, warn and protect you from negative forces. I'll end by how I started with the ten magical two letter words...

IF IT IS TO BE, IT IS UP TO ME.

Davis Williams

"A flower does not think of competing to the flower next to it. It just blooms."

Essay Nine

5th March 2009

N.I.G.G.A.

Written by Davis J. Williams

"Death is not the greatest loss in life. The greatest loss is what dies inside while still alive. Never surrender."
Tupac Shakur

"A coward dies a thousand times; a soldier dies but once."
Tupac Shakur

Tupac Shakur (2Pac) that crazy mofo' was and is one of the most influential yet misunderstood hip-hop artists of all time. He was born on 16th June 1971. On 7th September 1996, he was shot multiple times in a drive-by shooting and died a week later on Friday 13th September. He was born on the east coast of America and died on the west coast (the sun rises in the east and always sets in the west). What a wasted talent! He was only 25 years old when he died, yet to reach his prime. When I was 25 years old I was still growing; I made many mistakes, still finding my way in this crazy world. As far as spirituality was concerned I was lost and totally unaware of my true potential.

At the age of 25, many great leaders had failed to discover their true purpose. Malcolm X for example was still called Malcolm Little (known as Satan by some) and he was just a small-time street hustler.

Martin Luther King at 25 years of age was a young preacher and had a long way to go before becoming the colossal figure many know and love.

At the tender age of 25 years, Tupac managed to influence most of the people that listened to his music. From Mexico to Cairo; from Nepal to Moscow; and from Germany to England, Scotland and even Iceland. Tupac's influence caused people all around the world to dress and talk like him. Being a young pup he was bound to make some mistakes and utter some questionable statements, but spending eleven months in a maximum-security prison whilst innocent (his words) can do something to your psyche.

Tupac's talent was clear from a very young age. His rawness was so natural, that he inspired many artists like the Notorious BIG, 50 Cent and Kendrick Lamar to take their lyrics seriously. People loved Tupac's realness, the way he viewed the world, his knowledge, and his ability to channel his philosophy through his music, acting and poetry.

But to me, Tupac represented so much more that that!

"There should be a class on drugs. There should be a class on sex education, a real sex education class, there should be a class on scams, there should be a class on religious cults, there should be a class on police brutality, there should be a class on apartheid, there should be a class on racism in America, there should be a class on why people are hungry,   but there is not, there are classes on gym, 'physical education', 'let's learn volleyball'."
Tupac Shakur, aged 17

In my opinion, Tupac Shakur was one of the greatest rappers of all time. He was passionate and creative. His performances ignited that fire within, regardless of how cold-hearted you thought you were.

Through this essay, I hope to present Tupac in a different light. I am not going to focus too much on the media propaganda, the East Coast vs. West Coast drama, the shooting at the police and all the hype on the internet; I am going to focus on what made him so different to the others. I want people to recognise Tupac's genius; a creative who could spread a message that had been handed down to him. Tupac was a messenger and this essay aims to show you who or what he was a messenger of.

"There are always three sides to a story: your version, his version and the truth."

With most rappers, what you see is pretty much what you get. Tupac was unlike any other rapper out there. He was far from shallow, one dimensional or boring. Nor was he created in a boardroom like 50 Cent, Lil' Wayne or Rick Ross. Tupac is a cultural icon, manufactured on the streets of America. To me, he represents a deep-rooted and mysterious aspect of our culture, our struggle and our ideals that are rarely spoken about.

"History is HIS – STORY, his version and his perspective, my story is a mystery."

It is time to tell the story of Tupac from another perspective. **Perspective** = Standpoint, an attitude towards or way of regarding something; a point of view.

I would like to take you on a journey. What you are about to read may make sense to some, and to others it may seem like total nonsense. Whatever your position, remember that we are all at different places on this journey called life.

Perspective 1: New Age Warfare

'All war is based on deception'

The reason why so many young people gravitate towards Tupac is because he spent time in jail; this made him even more popular. But whilst in jail, Tupac didn't waste a second. He took advantage by studying the works of world-renowned scholars and strategists, analysing their philosophies and methods. One author amazed him; his name was Niccolo Machiavelli, an Italian who believed that he could eliminate his enemies through deception. After becoming engrossed with his works, in1996 Tupac assumed the alias *Makaveli*.

*"Niggaz is tellin me about this Illuminati shit while I'm in jail like the dollar sign, that's another way to keep your self-esteem low, that's another way to keep you unconfident, and I'm puttin' a **K** cos I'm killin' that illuminati shit, trust me if these muthafuckers wanted to kill you why the fuck are they gonna tell Farrakhan, why they gonna tell the Nation of Islam, why they gonna tell this nigga in jail about the plan, how did he know? How did it lead to him, who told him, who? The Pope? h come on man get the fuck outta here, you so thinkin' about the money you not gettin' the muthafuckin money, get the money nigga I don't care whose face on there…put that money out they accept it, and they do believe me, I tried it. I tried it to see if it was a white thing … everywhere I go with money they let me in everywhere I go. With none they don't let you in, trust me that's all it is, it's about money, when you got money you got power."* **Tupac on the Illuminati**

Tupac loved his people, but hated seeing them weak and powerless against the Illuminati. Tupac wanted people to wake up and fight with him against the powers that be and that motivated him to name his last album 'The Don Killuminati: The 7 Day Theory'. He was no longer 2Pac but Makaveli.

Study the works of Niccolo Machiavelli to get a full understanding of Tupac's attitude towards The Art of War.

People who tend to expose the Illuminati lose their life, or their mind. Tupac blatantly exposed them but had no intention of dying. He had a vision of making enough money through his music and his acting career, to build a global empire giving him and his army political strength, something that people lack.

He grew up in extreme poverty and was aware that the more money you have, the more you can influence change as POLITICS is based on money and money is POWER! Tupac was a world changer and he came from a long line of revolutionary soldiers.

Perspective 2: The 7 Day Theory

Why did Tupac name his last album *The Don Killuminati: The 7 Day Theory*?

Bearing in mind that Tupac read books on many topics ranging from religion, politics and astrology to art and civil rights, he was very much aware of the power of numbers and the ancient science of numerology.

Numerology is the name for the study of numbers, dates, cycles and astrological references. There are people in influential, high-status positions governing our political and societal affairs, who understand the power of numbers, dates and their symbolic references and use this knowledge to their advantage.

Let's apply this code to Tupac's life:

Tupac (5 letters)

Amaru (5 letters)

Shakur (6 letters)

5 + 5 + 6 = 16

1 + 6 = 7

Tupac was not born Tupac; his birth name was Lesane (6 letters) Parish (6 letters) Crooks (6 letters).

6 x 3 = 18

8 - 1 = 7

And he was born on the 16th September.

1+6 = 7

And he died when he was 25 years of age.

2+5 = 7

The time of death was 4:03pm.

4+3+0 = 7

The name of his last album was The Don Killuminati: The 7 Day Theory.

Tupac was killed in the month of September, which is the REAL

7th month (Latin *September*= seventh month), from *septem* ('seven'), from Proto-Indo-European; September was also the seventh month in the Roman calendar.

October is the original 8th month, it was never supposed to be the 10th October in Latin means eight and 'octo' features a lot in English language about the number eight.

After leaving the Mike Tyson fight on Saturday September 7, 1996 Tupac was shot several times in a drive-by shooting. He was immediately taken to hospital after sustaining four bullet wounds. The 7 Day Theory relates to Machiavelli surviving on the 7th, 8th, 9th, 10th, 11th, 12th, but "died" on the 13th, 7 days in total.

The album, 7 Day Theory is littered with sevens. I recommend you listen to the album and study the album art work as well.

Tupac was aware of numerology and applied its magic! Are you aware? Remember, all warfare is deception, don't let them deceive you!

Perspective 3 – The importance of his name

As I mentioned in perspective #2, Tupac was not his birth name, Shakur was the family name of his stepfather, Mutulu Shakur, a certified Black Panther who became famous when he helped his sister Joanne Chesimard (now known as Assata Shakur) escape to Cuba. The FBI had both on their 'Most Wanted List' because of their alleged crimes against the State. Tupac was named after an indigenous leader who led the revolution against the Spanish who were trying to control them. He was from Peru and became a symbol of strength, struggle and human rights.

The name Tupac was carefully chosen. Why did his mum choose that name?

What does your name mean?

Tupac's mother was born Alice Faye Williams and as she grew and developed through the ranks of the Black Panther Party (BPP), she changed her name to Afeni Shakur.

Tupac's parents had strong links to the New York Black Panther Party in the late 1960s and early 1970s and this foundation had a strong influence on him.

Perspective 4: His Values

> "*Thug Life hit me like the Holy ghost.*"

Tupac was a fan of backronyms

Acronym is a word that are developed from the initial letters of a word.

For example, R.I.P comes from Rest in Peace or LMAO means Laughing My Ass Off. BACKRONYMs are like acronyms, but they use a word that already exists and creates a new word.

For example:

N.I.G.G.A
Never Ignorant About Getting Goals Accomplished

O.U.T.L.A.W.S
Operating Under Thug Laws As Warrior

T.H.U.G L.I.F.E
The Hate U Gave Little Infants Fucks Everybody

People believe that THUG LIFE is about gangs and looting, but if you thought that, you were wrong. According to Tupac's perspective, Thug Life is a statement, a mind-set and attitude that AWARE WARRIORS adhere to.

Tupac believed that if you teach children to hate another group of people because of the colour of their skin, that attitude "fucks everyone". THUG LIFE believed in addressing this issue.

> "I didn't create T.H.U.G. L.I.F.E., I diagnosed it."
> **Tupac Shakur**

In 1992 at the 'Truc Picnic' in **Cali**, Tupac organised rival gang members and encouraged them to sign a peace treaty because he was tired of all the black on black senseless killings and wanted to put an end to it.

He called this Treaty (agreement) The Code.

Code OF THUG LIFE:
(Source: www.thuglifearmy.com/code-of-thug-life.html)

- All new Jacks to the game must know:
  a) He's going to get rich
  b) He's going to jail

c) He's going to die

- Settle disputes without conflict. In unity, there is strength!
- Carjacking in our Hood is against the Code
- Slinging to children is against the Code (selling drugs to kids).
- Having children slinging (selling) is against the Code.
- No slinging in schools.
- The boys in blue don't run nothing; we do. Control the hood, and make it safe.
- No slinging to pregnant sisters. That's baby killing; that's genocide!
- Know your target, who is the real enemy.
- Civilians are not a target and should be spared.
- Harm to children will not be forgiven.
- Attacking someone's home where their family is known to reside, must be altered or checked.
- Senseless brutality and rape must stop.
- Our old folks must not be abused.
- Respect our sisters. Respect our brothers.
- Sisters in the life must be respected if they respect themselves.
- Military disputes concerning business areas within the community must be handled professionally and not on the block.
- No shooting at parties.
- Concerts and parties are neutral territories; no shooting!
- Know the Code; it's for everyone.
- Be a real ruff neck. Be down with the code of the Thug Life.
- Protect yourself at all times.

As you can see, Tupac was very realistic with his visions. In London, community leaders will encourage young people to stop selling drugs, even if these boys, who have become the man of the house due to their absent father, have adopted huge responsibilities. These leaders expect these young lions to stop their hustling antics, which is unrealistic. Tupac understood that they would never stop 'Road Life' however, getting them to operate within certain boundaries, like not selling to children was a compromise and realistic.

Tupac already had his soldiers, the gang members who would assist him in cleaning up the community; the powers that be saw him as a massive threat. If you think he was killed over some dumb East Coast vs West Coast shit you have been greatly misinformed and deceived.

Tupac had way too much power for a black man and the establishment killed him and used the beef with himself, Death Row records and Bad Boy Entertainment as a smoke screen. The saying "All warfare is based on deception" now has a clearer meaning.

Tupac and Biggie were both under FBI surveillance when they died; this tells you something about their influence.

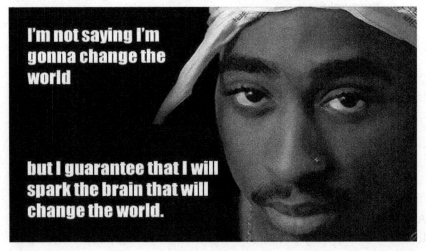

I'm not saying I'm gonna change the world

but I guarantee that I will spark the brain that will change the world.

Perspective 5 – What is a THUG?

THUG LIFE has played a massive role with Tupac's purpose but as you can see, he wasn't an easy person to understand. He was very deep and cryptic and for someone who read so much that is to be expected. Tupac studied books ranging from *The Art of War*, which is an ancient Chinese military treatise attributed to Sun Tzu, The **Prince** written *by: Niccolo Machiavelli,* plus books on meditation, communication, telepathy, civil rights, Shakespeare and many more.

His death is covered in so much mystery that many people believe he is still alive. It is not only fans who think this, but also journalists, researchers and observers who stumble across the circumstances of his death with many questions left unanswered.

So why did Tupac decide to call his movement THUG LIFE?

The first thing I decided to do was to Google the word 'THUG'

This is what came up.

Definition of a 'thug':

- *Thug, a common criminal, who treats others violently and roughly, often for hire.*
- *Thug, (proper noun), a member of the former Indian cult Thuggee, Thug Behram, a leader of the Thuggee cult.*
www.etymonline.com/index.php?term=thug

THUGEE...CULT...what the hell is this?

I was slightly confused, so I decided to do some more research into the THUGEE. I was interested in its etymological meaning, its root and where it was first used.

This is what I found.

1810, "member of a gang of murderers and robbers in India who strangled their victims," from Marathi thag, thak cheat, swindler, Hindi thag.
Source: *Google*

Who were the THUGEES? Where did they come from? What did they believe in? Were these the first thugs? Why did Tupac get THUG LIFE tattooed on his mid-section?

"My mother was pregnant with me whilst she was in prison (in 1971) and a month after she got out of prison, she gave birth to me, so I was cultivated in prison, my embryo was in prison," reflected Tupac Shakur during a 1995 interview.

Perspective 6 – About the THUGS / THUGEE

We mentioned how Tupac's family was associated to the Black Panthers, a community-based organisation who w*anted freedom and power to determine the destiny of the black community amidst severe police brutality and racism.* They had a ten-point programme similar to THUG LIFE's code. The way the Black Panthers protected their community and the way they stood up against those who made their life a living hell, gained respect and admiration from around the world.

The FBI wanted key members from the Black Panthers in jail, and placed them on America's Most Wanted List.

Osama Bin Laden was on the Most Wanted List!

Many of Tupac's family - his mother, step-father, uncles and aunts - were heavily involved in the Black Panthers' Ten Point Programme. The vision of the Black Panther Party was simple; they wanted to cater for all the needs of oppressed people and to defend them against their oppressors. They regarded the American government as the most-evil on the planet and they did not expect for one moment that they would ignore their efforts to protect and provide for their community.

Their Ten Point Program stated:

- We want freedom. We want power to determine the destiny of our Black community.
- We want full employment for our people.
- We want an end to the robbery by the white men of our black community.
- We want decent housing, fit for shelter of human beings.
- We want an education for our people that expose the true nature of this decadent American society. We want an education that teaches us our true history and our role in the present-day society.
- We want all Black men to be exempt from military service.
- We want an immediate end to POLICE BRUTALITY and MURDER of black people.
- We want freedom for all Black men held in federal, state, county and city prisons and jails.
- We want all Black people when brought to trial to be tried in court by a jury of their peer group or people from their Black communities, as defined by the Constitution of the United States.
- We want land, bread, housing, education, clothing, justice and peace.

The Black Panthers took on the United States of America. Tupac's mother was known for defending herself in court after she was accused of taking part in several bombings, which were blamed on the Panthers. She was accused of 156 acts of terrorism but was found NOT GUILTY. This achievement gained the respect from Namdeo Laxman Dhasal, a Marathi poet, writer and Human Rights activist from Maharashtra, India. Through studying the methods of the Black Panthers, he created his own version of the Indian Dalit Panther who also represented strength and might against their oppressors.

So, the Indian Black Panther and the American Black Panther were connected in terms of vision, methods used and attitudes towards the State.

In India, there was a brotherhood called The Order of Thugee; this was the original Thug, and they were a brotherhood of men who were considered a secret society. The Thugee's main enemy at the time was the British, who wanted to exert their global dominance and they had to oppress the indigenous population to achieve this.

Does this sound familiar?

Are you not considered a THUG?

Are black people often depicted as public enemy number one?

Ask Smiley Culture, Mark Duggan or Trayvon Martin.

The Thugees were known for spending their time stealing from and terrorising the rich elite class. Even though they did this, they still followed a code of conduct: they would not harm anyone; they would not bring harm to their own community nor to those who were in the same position as themselves. The Thugees were known for killing the rich without shedding blood. Strangling their targets to death was their chosen method to kill.

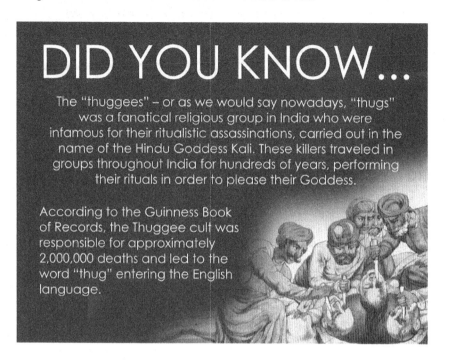

DID YOU KNOW...

The "thuggees" – or as we would say nowadays, "thugs" was a fanatical religious group in India who were infamous for their ritualistic assassinations, carried out in the name of the Hindu Goddess Kali. These killers traveled in groups throughout India for hundreds of years, performing their rituals in order to please their Goddess.

According to the Guinness Book of Records, the Thuggee cult was responsible for approximately 2,000,000 deaths and led to the word "thug" entering the English language.

Perspective 7 – The Feminine Energy

The Thugee exalted the woman just like Thug Life and Tupac respected the sisters.

"Since we all came from a woman, got our name from a woman, and our game from a woman. I wonder why we take from women, why we rape our women, do we hate our women? I think it's time we killed for our women, be real to our women, try to heal our women, 'cus if we don't we'll have a race of babies that will hate the ladies, who make the babies. And since a man can't make one he has no right to tell a woman when and where to create one." **Tupac Shakur**

Not only did Tupac respect the sisters, but he also had a tattoo of Nefertiti on his chest and for those who don't know, she was a beautiful African queen.

The Thugee also respected and worshipped an Indian goddess. Her name was Kali-Ma.

One of Tupac's biggest tracks was 'California Love'. Why did Tupac, the originator of THUG LIFE, have so much love for CALI / KALI? Tupac was not born in California, he was born in New York! The Code of THUG LIFE was also founded in city known as Cali.

Can you see the link?

THUG LIFE was also born in Cali-fornia, which makes his connection to Kali-Ma even clearer.

Perspective 8 – Kali-Ma, the Black Mother Goddess

Kali-Ma is recognised throughout India; she is known for her ability to empower her followers. This Hindu goddess is known to have been Black, having smooth skin and of having a loving nature. The very word Kali-Ma comes from the word *Kala*, which means black time and the Lord of death.

If you associate India with Asian-looking people, then it may be harder to accept that Kali-Ma was in fact a black-skinned African goddess. Africans were known for travelling to Asia and building civilisation. Pyramids are found in China and India, early images and statues of Buddha feature full lips and broad nose with woolly hair, even though people in that region do not have these features. Images of Kali-Ma can be found on the internet; she is often depicted as being sinister and violent and because of this, she is massively misunderstood. In fact, she is the most misunderstood of the Hindu goddesses. Does this sound familiar? The only images black people tend to see of themselves in the media are negative, violent or degrading.

The images found of the Black Goddess Kali-Ma were known to bring death to the ego because the ego is an illusion and a hindrance to mankind's progression. Kali-Ma and her followers wanted to bring death to anything anti-nature and she was the force needed to restore balance in the world. The Goddess Kali-Ma is seen with four arms which represents immense strength. In two of her hands, she has a sword in one hand and a severed head in the other. This represents a great battle where Kali-Ma defeats a demon. The other two hands are not associated with violence or death but are seen showing love and charity to her followers. Remember, these images are symbolic, so no, she did not actually have four arms.

Remember what I said about Kali-Ma disliking illusions?

Well, what is interesting is that Dr Dre and Snoop Dogg performed a live stage show in Cali-fornia at a music festival called Coachella. This performance received global attention because it featured a hologram of Tupac. People at the concert were crying whilst they watched a life-like Tupac grace the stage 16 years after his death (1+6=7) his death. Holograms are optical illusions and Kali-Ma destroys illusions. Holograms are also very expensive. Digital Domain, the visual effects company who were responsible for tricking millions recently filed for bankruptcy. Perhaps Kali-Ma got her revenge!

The THUGEEs were a brotherhood that followed Kali-Ma and they were anti-corruption and money-hungry government structures created by man to oppress people of colour.

Perspective 9 –The Brotherhood

Young people rarely identify themselves as being in a gang because the term does not represent what they stand for. The term brotherhood is one that is on the rise, especially by young people entering the criminal justice system as confused non-believers of any religion and leaving prison as Muslims, associated with the Islamic brotherhood. Many may frown upon this conversion of young black men but they are desperate to belong to something deep, meaningful and spiritual.

The word 'brotherhood' is a compound word consisting of two words, 'brother' and 'hood'. Have you ever asked yourself what does the 'hood' represent?

'Hood' can be associated with other words such as neighbour – **Hood**, brother – **Hood**, sister –**Hood**, priest – **Hood**, father – **Hood**, man – **Hood, Hood**-lum and **Hood**-wink.

According to the online etymological dictionary the word Hood means

"Covering," Old English *hod* "hood," from Proto-Germanic **hodaz* (cf. Old Saxon, Old Frisian *hod* "hood," Middle Dutch *hoet*, Dutch *hoed* "hat," Old High German *huot* "helmet, hat," German *Hut* "hat," Old Frisian *hode* "<u>*guard, protection*</u>"), from PIE **kadh-*"cover" (see *hat*).

The words 'guard' and 'protection' jumped out at me because that is what a Hood does –it protects you from someone or something.

The Brotherhood was formed to protect its members from something seen as a threat.

Young people, who are seen as gangs, form a brotherhood to protect themselves from threats from the police, other gangs, or to protect themselves from the trauma of family abuse or even to protect themselves from their own insecurities.

"Birds of a feather, flock together"

In 2006 David Cameron who would become British Prime Minister years later made a speech about young people wearing hoods.

"We, the people in suits - often see hoodies as aggressive, the uniform of a rebel army of young gangsters, but hoodies are more defensive than offensive. They're a way to stay invisible in the street. In a dangerous environment, the best thing to do is keep your head down, blend in."

It is not only young people who wear a hood when feeling threatened. There is only one animal in the world that has a hood, and that is The King Cobra, the world's largest venomous snake. Many cultures see snakes as royal and special, especially in Kemet (Egypt) where the cobra can be found on the crown of King Tut as well as other kings. In Ancient Greece, the use of snakes was also respected as it was thought they had healing properties. Even to this day you will find the symbol of two snakes wrapped around a wand on the side of ambulances or in chemists.

Young people are the modern day THUGEE.

There is no mistaking that young people today love wearing hoods. Rest in Peace Trayvon Martin. You were targeted because you wore a hood and society sees the hood as a sign of aggression, when in fact it is a sign of PROTECTION.

Young people need to realise that they are the BROTHERHOOD,

Young people need to realise that they are the BROTHERHOOD, they are the THUGEE and they need to understand why they are targeted and portrayed as a threat and why the media pumps BILLIONS of pounds into trying to keep the self-esteem of these young lions low and their attention distracted.

Here is a speech from the 1979 film 'The Warriors'. In this scene, a local gang leader appears in front of hundreds to deliver his keynote speech.

Cyrus, the main gang leader addresses the crowd:
"Can you count, suckers? I say, the future is ours... if you can count!"

Now, look what we have here before us. We have the Saracens sitting next to the Jones Street Boys. We've got the Moon-runners right by the Van Cortlandt Rangers.

Nobody is wasting anybody. That... is a miracle. And miracles are the way things ought to be.

You're standing right now with nine delegates from one hundred gangs. And there's over a hundred more. That's twenty thousand, hard-core members. Forty-thousand, counting affiliates and twenty-thousand more, not organised, but ready to fight. Sixty thousand soldiers! Now, there ain't but twenty thousand police in the whole town. Can you dig it?

Can you dig it?

Can you dig it?

Davis Williams

Now, here's the total: One gang could run this city! One gang. Nothing would move without us allowing it to happen. We could tax the crime syndicates, the police, because WE got the streets, suckers! Can you dig it?

The problem in the past has been **the man** turning us against one another. **We have been unable to see the truth**, because **we are fighting for ten square feet of ground**, our turf, our little piece of turf. **That's crap, brothers**! The turf is ours by right, because it's our turf. All we have to do is keep up the general truce. We take over one borough at a time. Secure our territory. Secure our turf, because it's all our turf!

With unity comes strength

Final words

We need to stop relying on the media to tell the stories of our heroes and we must learn to investigate things for ourselves.

Asking questions is essential as they give a better, more in-depth understanding of a chosen topic. We are living in a society where the media feeds us information and disinformation and more often than not, we accept it without asking questions. We regularly use words without knowing their true meaning and we fight for causes thinking that they are righteous, oblivious to the fact that we have been lied to. We are now living in the information age; it's time to wake up.

We all know that Tupac was a great rapper; we have read about his family connection to the Black Panthers who fought for freedom and equality. Many of us remember his transformation from a mere dancer to a Hollywood actor. We have engaged in debates about who was better, Tupac or Biggie or in conversations around Tupac's current location. Many people believe that Tupac is alive, others don't.

Was Tupac a THUGEE? Did Tupac read about them and adapt their philosophy? Did Tupac worship Kali-Ma? And was he trying to convert the masses unknowingly to this ancient Brother-Hood just like performers today such as Jay Z and Beyoncé who are often accused of pumping subliminal, cryptic messages into their music and videos?

Some of Tupac's famous quotes

"Ain't a woman alive that can take my momma's place."

"Was Tupac talking about his mother or The Great Black Mother Kali?"

"Only God can judge me."

We know Tupac was not a Christian. Was he telling people that he was devoted to the God Kali?

"They got money for the war but can't feed the poor."

Tupac made it crystal clear that he had issues with the political powers that be.

"Wars come and go... but my soldiers stay eternal."

Soldiers fighting the righteous war.

"You gotta make a change. It's time for us as a people to start making some changes. Let's change the way we eat, let's change the way we live and let's change the way... we trea

each other. **You see the old way wasn't working so it's on US, to do what we gotta do to survive.**"

"I'm not sayin I'm gonna rule the world, or that I'm gonna change the world, but I guarantee that I will spark the brain that will change the world."

Did Tupac SPARK something in your brain? Are you the one he was trying to motivate into action? It is time to ROAR young lion and change the world like Tupac tried to. Find others who feel like you and familiarise yourself with basic CODES. Wear your hoods of protection with pride.

Tupac was the realest rapper I know, the smartest and without a doubt, the most misunderstood. I hope that this essay inspires many to know that they too can become a THUG. Not everything is what is seems.

I honour and salute Tupac Shakur, the urban THUGEE

R.I.P

Roar In Paradise

Essay Ten

14th October 2003

A Reality Check

Written by my mentor Dr. Suzella Palmer

"How in the hell could a man enjoy being awakened at 8.30am by an alarm clock, leap out of bed, dress, force-feed, shit, piss, brush teeth and hair and fight traffic to get to a place where essentially you made lots of money for somebody else and were asked to be grateful for the opportunity to do so?"

Charles Bukowski

You don't have to agree with me, but I think that human beings can be divided into two categories – they can either be leaders or followers. I like to think of myself as a leader, not because I believe that I lead people, but because I go out of my way to lead myself. By that, I mean that neither my parents, my school, my friends or any religious teachings dictate the things that I do. For example, I respect people who respect me rather, than respecting them because of their status. I question a lot of what I've been taught at home, in school and at university and I won't accept religion based on faith alone.

While some of the people that have tried to guide me in life have done so with good intentions and may have given me some good advice about life in general, I think it would be foolish to think that they can't be mistaken. This enabled me to learn to hear what People don't always like it, but I can live with that. I try not to 'go along' just to 'get along'.

Davis Williams

others have to say but come to my own conclusions about whether I agree or not, no matter how unpopular my view is. This also enabled me not to do what others do or what others expect. Sometimes we should obey those in authority for our own good, because they know things that we don't. If a parent warns a child about the danger of fire, they are acting in the interest of the child by protecting the child from being burned. But when a parent tells a child that when they are in adult company they should be 'seen and not heard' or that they should believe in a particular religion, should the child always comply? What if most adults are followers who don't know if what they believe is true or understand why they do what they do? Rather than question what the media, politicians and religious leaders tell them, most adults seem to believe what they're told without question and often ignore the fact that many politicians are corrupt, that the mainstream media is dishonest and that religious leaders are not always as God-fearing as they make out. This culture of ignorance is then transferred to their children who are conditioned by their parents, their schools and the media to follow, rather than lead.

Those who study psychology know that people can easily be influenced which is why we have an advertising industry that's worth approximately £16 billion a year. If advertising didn't influence people, then companies wouldn't spend so much money on a 30 second advert. We trust and allow the media to tell us what is important, what looks good and what will make us happy. This may explain why every year, 'poor' people struggle to find hundreds or even thousands of pounds celebrating Christmas, because it's what everyone else does. It may also explain why we struggle to buy expensive brands so that we can feel good or even comfortable around other people because our status in life is now decided by what we own and wear rather than what we do.

Having 'things' gives us a 'feel-good factor' it would seem.

A few smart people in the world make a lot of money by making most people, who are not so smart, believe that by buying a particular product they will be somehow better off. Many end up spending most of their lives struggling to keep up with the latest trends which lines the pockets of the smart people who decide what the trends will be. The majority are left trapped in a world where they feel material things give them status.

As a criminologist and my role as a parent this causes me to be particularly concerned about the impact pressure to consume has on young Black people today. They are culturally included yet economically excluded. In other words, they share the same mainstream media-driven material expectations but are often unable to meet these aspirations through legitimate or legal ways. In some cases, young people will resort to violence for material gain and too often, the victims are people who look just like them.

Whether we believe that any links between Black males and crime are exaggerated by the media, the police and politicians, it would be unhelpful to deny that today, the number of young Black males who have been attacked and even killed by other young Black men is a problem we must admit and confront. However, to successfully deal with the problem we must understand it. Although many organisations in the UK are already involved in work that is geared towards preventing crime and violence amongst young Black males and steering them away from gang involvement, in many ways, many of these organisations are failing us and our young people. Although they may be well intentioned, they are often part of the problem rather than the solution and are based on weak belief systems.

These dodgy organisations assume that young people simply need something to do and believe that the solutions to our current problems lay in the creation of more youth centres and programmes that facilitate music and sports activities to divert young people from gangs and criminal activities. Others push the idea that 'positive role models' will somehow give our young people hope and ambition. It concerns me that the adults that run these places have been conditioned to believe that Black young people are the problem rather than the 'sick' psychopathic societies that they live in. Along with well meaning (or sometimes not) teachers, youth workers and social workers, they think that getting young people to conform to mainstream values (which incidentally, no other groups adhere to) is the solution. The continuous violent incidents between young people from different 'ends' or postcode areas in towns and cities across the UK however, suggest that we have not got to grips with the problem.

The main source of these problems is not new. We've just stopped talking about it. This is the result of racism - the same racism that has existed since at least the mid-15th century. Adults want to pretend that things are not as bad as they used to be and that in terms of 'race relations' we have come a long way. They'll highlight the fact that there are more 'Black faces in high places' but they'll sweep the issues of suspicious Black deaths in custody and police brutality under the carpet. Failing to understand and address the everyday realities of institutional racism in the education system, criminal justice system, and the media can impact the way that young Black people see the world. Other than keeping young people occupied, these organisations can do little in the way of providing any real solutions to these issues. Whilst the programmes and activities they offer may give young people the skills and opportunities to compete in music and sporting events; to find employment, they often fail to provide them with the tools they need to navigate the streets.

Many of the young people I have spoken too since I started

researching youth crime felt their teachers had labelled them as troublemakers and that they were unfairly victimised by teachers who fully expected them to fail. They were afraid their parents wouldn't believe them, they hold negative views about school. Rather than seeing school as an opportunity to advance their education, the school environment is a stressful one in which they're forced to share their space with adults who disliked them, disrespect and wield power over them. Likewise, young people often feel that telling their parents about incidents of police harassment, brutality and racism is also pointless. If their parents are unsupportive about their experiences in school, they feel that their parents would either think that they must have done something wrong in the first place; even if their parents are sympathetic, they're powerless to do anything about it.

Whether the view that Black parents are disconnected from their children and unable to support them is justified or not, what we must accept is the perception many of our young people have. Although this disconnection is not confined to the Black community, the daily risks they face which lead many of them to believe that they will not live beyond the age of 25, cannot be ignored. However, they can't solve this on their own and need the support of both parents and the wider community.

Whilst many organisations currently funded to work with young Black people do not recognise racism and injustice as a significant problem, those that do, think that it can only be challenged by Black integration into mainstream organisations and institutions. They will often argue that only by educating ourselves and getting into their institutions can we bring about effective changes. However, experience and history teaches us that the state and its institutions have no interest in empowering our communities and our young people. Black people have been dying under suspicious circumstances whilst in police custody since the 1960s and over 50 years later, their families have still not seen justice. Despite the introduction of laws against racism and discrimination, racism in the police and the criminal justice system, in mental health and education continues to affect Black communities disproportionately. Despite the obvious contradictions between the words and actions of those in power, the unthinking amongst us remain convinced that racism and justice for Black people can be fought for from the inside and are suspicious when they see Black people organise to achieve self-determination.

The impact and consequences of racism and the discriminatory treatment of Black people in the UK over the past 60 years is explored in detail in my PhD research paper. Whilst it is too complex to explain in detail here, what I essentially demonstrate is that in the 1960s and 1970s there was a greater sense of community, self-help and cultural pride. I show how this has been gradually eroded and how it has been replaced with a divided and selfish outlook. Increasingly, we are no longer looking out for ourselves and the community that we say we love.

By focusing on 'our own', we often make the mistake of thinking that if our children are alright then we are doing 'our bit'. However, what should to be considered is that when it comes to racism and injustice, Black people are more likely to be victims whatever their class, background, religious beliefs. Only being honest about what our young people are up against, by putting aside our ideological differences and coming together to work for the betterment of our communities, can we hope to make any progress in reducing the violence and other social problems. No matter how well some of us think we are bringing up our children and how much we think we are protecting them from the street, crime and negative influences, those of us who lack the resources to move away must bring up their children in the same environment as other young people who may not have the same guidance.

As a community, we need to begin to look at all young Black people as 'our' children and 'our' responsibility, because whilst we may be able to keep our children in school, college, work and other so-called 'productive' activities, they are bound to have negative encounters with their peers. A substantial amount of robberies and violence amongst young people take place after school rather than at night and a trip to the local shops, football practice, computer class, a youth centre or any other constructive activity could end up in a robbery or violent attack. A friend of mine describes it as sending a child into a jungle and expecting them not to get attacked. We also need to understand that victims and perpetrators are often the same people. It is no huge leap for a young person who is victimised to become a perpetrator, especially if they feel, rightly or wrongly, that they need to respond so they do not become a victim themselves.

Many young people that I speak to who are in gangs say that a positive aspect of being in a gang is the sense of family, belonging and protection which is extremely important to them.

Out of touch with the plight of its young people and lacking insight into their realities, the older generations of Black people and organisations that work with them, need to communicate more effectively, recognise, take seriously their concerns and begin to see all young Black people as *their* responsibility. Only then can they offer effective support to reduce the number of young people involved in self-destructive behaviour.

Until then 'real' will continue to recognise 'real', for the young people who are fortunate enough to become enlightened and empowered (by the very few organisations and individuals who give their time), I wish them more power and acknowledge that although it's on a small scale, the seeds of change are being planted.

Essay Eleven

5th May 2003

A question to the Pagan
Written by Davis J. Williams

"The Black skin is not a badge of shame, but rather a glorious symbol of national greatness."
Marcus Garvey

I was out with a few friends in this club on a Friday night. Everything was splendid, the girls were in full effect, drinks were two for the price of one and the music was causing havoc on the dance floor; I love my hip-hop, broken beat and anything else that contains that funk!

"Yo blood, yo <u>blood</u>,"

I was in unknown territory, in a post code that was foreign to me, so I was certain no-was hollering at me. Even though I travelled a lot, I knew for sure no one could be referring to me as "blood, yo blood" I am a grown-ass man!

The music continued to move me, I danced and grooved until my flow was interrupted by the sound of a bottle dropping on the floor followed by unexplainable commotion coming from a dark corner.

My few mates and I took no notice.

These things happen and being an older person gives you that '**steady**' in such situations. There was no need for any of us to act paranoid because we were not involved in foolish road drama. We remained cool, calm and collected.

The music switched up, and the tempo slowed right down. It was that time to find a chick to grind myself on. Everyone scattered to find their corner and their potential dance partner; it was like the January sales.

There it was again,

"Yo **blood**"

Those who were hanging out in the dark corner revealed themselves by flashing their lighters. There were several guys who were wearing hoods, black gloves and their eyes were piercing through the darkness, looking in our direction. Some of these suspicious characters remained posted in their corner, whilst others repeatedly went outside, only to return several minutes later. They must have made several journeys outside in the space of 10 minutes.

It was me and two others who remained, as we didn't find a girl that matched our specification. Whilst the others danced we went outside to search for that special girl.

"Mmmm, the breeze is nice and refreshing. I hate these sweat boxes, especially when certain people don't wash"

"What? Like your girl?"

"My girl is your mama."

My friend and I started laughing as we began to diss each other like the good old days.

"Yo blood"

It was that damn voice again! This time I knew he was talking to us. I noticed the eyes of an extremely short, dark-skinned dude fixed on me. I had enough of this bullshit so I decided to go and tell the guys what was going on, but these unsavoury characters blocked my route to the basement.

There was only me and one other, everyone else who came out with us was dancing in the corner with some hood rats downstairs. I began to feel paranoid and even though I assumed that my friends were dancing somewhere in the club, I hoped that they would come outside real soon.

"Yo, yo, yo!"

There he goes again… I really did not have a clue what was going on, all I knew was that I came here to have fun and these guys are trying to intimidate me. Why?

Out of the group emerged a short black boy who started walking towards me mumbling at the same time,

"Why you looking at my girl FAM?"

"Who is your girl?" I replied instantly.

"Don't play dumb FAM, why you watch her?"

(In my head, I said "it's watching her you dumb fuck.")

"Who is your girl?" I asked.

"Don't piss me off, I saw you clocking her! Where you from?"

This guy had a damn short temper why is he getting all aggressive over nothing? I knew I should have left this blue hoodie at home, now this guy thinks I am a pagan who got caught slipping. He was getting even more irritated as his friends quickly disappeared into the background only to re-emerge behind me. I had to act quickly because if these fools press my button then I will have to show them my age. Turning away was not an option, because I  was surrounded with nowhere to run and my friends were downstairs, not that I needed them but this was not a situation I had asked for.

"One last time blood, where you from? Are you a pagan? Talk you pussy pagan."

I could not take this anymore, as I had no choice but to give this matter some real attention and energy.

In a loud, articulate dictator-type voice I said

"Me? You're calling me a pussy? You guys are taking it too far now. I seriously thought I knew you from one of the schools I teach in. You're really being serious, right? You're really trying to stick attitude onto me like I am your age. Let me tell you something, I am old enough to be your dad, damn, I probably know your dad, I am a grown-ass man trust me."

I began to size up and screwed my face!

"Who the hell are you calling a pussy? I don't know about you, but I love the soft texture slide upon my dick, I would never call my enemy or someone I got issues with a pussy. Are you saying that you want to enter me bro? Do you seriously hate the woman's vagina like that?"

"Furthermore, who are you calling a pagan? You're there rolling up on me angling for a postcode? A postcode FAM? The Queen owns your postcode! You're rolling up on me, someone who looks *just like you*, someone you should be showing respect and solidarity towards, but like a true pagan you will happily and freely work for The Crown and her employees targeting young black males. You're an agent for the system mate! You're a traitor. You should be stepping to the people who placed you in shitty accommodation and litter your deprived area with betting offices, dirty chicken shops and off licenses everywhere you look."

"You should be stepping to the people who stop and search you at every opportunity, causing you distress with their early morning raids or their unjustified aggression when they arrest you for no reason at all. You should ask them why we are more likely to get stopped and search more times than anyone else, surround them and demand answers. About you're coming to me!"

"At the same time, go and ask your employers for a pay rise because you're not being paid enough. Your employer is the police because right now you're doing what they want you to do."

"But wait, you're looking at me like you don't know what the fuck I am talking about."

"Listen here, did you not know that you are working for the government? Unemployment is a myth, it is not real, and you are someone's cash cow, buddy."

"Did you not know that you are a pagan, an undercover, sleeper cell like Jason Bourne in that film? The system has you working for them. You make them huge amounts of money bro. Every time you or your clique get arrested and face a sentence in jail, you make them money. Understand that your black arse in prison costs £160,000 per year. That's right, £160,000 a year for one young person like you to be in jail! Didn't you know that prison is a private company, run by shareholders who are in it for a profit? Didn't you know? Someone lied to you; they told you that I was the enemy."

"But wait, there's more. When you go prison you are more likely to reoffend and live in poverty. The £160,000 that you're worth could pay for approximately three people to attend Eton School, the best school in this country, for a year. You're the pagan, pagan!"

"You should be stepping to the local business owners who set up shop in your area and sell you, your mum and grandma old, dirty and decaying meat. Meat that they would not feed to their dog. You need to protest and call them into account."

"You need to be challenging the education system. Why do young black males excel in primary school yet fail considerably in secondary school? African-Caribbean boys in particular, start their schooling at broadly the same level as other pupils, but during the course of their education fall further and further behind so that roughly 70% of African-Caribbean pupils leave school with less than five higher grade GCSEs. This represents the lowest level of achievement for any ethnic group of school children. In national examinations, African-Caribbean boys have been the lowest achieving group at practically every key stage for the past four years. Unsurprisingly the most recent census indicated that African-Caribbean men were the least likely of all men to have a degree or equivalent qualification."

"You need to creep up on the media and demand answers as to why teenagers are often portrayed as a hoodie, or a gang members who have no morals or values. Go and ask them. Furthermore, go to the Houses of Parliament and ask them to reduce your student tuition and give you more opportunities, centres and platforms for young people and their development because right about now, you have nothing."

"Why don't you take all that pent-up aggression you have and go on Twitter and ask Jay Z or Kanye West to stop putting subliminal satanic messages in their music? You know they are a part of a secret society, right? Go holla at Lil Wayne and ask him why he's wearing low batty skinny jeans with Uggs and then decides to kiss Birdman on the lips?"

"Oh wait, your jeans are skinny. Why can I see your boxer shorts FAM? That's not a sign of a true man, it's quite clear that the media and other external forces got you doing things that you are unaware of."

"I am not your enemy, I am your brother, here to protect, guide and advise. Your aggression is misdirected and right about now, you're being a pagan and a traitor to those who hustle everyday trying to escape the claws of a system that is oppressing us all."

As I continued to spout my frustration, one by one, the guys disappeared.

5

Take Break, Breathe, Inhale, Exhale and come again

What makes a young black male look at someone who could be his brother and feel such anger, distaste and animosity, that he will take a blade and shank him (stab)?

Or produce a gun and...

Bang...Bang!

What has happened?

Would a white guy get the same treatment?

Why do they call it black on black crime when white people kill each other too?

What is it about young black males that make them act in such a hostile and self-destructive way?

I am no researcher, nor a professional in this field, nor am I saying I have the answers; all I am saying is that there is something serious going on here.

When I was, younger I remember receiving an email about a story of a little boy named Michael, who woke up one morning and asked his mother, "Mom, what if there were no Black people in the world?"

His mother thought about that for a moment, and then said, "Son, follow me around today and let's just see what it would be like if there were no Black people in the world. Now go get dressed and we will get started."

Michael ran to his room to put on his clothes, and shoes. His mother took one look at him and said, "Michael, where are your shoes, and those clothes are all wrinkled, son. I must iron them." But when she reached for the ironing board, it was no longer there.

You see, Sarah Boone, a black woman, invented the ironing board and Jan E. Matzeliger, a black man, invented the shoe-lacing machine. "Oh well," she said, "please go and do something with your hair."

Michael ran to the room to comb his hair, but the comb was not there. Walter Sammons, a black man, invented the comb.

Michael decided to just brush his hair, but the brush was gone. You see Lydia O. Newman, a black female, invented the brush.

Well this was a sight, no shoes, wrinkled clothes, hair a mess, even Mom's hair, without the hair care inventions of Madam C. J. Walker, well you get the picture.

Mom told Michael, "Let's do our chores around the house and then take a trip to the grocery store."

Michael's job was to sweep the floor. He swept and swept and swept. When he reached for the dustpan, it was not there. You see, Lloyd P. Ray, a black man, invented the dustpan. So he swept his pile of dirt over in the corner and left it there. He then decided to mop the floor, but the mop was gone. You see, Thomas W. Stewart invented the mop.

Michael yelled, "Mom, I'm not having any luck."

"Well son", she said,

"Let me finish washing these clothes and we'll write a list for the grocery store." When the wash finished, she went to place the clothes in the dryer, but it was not there. You see, George T. Sampson, a black man, invented the clothes dryer.

Mom asked Michael to fetch a pencil and some paper to prepare their shopping list. Michael ran for the paper and pencil, but noticed the lead was broken. Well, he was out luck because John Love, a black man, invented the pencil sharpener. Mom reached for a pen, but it was not there because William Purvis, a black man, invented the fountain pen.

They made their way over to the car and found that it just wouldn't go. You see, Richard Spikes, a black man, invented the automatic gearshift and Joseph Gammel invented the supercharge system. Then they noticed that a few cars were crashing into each other because there were no traffic signals. You see, Garrett A. Morgan, a black man, invented the traffic light.

It was getting late, so they walked to the market, bought their groceries and returned home. Just when they were about to put away the milk, eggs and butter, they noticed the refrigerator was gone. John Standard, a black man, invented the refrigerator. So, they just left the food on the counter.

Mike felt a little cold. Mom went to turn up the heat, and what do you know? Alice Parker, a black woman, invented the heating furnace. Even in the summer time they would have been out of luck because Frederick Jones, a black man, invented the air conditioner.

It was almost time for Mike's father to arrive home. He usually took the bus. But there was no bus because its precursor was the electric trolley which was invented by another black man, Elbert R. Robinson.

He usually took

the elevator from his office on the 20th floor, but there was no elevator because Alexander Miles, a black man, invented the elevator.

He usually dropped off the office mail at a nearby mailbox, but it was no longer there because Philip Downing, a black man, invented the letter drop mailbox and William Barry invented the postmarking and cancelling machine.

Mike and his mother sat at the kitchen table with their head in their hands. When the father arrived, he asked, "Why are you sitting in the dark?"

Because Lewis Howard Latimer, a black man, invented the filament inside the light bulb.

Mike quickly learned what it would be like if there were no black people in the world. Not to mention if he were ever sick and needed blood. Charles Drew, a black scientist, found a way to preserve and store blood, which led to him starting the world's first blood bank.

You don't hear stories like this in school nor in mainstream media so we can only rely on stories from the elders, from mum or dad, or personal research.

Even though I showed little interest in my parents' stories they always made a point of telling me about when they came here on a boat from the Caribbean on November 5th 1965. They called this period 'Windrush' because people from the West Indies rushed Great Britain, like the wind (shu) in hopes of a better life. When my mother arrived here, she often recalled the Brits living in the Dark Ages. I heard that they never washed, the roads were littered with rubbish and they were racist and ignorant. Regardless of how immigrants improved Britain's standard of living, they never received any acknowledgement or appreciation for this from white people. Despite the racial hatred, discrimination and miscarriages of justice, those who came here managed to stay together, as a community, strived, schemed and progressed.

Nowadays, this community, and the families within it, seem fragmented, separated, diluted and impotent. There seems to be no commonality.

Things were not always this way.

They say when America sneezes, Great Britain catches the cold, so when I'm referring to GREAT BRITAIN, there are things that happened in the United States that could also apply here because the Black family in America is also fragmented, diluted and retarded.

Not so long ago in 1921, the so-called 'Black Wall Street' flourished in America. However, this thriving community was burned to the ground by scores of envious white people who believed in God and the bible and regarded blacks as slaves and saw themselves as the superior race. As a matter of fact, they saw themselves as the only race. In a twelve-hour siege, a once thriving black business district in northern Tulsa, USA, lay smouldering. The community was destroyed and a major African-American economic movement was snuffed out like a candle.

About 3,000 African-Americans died, and over 600 successful businesses were lost in an instant, all because of the colour of their skin. The white supremacists showed other black communities about the consequences of hope – the audacity of hope.

How dare these black animals try and make themselves

independent of the white man.

The thought of these former slaves organising themselves and becoming successful and independent petrified many white people and the only way to ensure their power structure remained INTACT and WHITE was for them to keep the Black man poor and dependent. A beautiful town blown up by people who hated us, because they believed that blacks were cursed with black skin and that blacks were not human, but animals.

If you're black, African and reading this, they saw you as an animal and treated you like one at every opportunity. No hiding, no discretion, no secret whispers. They would look you in the face and tell you how they felt.

Many people referred to this area in America, this "Land of the Brave", as little Africa or the mini-Beverly Hills. This city was an example of excellence, success and sustainability and proved to everyone that these former slaves had a successful infrastructure. That's what Black Wall Street was about. The black business owners took pride in *re-educating* their *children* to ensure that the next generation improved upon the foundations created by their parents.

The mantra of the community was to educate every child and return to greatness.

The dollar circulated 50 to 1500 times, sometimes taking a year for currency to leave the community. Nowadays, money leaves the black community in 15 minutes. Furthermore, how many black owned areas do you know of? I can name areas where all the businesses are owned by white, Asian or Chinese people, but not one area that is black-owned.

The audacity of hope. How can these niggers believe in

progression when they are black?

During this period, it was not unusual for black people to be burned to death; - in fact, it was very common.

Hundreds of white families used to leave their homes, dressed in their Sunday best, as they went to watch a human being of African descent, burned to death, murdered, humiliated, tortured and dehumanised for everyone to see.

Lynching was the practice of killing people by hanging and was carried out by racist mobs in the United States from the late 18th century through the 1960s. Lynching took place most frequently in the southern American states from 1890 to the 1920s. Lynching was used to maintain white supremacy in the South to prevent African-Americans being granted civil rights, including the right to vote.

In their minds, niggers are not seen as human so no human rights need to be given!

As a result of this type of thinking, black people were lynched on a regular basis.

Lynchings were never enough though.

"Whilst these burned, dead and lifeless niggers hang there, on fire, onlookers used to wait for the corpse to cool down so the children in particular could approach the crispy burnt nigger and begin to take body parts for their collection. If it was a male who was burnt, the penis was always the first thing spectators would take to place on their fireplace. Fingers, ears, toenails, eyelids, pieces of skin, you name it, it was claimed as memorabilia."
From the book, Without Sanctuary

In May 1918, a 31-year old white plantation owner named

Hampton Smith, known to abuse and beat his workers, was shot and killed on the plantation by one of his black workers a 19-year old Sydney Johnson. Earlier that day Johnson had been beaten by Smith for not working while he was sick.

Smith's death was followed by a week-long mob-driven manhunt in which at least 11 people were killed. Among those killed was another black man called Hayes Turner. Distraught, his eight-month pregnant wife Mary, publicly protested her husband's murder and threatened to have members of the mob arrested. The mob then turned against her.

She was dragged from her home by a mob of several hundred, who brought her to Folsom Bridge over Little River, which separates the Brooks and Lowndes counties; all this for one black woman who was grieving her husband and heavily pregnant.

They tied her ankles, hung her upside down from a tree, doused her in gasoline and motor oil, lit a match and set her on fire.

While Mary Turner was still alive, a member of the mob split her abdomen open with a knife.

Her unborn child fell on the ground, where it gave a cry before it was stomped on and crushed.

Crushed like a bug.

Finally, Mary Turner's body was riddled with bullets.

Image the impression this action left in the mind of Black observers. How likely would it be for them to step out of line?

Lynching was a popular and exciting pastime for many white families; for them, going to a lynching was a leisure activity, to help them relax and wind down in the great outdoors, whilst eating food and catching up. It was typical to have a picnic on a weekend in America, especially in the South. The word 'picnic' was short for 'pick a nigger' to lynch.

Black Wall Street flourished from the early 1900s until June 1, 1921. It was on that hot summer day when the USA allowed the largest massacre of non-military Americans in the history of the country. It was led by the Ku Klux Klan, local governmental officials and other murderers.

Yes, that's right, it remains as the largest massacre of non-military **Americans** in the history of the USA. They were American citizens.

White families stood by and watched innocent families get slaughtered. What kind of mind does that?

It was estimated that between 1,500 to 3,000 people were murdered and either buried or thrown in mass graves around the city. Ancestors owned 13 million acres of land at the height of racism in America and showed the world that we had our act together and that we could not be destroyed. In the face of adversity, we rose and we progressed.

The FBI, CIA, KKK and other groups pledged to never let Black America rise again.

ACHOOOOO... America sneezed.

What has happened to us here in Britain? Meat?

A man will murder someone who looks just like him over a postcode, a colour or an insignificant argument or beef.

We are such a great people.

A symbol of our greatness was the building of the pyramids, and I am not just referring to the Great Pyramids in Africa, I am talking about the ones in China and Mexico, by the Aztecs, Mayans and Ancient Egyptians. Different civilizations with one very large similarity, pyramids; structures that were built thousands of years ago. Structures that the most advanced engineers of this modern age cannot replicate.

Simple as that!

Yes, there are pyramids in China too, but the Chinese government is keeping it a secret because they do not want the world to link Africa to China, even though it is well documented that Blacks existed in that region long before those who inhabit that region now. Just Google 'Pyramids in China' and see what you find.

There are numerous pyramids in Africa, but the one that stands out in architectural achievement is the 'Great Pyramid of Giza', the only one of the 'Seven Wonders of the Ancient World' which still exists today. Its size spans more than six hectares and is constructed from an estimated **2.3 million blocks** in one solid mass of stone with corridors leading to different chambers.

According to the ancient Greek historian Herodotus the Egyptians took twenty years to build this pyramid However, if that is true, they had to place one block in five minutes for twenty years without any interruptions and installed approximately 800 tons of stone every day, which is highly unlikely. I would say impossible, but anything is possible.

These ancient African people, who white racists say were wild and uncivilized, built this Great Pyramid which is in the centre of the land mass of the earth, at both the longest longitude and the longest latitude. It is orientated at almost exactly North, South, East and West points and only removed a mere three minutes from true North. I know that was some technical information, but the point is the technology back then did not exist for the Egyptians to achieve such a mathematical feat.

Many architects, engineers and scientists who have studied the structure of the Great Pyramid for periods stretching over a decade have admitted that they could not duplicate the structure even with the help of modern technology we have available to us now.

This, amongst other findings proves that Africans, have a culture bathed in glory, inventions and outright genius. Today, the picture looks totally different as the descendants of these African gods rely on past glories. They are politically, socially and economically impotent, and on top of that, we cannot even get on with each other.

Sure, things could be worse, but compare what we are doing now to our past achievements and it's clear there is a huge problem. Where has, the love gone?

There is a saying, "When the axe enters the forest the trees say look, the handle is one of us."

WE are the ones we have been waiting for!

Essay Twelve

23rd December 2005

Bloods and Crips Remix

Written by the alter ego known as Sobek Trismegitius (Davis J Williams)

"I'm 23 years old. I might just be my mother's child, but in all reality, I'm everybody's child. Nobody raised me; I was raised in this society."
Tupac Shakur

"Do you know why Bloods wear red and Crips wear blue?"
(Blood and Crips are America's biggest street gangs)

Since I was a little whippersnapper I have heard about the Bloods and the Crips. More recently, I have watched documentaries and videos on YouTube and even attended meetings where 'gangs' were the topic of conversation. I was told that one would be able to identify what gang a person belonged to by the colour they wear. Some gangs would wear red, whilst others would wear blue but green, purple and black were also worn. People talk about gangs but very rarely, maybe never, has anybody given the reasons why certain colours are worn.

Why green? Why blue? Why are some gang members prepared to take a life for wearing the wrong colour? No one has been able to provide me with a worthwhile explanation, so I had to do some research into this matter and this is what I came across.

For a long time, the colours of red and blue have been rivals. This rivalry is seen in sports, food/beverages, entertainment, politics, science and others.

Some companies will have the red and blue combined symbolizing internal conflict, as with Spiderman (Spiderman v Peter Parker); Superman (Clarke Kent v Superman); the National Football League (NFL) and the American Football League (AFL). Sometimes there is external opposition, like with Pepsi and Coke, Raw and Smackdown, or Liverpool vs. Everton – two English football teams who are based in the same city.

Here are some more examples:

Blue Wearing forces		Red Wearing Forces
Manchester City founded in 1880	VS	Manchester United Founded in 1878
Everton founded in 1878	VS	Liverpool founded in 1892
Democratic Party founded 1792	VS	Republican founded – 1854
Crips1969	VS	Bloods – 1972
WWE Smackdown – 1999	VS	Raw – 2002
Conservative 1834	VS	Labour 1900

I have always seen young gang members in my area representing certain colours, but I never really understood the reason why they hold one colour above another I don't believe that the colours were chosen randomly.

Masons, the occult and the Illuminati are mainstream examples of how secrets are kept hidden from the public.

It is a fact that the Federal Bureau of Investigation (FBI) has over 50,000 secret pages on Malcolm X that still remain classified and undisclosed. They've hidden 9/11 CCTV footage and the truth behind the 'war on terror', they will never reveal everything known about certain events. Do a quick search on Area 51. In the 1940's, newspapers and witnesses saw a UFO (Unidentified Flying Object) crash-land in a place called Roswell, near New Mexico. But, just like in the films, the US Government arrived at the scene, marked the area as restricted, and informed the media that it was nothing more than a hot air balloon that crash landed.

They threatened to shoot anyone who tried to enter the restricted area and labelled the location Area 51. People have presented excellent research proving that this location is now being used to perform numerous tests on alien life forms and alien technology. The reason why these divisions use different colours can be classified as occult knowledge.

I had to find out more as I was convinced that the use of red and blue did not originate from the Bloods and Crips.

When I was young I used to wear red all the time. Was I being influenced by someone indirectly brainwashing me to wear his or her favourite colour? Was there another reason?

The first thing I did was check out some dates to determine who came first from the list above and what colours they wore. In nearly all cases where there is a clash between the red side and the blue, the blue side came first. The blue teams/organisations etc. were the original.

Red is almost universally seen as:

- Danger
- Death
- Passion
- Aggression
- Hot
- Representing blood

Blue seems to represent:

- Protection
- Safety
- Relaxation
- Calming

The meanings or the colours are opposites, therefore logical to use them to represent opposing teams. For me, it was interesting to know that the blue side came first, but what did this mean? What did the colour blue represent?

There is one thing that these colours have in common.

THEY ARE ALL A FORM OF LIGHT.

ROY. G. BIV is an **acronym** for the sequence of colours known as the visible light spectrum (red, orange, yellow, green, blue, indigo and violet). It is known as the visible light spectrum because our sight is limited. We are surrounded by radio waves, microwaves and infrared waves that we can't see, but know they exist because we see the effects.

Light comes in many forms, which sounds strange but is true. The human body literally glows, emitting a visible light in extremely small quantities at levels that rise and fall within the day.

Research has shown that the body emits visible light, 1,000 times lower than the levels which can be seen with the naked eye. In fact, virtually all living creatures emit a very weak light.

To learn more about this faint visible light, scientists in Japan carried out an experiment. They found five healthy male volunteers in their 20s who were placed bare-chested in front of cameras in complete darkness in light-tight rooms for 20 minutes, every three hours.

The researchers found their body glow rose and fell over the day, with its lowest point at 10am and its peak at 4 pm, and then dropping gradually after that. These findings suggest there is light emission linked to the body clock, most likely due to how metabolic rhythms fluctuate over the course of the day.

Every living thing on this planet is made up of light. This is a fact that all scientists will confirm. Even plants absorb light from the sun and turn it into life in a process called photosynthesis. The sun is responsible for light.

This is when I began to realise how amazing the human body is. Through research, I found that the human body has its own energy field, sometimes referred to as the aura. How the sun can affect people's moods with how much light it produces, people too, produce light and this can influence other people. How many times have you been around someone, and for a strange reason, you just did not like their vibe? They haven't done anything, but you just did not like that person. What is all that about?

The human aura is the electromagnetic field that surrounds the human body, like Magneto from the X-Men series. The Human Energy Field is a collection of magnetic energies of varying densities that radiates (like the sun) from the physical body of a living person. Machines can measure this energy field and some humans can see auras with their naked eye. Auras are particles of spiritual, emotional, and mental energy that are suspended around the healthy magnetic human body. Check out these images.

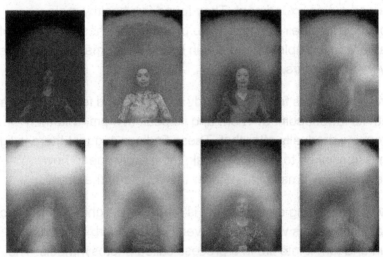

Other methods that can be used to highlight this energy include Kirlian photography, which captures the various light colours that a person radiates. It is truly amazing. As Bob Marley said, "Teach the youth the truth."

We are being lied to daily. Not only are we being lied to, but valuable information vital for our development, is being kept from us.

What I am about to reveal now requires extra study from you, because it is something that is not common knowledge. I am going to give you a crash course on the Chakras which are related to the colours red, and blue, and worn by the Bloods and the Crips.

Blue is protection, and blue is spiritual. In most cases, it seems as if blue came first when manifested through groups or occupation. Manchester City, the C.R.I.P.S, the Democratic Party and the Conservative Party all came before their opponents.

Those who subscribe to the principles of the colour blue were approached by those who preferred red, i.e. those who were carnal, angry, jealous and passionate.

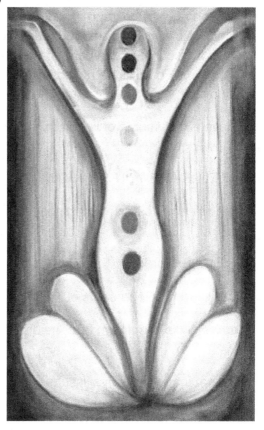

The true opposition of these colours can be seen in the Chakra system from Africa and the eastern world. Every ancient culture referred to this system which states that the human body has energy centres, called chakras which function like pumps regulating the flow of energy.

The seven chakras are

not visible to the human eye.

Microwaves are a type of light; infra-red and radio waves are a type of light, even though we cannot see them or acknowledge their existence.

Near your heart is a region called the solar plexus. Why did they call this area the solar plexus? We know that the solar is a reference to the sun. The same principle applies; you cannot see the solar plexus, and you cannot see any flames but just because you cannot see something does not mean it does not exist. You have a sun in your chest, an invisible sun that needs oxygen to survive and releases carbon dioxide. Just like a real fire. Only fire can produce carbon dioxide. Your body can produce natural heat. Where is the source of this heat? If you drink whiskey your solar plexus area will burn like a naked, visible flame when alcohol is thrown over it.

You have a real source of light within your chest that you cannot see. Cool, right?

WHAT ELSE ARE YOU NOT BEING TOLD?

As I am referring to these energy centres I should explain what they are.

The 7 Chakra's are:

1. Root Chakra: Represents our foundation and being grounded.

Location: Base of spine in tailbone area, near your sexual organs.

Emotional issues: Survival issues such as financial independence, money, and food.

This chakra is also associated with passion, anger, love and danger. There is a reason why you see red when you are angry. This is the lowest, most basic chakra.

Colour: Red.

2. Sacral Chakra - Our connection and ability to accept others and new experiences.

Location: Lower abdomen, about two inches below the navel and inches deep.

Emotional issues: Sense of abundance, well-being, pleasure, sexuality.

Colour: Orange

3. Solar Plexus Chakra - Our ability to be confident and in-control of our lives.

Location: Upper abdomen in the stomach area.

Emotional issues: Self-worth, self-confidence, self-esteem.

Colour: Yellow (like the sun).

4. Heart Chakra - Our ability to love.

Location: Centre of the chest, just above heart.

Emotional issues: Love, joy, inner peace.

Colour: Green

5. Throat Chakra - Our ability to communicate.

Location: Throat.

Emotional issues: Communication, self-expression, the truth.

Colour: Blue.

6. Third Eye Chakra - Our ability to focus on and see the bigger picture.

Location: Forehead between the eyes. (Also called the Brow Chakra)

Emotional issues: Intuition, imagination, wisdom and ability to think and make decisions.

Colour: Indigo.

7. Crown Chakra - The highest Chakra represents our ability to be fully connected spiritually.

Location: The top of the head.

Emotional issues: Inner and outer beauty, our connection to spirituality, pure bliss.

Colour: Violet.

Only root and the throat chakras are able to create, give birth, express and reveal to the visible world.

How so? The throat (blue) and the root (red) chakras are both able to reveal themselves through one's self-expression. These chakras are the only two that can do this.

These chakras are actual gateways and are in natural opposition. Through the root chakra one can create life though the power of sexual intercourse and sexual expression. However, the throat chakra is responsible for sound, words, song, communication and other forms of self-expression.

We are light beings, having a human, physical experience. The war on gangs is not a physical war, it is a spiritual war.

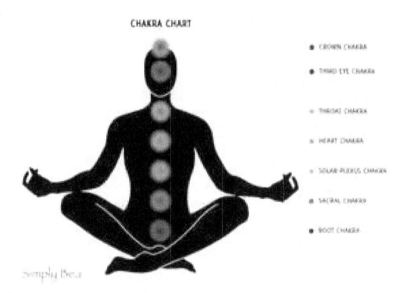

CHAKRA CHART

- CROWN CHAKRA
- THIRD EYE CHAKRA
- THROAT CHAKRA
- HEART CHAKRA
- SOLAR PLEXUS CHAKRA
- SACRAL CHAKRA
- ROOT CHAKRA

Essay Thirteen

14ᵗʰ September 2012

Y is a letter with a long tail/tale

Written by the alter ego known as Dexter St. Jock (Davis J Williams)

"Too many people spend money they haven't earned, to buy things they don't want to impress people they don't like."
Will Smith

Police Officer

(Policy Enforcer)

An agent of a private corporation with a monopoly on force, employed to intimidate, harrass and abduct anyone who fails to obey their corporate policies.

Why. W.H.Y. Three little letters that can have a huge impact.

Why, why, why?

Why is a letter with a long tale!

Why don't people like me challenging the status quo? Why am I being deceived daily? Everywhere I turn I am being lied to, why? Why do people always claim authority over me? Telling me what to do, watching me, bullying me, forcing me to do things I don't wish to do?

Why do they want me to feel like a slave? Powerless and obedient? The police are the biggest enforcers of this.

Why am I told that I am British? No one asked me what I wanted to be.

Why am I told that Britain is a great nation whilst Companies House refers to Great Britain being a registered business, trading for profit under liability? That means McDonald's and the UK belong in the same bracket. I thought I lived in a country, not a corporation or company.

Why does Great Britain hail three lions, when lions are found in Africa, not England?

Why is my three year-old son referred to as a 'Master'? Seriously, he received a letter from the local doctor and he was not called Mr. Jones, they called him Master Jones. Why am I, the adult, referred to as Mister and they refer to my son as a Master?

Why is my little girl called Lady? And her mother a Ms.? Why are those under 16 years old referred to as Master and when they turn 17 years of age - or thereabouts - and receive a National Insurance card, their title changes to a Mr.?

Why am I given this National Insurance number?

Why am I told that I can't work without one?

Why have I been bonded to this number?

Why have I been branded like my mobile phone?

Why was I told that I had to register my child at birth and in receipt of that registration I received a birth certificate?

Why was I forced, under duress, to register my child to a company that trades for profit? What are they trading? Who are they trading?

Why do people say "God save the Queen?"

Why don't people say, "God save everyone?" Is the Queen's life more precious than my own?

Why do people claim to have power over me? Are we not all born free?

Why do I vote?

Nothing ever changes. When I speak, nobody listens and when millions march, nothing happens. Things remain the same.

Why do I need permission to protest?

Imagine, I am against the Government who increases tuition fees, so I decide to protest, but to protest I must ask the same Government permission to do so?

Why am I so powerless?

Why does this £20 note say 'I promise to pay'?

What the hell is that all about?

Why is it a promise and not actual payment?

Is that not an I.O.U? I promise to pay?

Why is it called a pound, as in a pound in weight, when it's just a piece of paper? £50 of what exactly?

Why do people kill for this piece of paper that is made in a factory?

Why is there debt? Why are there complaints about not enough money when they can print as much money as they wish... literally?

Why do I get fined for everything?

Dropping litter; parking on a yellow line; travelling without a ticket; driving with no seat belt; driving and walking through certain zones and why am I paying road tax and insurance? The roads are an utter mess, potholes everywhere?

Why do I pay tax on tax? I work, they take tax, I shop, and I get taxed again. I then open a letter and it says Council Tax! I thought I paid that already?

Why are we made to fund our own debt?

Why are police officers referred to as public servants?

Why are public servants, who swear an oath to the Queen to serve and protect my property abusing us?

Why is a public servant, a person employed to protect me, asking me where I am going, searching my personal belongings and refusing to answer my questions?

Why are police officers more interested in issuing fines instead of catching the bad guys?

Their roadblocks. Their bus raids. Always for money, or seizing people's property.

I remember seeing a father, his shopping, his three kids, buggy, car seat, ego and power dumped onto the sidewalk as the police repossessed his car because he had two unpaid parking tickets. It cost so much to get the car out of the car pound that he never saw his car again.

Why are young black males more likely to get stopped and searched than any other racial group?

Why are young black males more likely to stab someone that looks like them?

Why is it a big issue when the NHS kills more people than gang members? People don't march about that?

Why do black people refer to themselves as a colour that is not descriptive of them? They are brown, and various shades of brown, not black. Why do white people fall into the same trap?

You are neither white nor black.Why don't things make sense?

Why am I told to register my property? It's mine, I paid for it! But I can't use it until I register it. Why am I told that I must register my car with the DVLA to use it and driving it without being registered is an offence?

Why is someone offended by my actions? I am not hurting, so why is it an offence? Who have I offended? The car is mine, isn't it, so what's the problem?

Why do they take taxes? I don't 'pay' taxes; it's taken without my permission.

Why do they then take my money and go to war with innocent nations without my consent? They rob and pillage other countries with my money and I don't get a share of the loot.

Why do I wear £120 trainers made by a six-year-old child who is paid £1.50 a day? Yes, per day. Why do I wear trainers named after Greek and Roman gods, namely Nike? What the hell...?

Why do I see chemtrails in the sky and poisonous ingredients in foods? Why isn't anyone marching and protesting this?

Why are they keeping DNA samples of innocent people who enter police stations unwillingly, on a massive database? They are innocent, they should be removed at once!

Why do I accept their poisonous vaccinations? Am I mad? Or just gullible? Am I afraid?

Why is fluoride in my toothpaste and mercury in my tooth fillings? Don't people know that fluoride was used in World War I as a weapon? Mercury is highly toxic, so much so that countries like Sweden and Austria\ have banned amalgam mercury fillings. Why does my favourite drink have aspartame in it? An artificial sweetener that, in the 1970s, was banned food due to its toxic effects. Aspartame which is found in sugar free food beverages and is 150 times sweeter than white sugar.

Why do people not seem to care about their health?

Records show that there were over 50,000 pages, yes, that's right, 50,000 pages of FBI documents on Malcolm X. Imagine for a second that you are being interviewed by the Police and they drop a massive 50,000 page document of evidence on the table! But check this though, the majority of the pages are not allowed to be seen by the public. They have been labelled classified! Now ask yourself, what are they not telling you? why are they not telling you?

Why?

Why do people pay to get sick eating rubbish, then when they are sick, pay to get better?

Why do these companies produce items that are harmful to our health? Surely that's immoral?

Why are people tricked into playing this game of tricks, a scam and a massive deception, whilst at the same time politicians claim everything is ok?

You've got your smartphone, television, money, your gadgets and Jerry Springer to keep you busy and distracted. Is this why you don't have time to address the things that really matter?

Why are humans dumb as fuck? It annoys me how stupid we are. Why do people smoke cigarettes knowing that it kills them? Damn, even on the cigarette box it clearly says "Smoking Kills" in big bold letters. People read it and then light up!

The media has introduced a bright light to blind and confuse everyone. We call them 'Superstars'; the so-called illuminated ones.

Why are some people so blind to the truth, regardless of what you tell them?

There was no letter J in the English alphabet until the 14th Century. That means his name could not have been Jesus. It's impossible and factual. Why don't you care?

Why are people screaming YOLO? Is this an excuse to do self-destructive things?

People are not afraid to die, they are afraid to live, why is that?

Why are people so fearful by nature? In 1999, the world was going to end. On 21st December 2012, the world was going to end and at the London Olympics aliens were supposed to come and destroy the planet?

Why do people focus so much on what they DON'T want instead of what they do want?

Who is responsible for this?

Why am I not taught that I have potential or about history or the power of the subconscious mind?

Why do I feel trapped? I have no chains or shackles on my body but I can't seem to free myself from the shackles of my mind.

Why do some people show love for their oppressors? I know my enemy hates me and does everything in their power to bring me down but I, for some strange reason, love and focus on them. It's similar to 'capture-bonding' otherwise known as the Stockholm syndrome; this is a psychological condition where a people in a hostage, prisoner or abusive situation.

Why do people who despise the system send their children to be educated by it?

Why don't people understand that Legalese is a language? It may sound like English but it is not.

Why are people oblivious to the language Legalese? Legal is the idea, the doctrine, the application, the codes and guidelines. But legalese is the language used by those who belong to the Law Society, those who administer legal processes.

Every legal professional owns a dictionary called Black's Law Dictionary; we might think the word 'person' means one thing, but in Black's Law Dictionary, it has a totally different meaning. So

much so that if you call yourself a 'person' in certain circumstances you might find yourself in trouble.

Why did a guy stop me randomly the other day and say that I owed him £230? I was like why, who are you and what do you want? He said I stepped on his shoe and under the Shoelace Act 2012; I was required to pay him for the offence. I was unaware of this act, but he showed it to me and asked me if I understood what it says. I read it and said, "Yes, I understand", and paid him his money, reluctantly.

If you believe that the Shoelace Act is real please put this book down!

Why do we willingly stand under various statutes and acts, even if we don't know what they are?

Why do they insist on governing over me, inspecting me regulating my activities?

Why do governments and their cronies assassinate anyone who reveal their hidden agenda? Tupac dead, Patrice Lumumba dead, Malcolm X dead, Michael Jackson dead, JFK and Robert Kennedy dead dead dead dead!

Why does Bill Gates want to eradicate BILLIONS OF PEOPLE because of his theory that the planet is over populated and because of this, the planet's temperature is increasing? IT'S TRUE! He spoke at TED's innovative conference where hundreds of people attended and heard him say that through health care, vaccines and reproductive services he plans to reduce the world's population.

Why are you even here? Why?

Why is a letter with a long motherfucking tale!

What is your WHY?

Essay Fourteen

14th December 1976

I am 5ive

Written by the alter ego known as 5ive (Davis J Williams)

"This is my simple religion. There is no need for temples; no need for complicated philosophy. Our own brain, our own heart is our temple; the philosophy is kindness"
Dalai Lama

There lived a person called 5ive. I know, it's a very unusual nickname and one can only assume that 5 is his lucky number, or something significant happened on that day. Or maybe he stutters, and on the 5th time trying, he manages to release the word he was trying to present on the four previous occasions.

One can only assume.

From 50 Cent, U2, 98 Degrees, Soul II Soul to Wretch 32, Three Six Mafia and UB40. There are many groups and individuals who use numbers as a part of their name. Even though the words are obvious, the numbers are often symbolic.

Words and numbers; heads and tails; hot and cold; two sides of the same coin.

Most people understand one side of the coin (words) but when it comes to the other side (numbers) many are left to assume and presume. Numbers, like words, also have value, history and etymology.

Numerology is the study of numbers, dates, cycles and astrological references and these sciences give a clearer meaning to random numbers, because in fact, there is no such thing as a random number.

There are people in prestigious positions, governing our affairs, who understand the power of numbers, dates and they use that knowledge to their advantage.

Barack Obama, George Bush, Bill Clinton and many other presidents and influential people around the world enlist astronomers to inform them of the best time to make a deal, or to go to war, to travel or to pass certain laws. They never choose random dates, NEVER.

The release date of this book also has astrological undertones.

The continuous use of this method is known as a ritual.

Rituals have a religious undertone, but rituals are not always religious.

Brushing your teeth in the morning is a ritual. Michael Jordan extending his tongue whilst in mid-air is a ritual. David Beckham's stance before he takes a free kick is a ritual. Damn, the way you close your eyes to think every time you're confused is a ritual. Rituals have existed since the dawn of time. Most of us have rituals, whether it is your morning tea and newspaper to get your day flowing, or going to church every Sunday to wearing pink gloves in the belief that it will give you luck.

It's just a series of actions performed to achieve a particular response.

When you begin to study this subject, you will begin to notice that there are many people who believe in the science of numbers;

with words things are pretty obvious, but when it comes to numbers, a person needs to have an analytical mind.

As a youngster, I was never into numerology or astronomy and to be honest, I didn't even know what it was. As I have grown older and gained more knowledge, read certain books and paid attention, I have seen certain patterns in dates, times, and numbers corresponding with historical events.

This information can easily be researched on the internet or in various books.

Understand this; there are 26 characters in the alphabet, commonly referred to as A-Z. We can say with confidence that there are 26 letters in the English alphabet however, how many numbers exist?

Infinity, right? Numbers are unlimited.

That is in fact a myth!

It is important to understand that there are only 9 numbers.

That's right, only nine (9) numbers exist.

They are 1,2,3,4,5,6,7,8,9

Every number after 9 is called a compound number, that is, a number consisting of a combination of other numbers. So 10 is a combination of 1 and 0.

23 is a combination of 2 and 3.

So the highest number known is 9 and the lowest is 1.

The same rule also applies to letters. There are 26 letters in the alphabet however these letters are also combined, just like numbers, to form words. The more letters you combine, the more complex the word becomes, forming sentences, paragraphs or books.

Letters and numbers are opposite sides of the same coin.

The understanding and decoding of numbers is referred to as numerology, which studies the relationship between numbers, words and life.

Within this system, numerologists present the numbers, and what each number means. For example, the number six is said to represent death. Why? Keep on reading and you will soon discover why many believe this to be the case.

Let me share something I discovered, which took me ages to unpack. I still don't understand its full significance, but one thing is for sure, there is a blatant pattern.

Try this at home. You need a chart that gives each letter a corresponding number, why? Because letters and numbers are both sides of the same coin; in numerology, letters are given a numerical value.

A-1	B-2	C-3	D-4	E-5	F-6
G-7	H-8	I-9	J-10	K-11	L-12
M-13	N-14	O-15	P-16	Q-17	R-18
S-19	T-20	U-21	V-22	W-23	X-24
Y-25	Z-26				

So let's decode my name, my date of birth and everything else about me.

The name of my road is Middle Road.

5 is the number that sits in the middle, with 1 to 4 to its left and 6 to 9 to its right, making number 5 the gate.

123456789

Also Middle Road has 10 characters, and the MIDDLE of 10 is 5!

My house number is 14.

Remember, there are only nine numbers, everything else is a compound number, therefore, in numerology 14 becomes 1+4 = 5.

We always want a single digit.

Davis has 5 letters.

Davis J Williams has 14 letters (1+4=5).

Davis John-Athane Williams has 23 letters (2+3=5).

D is the 4th letter in the alphabet, and J is the 10th, mum sometimes called me DJ.

DJ (4+10=14) 1+4=5.

W (2+3=5).

Davis (4+1+22+9+19) = 55.

John-Athane Williams
(10+15+8+14+1+21+8+1+14+5+23+9+12+12+9+1+13+19= 195).

19x5=9+5= 14, 4+1=5 (ok I broke the rules but who said there were rules?).

In a nutshell, my given name, Davis John-Athane Williams is 5.

My child, Makaylah Safiya Williams was born on the 5th October.

There are different ways you can add up 52 + 11.

You can add 5+2 +1+1 or 52 + 11.

Below I tried both.

Makaylah.

13+1+11+1+25+12+1+8 = 72 (7 minus 2= 5).

Or

1+3+1+1+1+1+2+5+1+2+1+8 = 27 (2 minus 7 = minus 5).

Safiya 19+1+6+9+25+1 = 61.

Makaylah Williams = 16 letters (6 – 1= 5).

Ma'Kai has 5 letters.

Makai's weight was 7IL 7 (7+7=14) 1+4=5.

The gap between Makai and Makaylah (my two children) is 5 years.

I am 5 foot 9 inches (14, 1+4=5).

Makada and Micah were expected on the 23rd October 2010 (2 + 3 = 5).

I was born on the 14th day (1 + 4 = 5).

My year of birth is 1976 (1+9+7+6 = 23 2+3 = 5).

My shirt number at football is 14.

My dad was born on the 5th month and 5th day.

His birth year was 1933 1+9+3+3= 16 and yes, 6-1=5.

I am the 5th member of my family.

My mobile number is 07939396465 (61, 6-1=5).

My dad's sister, the only one in this country also has five members in their family.

Before my dad made the transition, he was in hospital for five weeks.

My dad could not read or write, but he was a master mathematician and taught me to draw this picture from a very young age; this picture consisted of five vertical lines next to each other. When you joined the lines up, it would form a number five.

Why he taught me this?

I don't have a clue!

5
Take Break, Breathe, Inhale, Exhale and come again

I don't understand why five occurs numerous times throughout my name, my children's name, or the daily occurrences where the number five reveals itself to me.

Despite all this, I don't understand the significance of five, I just know it's here, there and everywhere.

Based on numerology, the number 5 is prominent in my life,

#iamjustsaying.

What secret does this hold?

We shall see.

But wait, there's more.

Let's talk about world events for a moment, because the calculations I made didn't just apply to me.

I could actually write a whole chapter or even a book on September 11th and the wars in Iraq and Afghanistan. I've watched dozens of YouTube clippings regarding September 11th, what was said about what happened and what really happened. The footage and testimonies from people at Ground Zero is astounding, but for me the thing that really caught my attention was the hidden meanings behind the dates.

Let's take a little look at these dates and decide if it this is all just a coincidence.

The Date of the Attack: 9/11 (9 + 1 + 1= 11).

September 11th is the 245th day of the year (2 + 5 + 4= 11).

After September 11th there are 111 days to the end of the year.

911 is the Emergency Services Number. For USA: (9 + 1 + 1 = 11).

119 is the area code to Iraq/Iran (1 + 1 + 9 = 11).

Twin Towers – standing side by side looked like: 11.

The first plane to hit the towers was Flight No. 11.

The state of New York – the 11th State added to the Union.

New York City (11 letters).

Afghanistan (11 letters).

The Pentagon (11 letters).

Ramzi Yousef (convicted of orchestrating the attack on the World Trade Centre has 11 letters).

Flight 11 - had 92 people on board: (9 + 2 = 11).

Flight 77 - had 65 people on board: (6 + 5 = 11).

Revelation Ch.9 verse 11 means "Destruction".

What do you think about that?

Remember when I said that in politics, nothing happens by accident?

Everything is planned and coordinated weeks, months and even years in advance.

Check this information sent to me about US Presidents. Again, notice the dates and the relationship between them.

Abraham Lincoln was elected to Congress in 1846.

John F. Kennedy was elected to Congress in 1946.

Abraham Lincoln was elected President in 1860.

John F. Kennedy was elected President in 1960.

The names Lincoln and Kennedy each contain seven letters.

Both were particularly concerned with civil rights.

Both wives lost a child while living in the White House.

Both presidents were shot on a Friday.

Both presidents were shot in the head.

Lincoln's secretary was named Kennedy.

Kennedy's secretary was named Lincoln.

Southerners assassinated both.

Both were succeeded by Southerners named Johnson.

Andrew Johnson, who succeeded Lincoln, was born in 1808.

Lyndon B. Johnson, who succeeded Kennedy, was born in 1908.

John Wilkes Booth, who assassinated Lincoln, was born in 1839.

Lee Harvey Oswald, who assassinated Kennedy, was born in 1939.

Both assassins were known by their three names.

Both names are composed of fifteen letters.

Lincoln was shot at the theatre named "Kennedy."

Kennedy was shot in a car called "Lincoln."

Booth ran from the theatre and were caught in a warehouse.

Davis Williams

Oswald ran from a warehouse and was caught in a theatre.

Booth and Oswald were both assassinated before their trials.

A week before Lincoln was shot, he was in Monroe, Maryland.

A week before Kennedy was shot, he was in Marilyn Monroe.

It is said that every political event, from Barack Obama being elected, to Princess Diana crashing in that tunnel in Paris, took place at the right time, date and location. It was planned and coordinated.

But if we don't ask the right questions, we will never get any answers. If we choose to be lazy and robotic we will miss the warning signs. We are being manipulated every second of every day by agents of the system who wants us to remain blind.

We take things for granted and we show too much trust. Would you trust the person who attacked your mum? Would you confide in your enemy?

They told us the year is 2015. How do you know? I mean really? How do you know you're being told the truth?

They said Jesus is the Lord and Saviour. How do you know?

We are told from a young age that September is the ninth month of the year in the Gregorian calendar, but once you're aware of letters, language and numerology, you will understand that, in Latin, *septem* means "*seven*" and *septimus* means "*seventh*"; September was in fact the seventh month, not the 9th month as we are led to believe.

October is the tenth month of the year in the Gregorian calendar but its name, from the Latin 'Octo' means eight. But we say it's the 10th month (an octopus has how many legs?)

November is the eleventh month of the year in the Gregorian calendar. November got its name from the Latin *novem* meaning "nine", but we are told it's the 11th month.

December is the twelfth and last month of the year in the Gregorian calendar.

In Latin, *decem* means "ten"i.e. decimal means a number or system based on the number ten.

We never ask questions such as why they call it 'sweet 16'.

Why are 16th, 18th and 21st birthdays so significant?

People don't care about their 19th birthday, or their 20th, but when someone turns 21 years old, they go all out.

We need to pay attention because there's a war going on. Mental warfare. If someone can control the way you think, they can control you. Those who want to control you, understand the power of words and how they can trap your mind.

We've seen how letters forms words and various combinations of these words, forms sentences.

I have already explained how words are obvious, and numbers are symbolic. However this is a belief. Someone wants you to believe that words are obvious.

We are led to believe that words are self-explanatory, easy to understand, obvious and not symbolic. A PINEAPPLE is a PINEAPPLE. A PHONE is a PHONE, simple as that, right?

But, just like numbers, words can also contain hidden messages. Contradictory meanings and dual explanations.

Let's begin with the word 'SENTENCE'.

We are taught that a sentence is a combination of words grouped together to express a statement, question, command or a suggestion.

We also know that the word sentence is the same word used by a judge in a court of law.

Mumia Abu Jamal was **sentenced** to life in prison. Google him.

So here a single word means 2 different things.

1) Sentence = Combination of words.

2) Sentence = Period of time in jail.

Walk with me...

A child, 5 years old, who is very creative, <u>bright</u> and confident. His mother is proud and loves him to bits.

But at the age of 5, just before his 6th birthday, daddy left, never to return. He left his home, three children, his money, his stability and he leaves the mother devastated and with the burden of raising three children alone. Mother is bitter and angry; the love she once had for her little boy soon turns to rage. His creativity and confidence disgust her as these qualities remind her of the man she now hates, his father. The child is the splitting image of his pops, with the same nose, lips and complexion.

Mother directs her hatred for the father towards the little boy, regularly telling him he's stupid and useless just like his father at every opportunity.

She repeats this statement daily, with energy and intent:

"You're ugly, you're stupid and useless, just like your dad."

"You're ugly, you're stupid, and you're useless, just like your dad."

"You're **ugly**, you're **stupid**, and you're **useless**, just like your **dad**."

"**You're** ugly, you're stupid, **and you're** useless, just like **your** dad."

"You're ugly, you're stupid, and you're useless, just like your dad."

A mother's words along with the tone of her delivery just sentenced a young boy's mind to a life in prison.

From being a grade a student, he has now become useless and angry, thinks he is ugly and stupid and stopped living and achieving.

He is now 16 years old, on drugs and poorly educated, with a bleak future.

One of the most powerful tools used to control the mind is that of religion. In the past, the Roman Catholic Church would kill those who did not accept Jesus Christ. If you had beliefs that differed to that of those in authority you would be killed, publicly. Without labouring on this point, let's see if there are any encrypted words or messages within God or Jesus.

Let's have a little fun.

What is God spelt backwards? It's dog right?

Dog is man's best friend.

What does a Roman Catholic priest wear around his neck? A dog collar.

What is the attire of someone who is successful? Tie and collar.

When taking a dog for a walk what do you need? A lead (tie) and collar, essential for control. These same items are also used to imprison someone, be it slaves or alleged criminals.

What is a dog's favourite food? Sausage.

What is Jesus spelt backwards? Susej.

We are now in the year 2015AD, AD meaning Ano Domini or 'After the Death' of Jesus. A lot of people argue over the name Jesus Christ. But these are the facts.

There was no letter 'J' in any language prior to the 14th century. The letter J did not become widely used until the 17th century. The letter J is a new sound! James, Jack and Jill are new names. The language they spoke back then did not have or use the letter J. So what name were people calling 2015 years ago? His name definitely wasn't Jesus, so who is Jesus?

They say "sticks and stones can break your bones, but names can never hurt." However, according to this, words can cause harm and confusion. Words can definitely cause trauma, a lifetime of suffering, especially when the words formed create lies, deception and single, dominant stories.

I was taught in school that if I did not know what a word meant I should refer to the dictionary.

Now a dictionary, made famous by Noah Webster the lexicographer, is a tool used by the world to help us better understand the English language.

Dictionaries deal with diction, which is a style of enunciation in speaking. With this in mind, dictionaries focus on how the word is said, not what it means. It does not define what a word means, because if it did it would be called a DEFINEARY, a book that defines words, but a dictionary dictates. It instructs you how a word is pronounced and explains what a word means.

English is a very symbolic and carefully constructed language. The people who put it together invested many years to get it the way it is.

I heard stories of Merlin the magician who was supposedly involved in the creation of this dialect that we use now. Maybe it's true, maybe it's nonsense, who really knows? The bottom line is this; the English language is pretty strange.

Earlier in this chapter you were given two words. PINEAPPLE and TOOTHPASTE.

Now, I want you to SPELL them out loud to yourself.

Spell the words.

SPELL them.

SPELLING WORDS many people say is a **_spell_** in itself.

When you use certain words that are SPELT correctly and uttered in certain tones, the results CAN BE DEVASTATING.

To help us SPELL words correctly we use a dictionary.

PINEAPPLE and TOOTHPASTE.

These two words, pineapple and toothpaste are compound words. Just like 11, 12, 134 are compound numbers, two separate words, sometimes three or four different words can be combined to make a new word. Tooth and paste combined makes toothpaste, or pine and apple.

To drive this point home the dictionary has a sister book, called a thesaurus, which is another tool that we can use to better understand the English language; it provides a variety of different or similar words that all have the same meaning.

Keeping in mind everything that I have already said about the English language and its hidden meanings and subliminal suggestions, you may have noticed something strange about the word thesaurus. Upon closer inspection it is clear to see that thesaurus is a compound word.

THE-SAURUS.

The Saurus.

We all know what 'the' means, but what does 'SAURUS' mean?

I will give you a clue, Brontosaurus, yes that's right, it is a type of lizard!

Google the word 'Saurus'.

The LIZARD, why are our children referring to a book called The Lizard to help them in their English lessons?

Remember, the snake in the Garden of Eden was a type of lizard, or reptile, and we know that a lizard has a split tongue, meaning the snake is a liar.

"White man speak with forked tongue" **Tarzan**

The snake in the Garden of Eden was the Devil, many believe. God's number one enemy.

And to connect the dots, what is the Devil's number?

When you're dead you are buried, how many feet below the

earth?

What's that number?

English is not a language, it is a modified dialect created for a purpose; and just like slang, and people speak in code. English is a language full of hidden meanings. You may think you're saying one thing, but to the learned man or women, they hear something else.

Why is a snake associated with a liar? Because it has a forked tongue, the muscle responsible for speech and when some people speak they use deception, trickery and contradictions.

And why do people say "good morning?"

'Good morning' is the greeting many people use in the morning, but upon closer investigation, **good morning** actually means good mourning. I am now wondering if it is good morning or good mourning which is synonymous with grief over the death of someone.

Another word that is associated with mourning/morning is the word WAKE.

Its 5am and you hear your mum calling you, asking several times "are you awake, are you awake?" Wake up. Now, we all know what 'A wake is'. A wake is a ceremony associated with death. Traditionally, a wake takes place in the house of the deceased, with the body present.

Need I say more? How much do we know about this language we call English?

Let me get a quick drink, almond milk, banana, Irish moss and ginger it is.

5
Take Break, Breathe, Inhale, Exhale and come again

Ohhh kayyy, I have reloaded!

You can tell a lot about a person by what they create, because their creation is a reflection of their beliefs, ideas and values.

I am not a religious person, but people identify the 'Mark of the Beast' with something evil, demonic and ungodly. People who read the Bible are aware of the quote that makes reference to this mark.

The Bible makes it very clear and even though not everyone believes in Christianity, the ruling classes do and they have based a system on it, a system that governs us all. Whether the Bible is a book of fact, myth or allegory the issue remains: **The origins of religion is so dodgy, there are too many discrepancies to simply ignore.**

Many ignore gravity, but it exists, whether the doubters believe it or not, they are still governed by gravity. They might refer to the force as something else as this eases their ego, but that force, by whatever name still exists. The Bible says:

[16]And he causeth all, both small and great, rich and poor, free and bond, to receive a mark in their right hand, or in their foreheads. [17]And that no man might buy or sell, save he that had the mark, or the name of the beast, or the number of his name. [18]Here is wisdom. Let him that hath understanding count the number of the beast: for it is the number of a man; and his number is six hundred threescore and six.

At some point this 'mark' became the controlling factor in one's ability to survive economically or even physically on Earth. Also, the 'mark' was thought to carry the curse of God to the point of one even being cast into 'Hell', itself. Quoting from Revelation: (13:16 to 18).

What is the historical meaning behind the number '666'?

Long ago, a numbering system was established called the Roman numeral system. In that system 666 is deciphered as VI VI VI. In the Latin language, this refers directly to: Vini, Vidi, Vinci. These words have the distinct meaning -"I came, I saw, I conquered."

Are you following this?

The Latin word "Vini", has since been re-spelled as "Veni."Thus, the abbreviation of Vini (Veni), Vidi, Vinci, is VI VI VI or 666.This number also appears on the front or forehead of the Pope's hatband as testimony that he, indeed, is the present Emperor of Rome. Long story short, the Pope has the mark, 666 on his forehead. He came, he saw, he conquered. Understand that the Pope and his country The Vatican, is the most powerful country on this planet, making the Pope the world's most powerful person. Research The Vatican for more details.

It has been well documented that we are heading for a cashless society, as the book of Revelations states. The Rothschild's are one of the families that is currently ushering in this New World Order. I urge you to Google the Rothschild's if you've not heard of them before. These ruling families are trying to establish One World Order where the world will be totally dependent on an electronic monetary system. To accommodate this, massive corporations (owned by these same ruling families) around the world have already made plans to ensure all bank customers have access to the chip and pin.

Today, this microchip can be found in everything from bankcards to mobile phones and it's now possible for these chips to be implanted in the human body.

At some point the plan is to have absolute control so that people will be unable buy or sell without an implanted microchip. Many people now are already living in a cashless society as they get paid monthly direct into their bank account, and only pay for things on a credit or debit.

Very rarely do they use cash.

"90% of the world's wealth is owned by approximately 5 families."

- Unknown

As far as I am concerned, the 'Mark of the Beast represents a system that influences the way people think and act. The word 'mark' when used in the expression of "leaving one's mark" means leaving an impression as an effect on another's mind or way of thinking.

Every subject matter discussed in this book requires further research; at the end of this book I have included some references so you can carry out your own investigation.

The Bible indicates that 6 is the number of a man or Satan (666). Man was made on the 6th day, according to the Bible. Using the alphabet and assigning man's number '6' to the first letter of this alphabet, a system has been constructed by giving each succeeding letter an increasing value of six. For example:

A is the 1st letter, so multiply 6 by 1 (6x1=6).

B is the 2nd letter, so multiply 6 by 2 (6x2=12).

C is the 3rd letter, so multiply 6 by 3 (6x3=18).

Here is the full breakdown;

A -6	B- 12	C-18
D - 24	E - 30	F – 36
G - 42	H - 48	I – 54
J - 60	K - 66	L – 72
M - 78	N - 84	O – 90
P - 96	Q - 102	R - 108
S - 114	T - 120	U - 126
V - 132	W - 138	X - 144

We said earlier that a 'mark' might influence thought. One such 'mark' in our society is the dictionary. The dictionary explains the meaning of words, then the author tells us what he wants us to believe about the meaning of the words in our language.

The most commonly used English dictionary today is *Webster's Dictionary.*

Let us tally the value of the letters in the name 'Webster's'.

(W-138, E-30, B-12, S-114, S-114, T-120, E-30, R-108, S-114)

We arrive at '***666***' the Mark of the Beast! We accept Webster's word definitions and place them in our minds in the frontal lobe of our brain or forehead and we carry Webster's dictionary as a constant reference to verify the meaning of given words. And so we have the Mark of the Beast in our forehead and in our hand.

How very clever!

Previously, I mentioned the Rothschild family vision of a cashless society. None of this would be possible if it weren't for the computer. In fact, the contribution computer is huge. The computer is central to everything we do in the modern, Western world be it work; business and commerce, entertainment; politics or security and governance. Some people say that the computer is the biggest invention since the wheel, books, the locomotive and the automobile.

However, if you apply the same system to the word COMPUTER you come up with:

C=18

O=90

M=78

P=96

U=126

T=120

E=30

R=108

You will find that it also equals 666.

Homework

How many books are there in the Old Testament? 66 right? If you can find the third "6" please let me know. Sometimes the answer is not so obvious and you have to do some code breaking.

Is the bible also 666? You tell me.

I love Apple Macintosh.

I think they are slick, trendy and highly effective. I am actually using a MacBook right now to write these words. I also have an iPad, an iPhone and an iPod Touch.

Apple's logo is the half-eaten apple and we all know that Eve ate the apple in the Garden of Eden, don't we?

Why did they choose that logo? We understand that the apple in the garden represented 'knowledge'; well that's what they say anyway. I don't take anyone's word for anything and enjoy forming my own conclusions.

Did you know, that the name 'Jesus' which is commonly known in Christianity today, actually did not exist until about 500 years ago!

In fact, the letter 'J' does not even exist in the Hebrew, Latin or Greek.

There was no letter 'J' in any language prior to the 14th century in England.

The letter did not become widely used until the 17th Century

Apart from fruit, where else is the apple used?

What city in the world is related or associated with an apple?

The Big Apple is a nickname for New York City. John J. Fitzgerald popularised the term in the 1920s. I don't have too much information about John J. Fitzgerald, but I did notice that his name contains 15 letters.

1+5 is 6 that dreaded number again and the 1920s also equals 6, you work that one out on your own, (the clue is to subtract), but that is not my point.

The state of New York includes New York City aka The Big Apple; this city is the most popular city in the United States and the centre of the New York metropolitan area.

Many would argue that New York is the most famous city in the world. A leading global city, New York exerts a powerful influence over global commerce, finance, media, culture, art, fashion, research, education and entertainment. As host of the United Nations Headquarters, it is also an important centre for international affairs.

However, upon closer inspection New York becomes

N=84

E=30W=138Y= 1500=90R=108K= 66

As you can see, New York is actually 666. Damn, I loved that city!

So you have the Apple, the devil who gave it to Eve and the number.

There may be hundreds or even thousands of words that equal to 666, and if you have the time, please compile them and forward them to me.

Before I finish this chapter, I wanted to leave you with a few words that I have come across that also calculate to 666 using the same method above. Once again, check out the relationship between the different words.

Digital ID Chip=666

VeriShield=666 (the company that makes Verichip)

Mark of Beast=666

Bio-Implant=666 Related to the buying & selling aspect of Revelation 13:16-18.

Verichip is a bio-implant. Note: Verichip is not evil unless it's used to control buying or selling).

Sorceries = 666

Necromancy = 666

Witchcraft = 666

Santa (Satan) Claus = 666

Corrupt = 666

Insanity = 666

Horrors = 666

Treacheries = 666

Slaughter = 666

Illusion = 666

Book of the Dead = 666

Vaccination = 666

Osama Bin Laden died May 1, 2011

Hitler died May 1, 1945

That is 66 Years Apart, and May (the 5th Month) and 1st is 5 + 1=6

666 again.

Wikipedia and other sources suggest The Illuminati were founded on May 1st. May is the 5th month, so 1 + 5 = 6. It was founded in Bavaria in Germany, by Adam Weishaupt.

5
Take Break, Breathe, Inhale, Exhale and come again

Davis Williams

Based on my research, it seems the language we call English was created by someone, or a group of people who were fond of serpents and snakes, the number six, death and control. They were, or still are, fond of clever word and number games. These techniques cannot be seen in any other language, as far as I know.

Sticks and stones may break your bones but WORDS can NEVER hurt you?

That is what they want you to believe. Words have the potential to be the most dangerous weapons we know.

Could this be a coincidence? According to the calculations above, the number 6 is the number associated with death and transition. When you die they bury you 6ft deep. Why not 7ft or 5ft? We all know that words form sentences and we know that the word sentence is what a judge gives to an offender to serve behind bars. The use of words forming sentence, or sequence of sentences has sentenced innocent minds to life in prison −the prison of the mind. I work with young people who are so intelligent, smart and amazing, yet victims of a closed, infected and imprisoned mind.

Under the microscope everything vibrates. Nothing is solid and everything vibrates at different frequencies and speeds. Even words vibrate and those vibrations hold a particular pattern, a mathematical signature that can result in a certain response or reaction.

Maybe the idea of words vibrating seems crazy.

Tables, phones and shoes are all made up of energy - even the molecules contained in a solid block of iron are vibrating with energy, only it is so dense and the movement of the molecules is so slow, that it appears to be still.

Words have energy and each word resonates at different frequencies. Not just the spoken word, but also the written word too. Words used when you write messages, the letters that you use, all convey the emotion you had when you wrote them.

For example, no matter how politely you word a text when you are feeling angry; the recipient of the text will sense the energy and the emotion from which it was written.

Professionals are skilled at masking the way they feel, they are taught how to ignore their personal feelings and to focus on the task at hand.

Words like HELL, DEATH, and PAIN FEAR all have negative and dense vibrations (generally speaking). These vibrations keep you low, sluggish and unmotivated. If you use these words in a sentence, directed at someone, the chances are, either your vibration or the person listening will be negatively affected. "I want you to feel pain", "you are the devil" or "I am fearful" all possess disempowering energy.

Words like LOVE, CARE, HAPPY, FREEDOM have a totally different effect! Try telling someone "I love you", "I am happy" or "I wish you peace and joy" and see what happens.

A Japanese scientist called Dr Masaru Emoto, proved that if water or food is exposed to a written word, it will respond to that word. Food and water exposed to words such as 'war' or 'hate' deteriorated quickly; those exposed to words such as 'love' and 'thank you' did not. Emoto's experiments exposed water to different words, pictures, or music and then freezing and examining the crystals with microscopic photography.

Emoto has sold over two million books; one of his best is *Messages from Water, Vol.1.*

Words, when used effectively, can affect the way you feel, think, behave and even the way you exist in life. Words can break your confidence and make you suicidal. On the other hand, words can make you feel like a king or queen. When you consider why Europeans took a great deal of effort to erase the language of enslaved Africans, you appreciate the impact and value of words. Not only were they forbidden from speaking their traditional language, they were not allowed to pray or call on their gods or allowed to play their music. They were even forced to adopt an English Christian name (yes Christian name) and a surname (the name of your Sir A.K.A your Master's name). These changes altered history.

In the beginning, was the word.

The English language. Whoever created it had a strange, perverse and crazy view of the world. What was their motive? Was it genetic survival? I could speculate, but one thing is for certain, the more you know about the English language and the power of words, numbers and certain sequences, the more you will understand what is really going on globally and economically.

Essay Fifteen

May 5th 2012

Shape Shifter

Written by the alter ego known as 5ive (Davis J Williams)

Perspective

"When the beggar asks for change, he is not always asking for your loose change, but for a CHANGE."
5ive

Let's jump straight into this!

When I left university, I was in serious debt. Even though I got my degree I couldn't find a job in my chosen field because I had no work experience. I studied for three hard years, making sacrifices, but I endured this because I thought that it would improve my chances of finding work.

No one told me that was a lie.

I was frustrated and felt hard done by, especially when I bumped into friends who opted out of the option to attend university. They were doing great. Most of them never bothered with university or college and some didn't even finish school, but they were successful managers and entrepreneurs. During the months of looking for a job in my specialist area, I was continually told that I lacked the experience needed.

A good friend gave me the number of a man who was employed by a local youth-focused charity aimed at helping young black males at risk of offending, into employment.

I decided to give him a call to arrange a meeting because by then, I was really desperate for work.

When I first saw him, I was pleased to see that he was black and had dreadlocks. He wore a trampy Tottenham Hotspurs shirt (I am a Gooner for life) but I had no doubt that I would connect with him and that he would be able to give me some practical advice. He helped me write a glowing curriculum vitae (CV) and we discussed interviewing skills, body language and pointed me towards their huge database of current vacancies.

After a dozen or so visits to this resource centre, I found a part time job working for London Underground as a ticket inspector at London Bridge Station. I was so excited that my hard work had paid off and even though it was only part time, it was a start at least.

This is where I was introduced to the Shape Shifters.

London Bridge ticket office was like a giant playground. I was young, bright and ambitious and that station had nuff gyal! Being a major interchange station there were all types of women. There were the office girl dem, the students, the shoppers and the 'I have just left my man's house' gyal.

It was inevitable, a standard procedure that these girls would get terrorised by us girl-hungry ticket inspectors on a daily basis. Sometimes they would give us attitude by fixing their lip like they had collagen stuffed in them or doing weird neck movements, but little did they know that we had the power. We would always refuse them exit from the station by inspecting their ticket and wasting their time if they were rude and try to correct their behaviour in the process.

I was the youngest ticket inspector at the station and was supervised by some of the older, more experienced members of staff. Even though they taught me their appalling habits on my very first day, their knowledge and experience was incredible. Another thing that I was exposed to on my first week was the internal politics, i.e. the bickering and segregation between the full and part time members of staff.

The full timers were privileged because they were seen as having more experience than everyone else and as a result they adopted the role of team leader.

I had only been working at London Bridge station for a week and could clearly see that those who worked part time were from the islands, Black British or in-between. Whilst the full-time staff were all Nigerian or from other parts of Africa. Why Africans only worked full time and the Jamaicans part time bewildered me, but being inquisitive, in time I would ask that uncomfortable question.

Being a part timer and from the Caribbean, I refused to adopt any learned behaviour, so, being young, savvy and sociable I decided to create peace and harmony between the teams. The first stage of my plan was to mingle between the teams, never taking sides and becoming familiar with everyone and establish striking up relationships based on professionalism, interest and love.

A few weeks went by and I actually remembered everyone's name so I stopped calling them 'brother' and 'boss-man'.

One morning while I mingled with the part time staff on the concourse helping customers with train times and ticket prices, and issuing the odd fine, I heard a massive...

"A wah di blooooooodclaaarttttt yu ah deal wid?"

Being a nosey parker I quickly took myself to where the

commotion was and I saw Tyrone (T-Boy) and Olusegan arguing.

T-Boy was a part-time member of staff and was fresh from Jamaica. Olusegan was a full-time member of staff originally from Nigeria (More about him later).

T-Boy and Olusegan went at it for at least twenty seconds before they realised they were at work. Twenty seconds is a long time when a train concourse of over 200 people freezes; a bloody long time. As soon as the twenty seconds were over, everything went back to normal as if nothing had happened.

At 11 o'clock the majority of staff had a break, as the rush hour had finished, this was the first time we had a chance to talk about the incident.

"Anton, wha gwan wid T–Boy man?" I asked in a cockney Jamaican accent.

Anton was another part timer who was close friends with T - Boy. I was concerned, as I didn't want anyone to lose their job over this disagreement so I thought that I could try and mediate.

"It's them dam Shifters - always trying to mess up man's operations", Anton replied sharply.

"What you mean 'Shifters'? Are them Nigerians on a fraud flex? Are they acting all shifty?" I asked confidently, thinking I knew what he was referring to.

Anton replied, "They're called Shifters because they do fraud all day, every day. The Shifters take the piss blood, they take man a man for idiots, you get me? (he said in slang) I ain't having it blood, you see me! Them Africans are shifty, deceiving people wid dem bad ways. Where me from, man die fi less, you get me?! Every morning we come into work, check two gyal and at the end of our shift we duss, nothing long. Remember blood, we are here every morning, we see the same girls, we catch jokes with them, some of the girls I met here are now my certified booty call, you get me? It's like that. Sometimes they bring us lunch, take us out, the man dem have a good operation here."

"For real, that sounds heavy, bring me in", I interrupted.

Anton continued...

"Of course it is blood, but check the drama now, what has been happening recently with T-Boy and Olusegun is deep. There was one gyal who use to pass through the station every morning like clockwork at 8:40am. Everyone knows the time. She was heavvvvvyyyy blooddd, trust. When she wore her tight suit, her back off was live rude boy. Every man wanted a piece of that. T-Boy was at the right place at the right time and he got with her and they had a little something poppin still. There is unwritten rule out here, DON'T COCK BLOCK! If someone has a certified, no-one interferes, as there are enough fish in this pond. Everyone knows to man their corner, their area and patrol that. I am known to hang around the clock tower, that's me all day long. Everyone knows to keep that spot for me.

"Everyone knows this law!"

Olusegun started acting funny towards T-Boy, always having him be positioned somewhere else in the station, which obviously meant that some mornings he would not get to see his beanie.

Then it happened. Olu did the unthinkable!

Bearing in mind T-Boy only works mornings, one evening, on her way home from work, Olu stopped T-Boy's girlfriend to inspect her ticket and whilst doing so decided to spark a conversation. He told her that he, as an African man, values women and therefore had to tell her that she was getting played. He then lied and told her that the reason she doesn't see him every morning is because he is checking a girl on another platform. He then started to move to the girl, trying to seduce her with poetry, compliments and promises.

"You're lying! Are you being for real?" I uttered.

Anton continued,

"Yeah man, I am being totally real, but Olu didn't know that the girl and T-Boy are tight, so she went back and told T-Boy everything. When T-Boy found out there was a big fight and there's been a divide ever since."

I was disgusted with Olu's behaviour but it also felt good to know the truth of how them man flexed. This knowledge would dictate how I'd with them in the future.

Months later, I was due a very important meeting with my manager to assess my progress and suitability to the company; this is called a probationary meeting. Olu, being my supervisor conducted this meeting. It was very informal, he basically asked me a range of questions about my role, how I thought I was developing and assessed my training needs. That meeting went according to plan. I kept my job and my performance was deemed A-star!

However, even though the meeting had officially finished Olu continued.

"Ah, I can see that you have a degree, very good, VERY good", he said in a strong Nigerian accent.

"You know Davis, I can see you are very intelligent. I see you getting along with everybody, never creating a fuss and I have received reports that your customer service skills are impeccable. It is clear you are very charming and popular. I do have some concerns about your choice of friends so please be careful, as some of them are just NO GOOD."

He continued,

"It is only because I respect you that I am telling you this! I know Tyrone and Anton profoundly misunderstand me, but they cease to grasp the concept that I am a man of African principles. I am God-fearing and speak my mind. If I see something I will say it, because God sees everything. They don't like the truth and that is why we clash and have conflict. I want us to get along; I do not want you to be influenced by lies and deception. The Devil speaks in many languages, tones and adopts various accents and customs, so don't let anybody confuse you! If you EVER want to ask me anything please do not hesitate."

"Thanks Olu, I appreciate your wise words and thanks for helping me pass my probationary period."

I was waiting for ages for an opportunity to speak, but this dude was just not stopping!

Olu interrupted,

"Wait, wait, before you continue, tell me something. Is there anything that you want to know? During our conversation, I noticed you absorbing everything I was saying. You are a good listener, but for us to get along, and build a relationship based on honesty and truth I want you to tell me what is on your mind. I told you what was on mine."

I thought for a minute and had an internal dialogue

"Mmmmmmm"

My instinct was telling me to bait him up about his off-key behaviour with Tyrone, but I already knew the state of affairs on that one, so I began to conjure up a storyboard. I did like Olu's approach, even though he was a charmer himself I had to use this as an opportunity. Earlier in our conversation he said he was God-fearing, but on the other hand he's involved in all sorts of fraudulent activity, hence the label 'shifters'.

It was clear that I had to confront him about his beliefs and of course exercise my ego a little bit in the process.

"Why does everyone call you guys the Shifters?" I asked, with a big smirk on my face.

I was expecting him to dig his own grave which would have given me the chance to get all righteous on him before walking off, leaving him with some food for thought; the unexpected happened. For once there was silence and the mood in the room changed. Olu's face became dark and fierce and his body language switched to that of a politician.

"Rahhh, sorry for asking Olu, but you did say be honest."

I was quick to defuse the tension, my ego was somewhat happy with the impact of my question. I obviously had him thinking deeply, forcing him to delve into his soul; my mission was done it seemed.

I stood up saying, "You don't need to discuss it if you don't want to. I know how it is. We've all done things that contradict our faith. So what if you do fraud, let no man judge you."

Olu started laughing uncontrollably, tears running down his fat, round cheeks and his hands waving around in the air as if signalling an airplane.

Slowly lowering his bellowing laughter, he composed himself.

"So Davis, you think we are called Shifters because we do fraud? I did tell you that the Devil's form would sometimes surprise you. You should not listen to them foolish, idiotic jokers, they'll believe anything. Let me tell you where that stupid term came from you gullible nincompoop."

He looked tense, a look I have never seen him pull before; it was the kind of look your dad gave you before a beating, so I sat back down, humbled myself and listened. I have been here before, so I could tell when it was lesson time.

"The Shifters thing started way before Anton and Tyrone had even started here. It stems back to 1987 when I first started working for the Underground. In1986 I arrived in the United Kingdom from Nigeria. Do you know that back home I was a young doctor? I had to leave Nigeria because I needed better pay and working conditions. Europeans call it the 'brain drain', where mass immigration of people with technical skills leave their home country in search of work elsewhere. Where I am from, there was a lack of opportunities, political instability, economic depression, health risks and a family who wanted me to improve my career prospects. I left my wife and six children in Nigeria and came to the UK in the hope of permanent employment in medicine. It was only supposed to be for twelve months, by which time I was expected to find employment in my chosen field, accumulate enough money and then bring my family over, but things did not work out due to the economic climate in the UK but I still needed money to send home. No matter what I did I just couldn't find any work. I searched for a job as a doctor or anything similar for two years; not a day passed without applying for a job, preparing my portfolio or networking with professionals who could potentially open up some doors for me."

Davis Williams

"My children back home were growing, that's what kids do. Their demands increased, my wife's demands increased and so did the weight resting on my shoulders. I had no choice but to find work, any kind of work."

"I've got mouths to feed so I needed to work as many hours as possible. I am one of many; you will notice that many Africans like me are highly educated and skilled and prepared to leave home looking for that break."

Until that time comes, I still need to send money back home to support my family. When I started working here, your people noticed that we would work long 24hour shifts, so they called us 'The Shifters'. Over time people made their own interpretation of what that meant."

I sat listening to him silently. I was actually quite emotional, because he was prepared to sacrifice everything to create a better world for his family. When Olu finished his story he ushered me out of the office reminding me to not always believe what people say.

I thanked him again and blessed him with a strong hand shake (you know them cultural West African handshakes where you click fingers at the end), and wished him and his family all the best.

Personally, the fact that Olu and the 'Shifters' could work 24 hours a day is not an issue for me, that is a minor. The killer was knowing that these guys are highly educated - some with a degree, Masters, PhD or similar - but they have the ability to SHIFT their mentality and their behaviour in order to respond to their situation.

There is a saying 'if nothing else moves you, life will'.

That interaction with Olu that day taught me something very

important about human development. There is always something in life that will make you shift. The 'Shifters' was merely a label that could be interpreted in so many different ways. My truth is this, the Shifters are a group of people who have the ability to shift their state of mind, their attitude, or shift their world view in order to accommodate the changes in their lives. It's called behavioural flexibility i.e. the ability to change your behaviour in order to thrive and succeed in any given situation.

I remember very clearly when my view of the world changed. The same thing was running through my head over and over again. I just could not believe what I was being told. The words contained in the Bible, a book that I respected, made no sense to me after having certain conversations with knowledgeable individuals. My whole belief system was turned upside down. I tried to ignore what was revealed to me, but that truth would not rest. It kept on eating away at my soul, whispering, screaming and growing like a virus. My mind was working overtime whilst I thought, analysed, questioned and tried to repair my shattered ego. After receiving my intellectual spanking at Luton carnival by that guy who called me a reptile, I vowed to research the areas discussed and return to set the record straight. I had no choice but to buy several books and DVDs so I could learn more. I became a student of life and research was my new fetish. I was encouraged to go away and not to believe a word he said, but to research it and prove him wrong. I have been trying to prove him wrong for over ten years now. Ten years of attending meetings and lectures, travelling the world, reading the words of renowned scholars, buying books and DVDs as well as reasoning and debating with people from all walks of life.

Most importantly I challenge, myself and my own perception of the world and why I think the way I do. I reached one simple conclusion.

The guy was right, but did I care enough to change?

Yes, I did.

Every facet of my life changed. I stopped eating meat, my habits changed; I became more self-aware, my environment and the people and things that occupied my space. I had more confidence, greater self-respect and actually felt powerful for a change.

Most importantly though, I stopped being afraid and insecure. Afraid of the truth, afraid of exposure, afraid of change and not being accepted.

I became a rebel. I became a Shifter.

I am sorry for those who are unable to shift their attitude, regardless of the countless warnings they've had. I know many people who refuse to change the way they dress, walk or talk because they claim that they are 'keeping it real'. Even though they don't own the road, many prefer to keep it road and gangster. They insist on remaining loyal to the streets, to the pavement and to a postcode.

Some people find it extremely hard to survive and succeed in the system and inevitably end up in prison, the betting office or dead, whether mentally or physically.

Being able to shift is essential for survival.

5
Take a Break, Breathe, Inhale, Exhale and come again.

Your thoughts shape your reality and if you can change the invisible (your thoughts) the visible (the things you want) will follow for sure.

The power of thought is the key to creating your reality. Everything you perceive in the physical world has its origin in the invisible, the inner world of your thoughts and beliefs. In order for you to become the master of your destiny and reclaim your power, you must learn to control the nature of your dominant, habitual thoughts.

Let's be honest, all of us do things that we should not be doing, but we do it because of habit.

Once we control our habits we will be able to attract the things we want.

Fear is nothing but a thought.

Change your thought process and fear disappears.

Love is a thought that creates an emotion, a feeling and initiates a series of responses, but, change those thoughts and love disappears.

Thoughts are more powerful than most people realise.

I was recently watching a documentary and they were talking about the power of the subconscious mind. Your mind is so powerful that if you tell it that you will be successful or that you can accomplish something, you will. Simple as that! If that were true, then everyone who worked hard and applied themselves would be successful with a nice career, fantastic relationship and nice home. But the truth of the matter is that some people make it and others don't.

It is because it's not what's in our conscious mind that determines what our lives will be like; it's what's in our subconscious mind.

Your conscious mind has got nothing to do with who you are as a person, nothing at all. The conscious mind is responsible for analysing information so that you can make decisions on a daily basis. The subconscious mind however is responsible for everything else, your beliefs, your values, your failures and successes are born from this portion of your mind.

The subconscious mind is the recorder, it forgets nothing and remembers absolutely everything.

Once you learn how to control your subconscious mind it's a wrap. Operation lock down. You will be in control of everything, just like Neo from The Matrix.

But here's a warning.

Your subconscious mind is a fertile ground.

Whatever seed is planted in your mind will grow, no matter what seed it is.

When you watch films like *The Bourne Identity* with Matt Damon or the *Manchurian Candidate* starring Denzel Washington you will see how the subconscious mind can easily be manipulated with suggestive instructions. Hypnosis and Neuro Linguistic Programming (NLP) are well known techniques used by politicians, police officers and the army.

There is such a thing as a 'Sleeper Agent'.

A Sleeper Agent could be anyone. Normally they are spies who are placed in a target country or organisation, not to undertake an immediate mission, but rather to act as a potential asset when activated. The activation code could be a special word, tone or picture. Imagine that.

You're working, minding your own business and your colleague just pulls out a gun and starts shooting everyone, randomly.

No motive, no warning, totally random.

Sleeper Agent.

5
Take a Break, Breathe, Inhale, Exhale, then come again

If you remember nothing else about your mind, remember:

The subconscious mind only thinks in the present.

It does not think in the past or the future like conscious mind. The subconscious mind only understands 'I AM', 'I HAVE', not 'I'm GOING TO BE', or 'I WILL have'.

The Subconscious Mind does not understand YES or NO, GOOD or BAD.

It just processes whatever command it is given. Remember, the mind is a holographic computer. It works with pictures and symbols, not words.

So if I were to say,

"Do NOT think about a cow doing press ups."

Your subconscious mind can't help but process the cow doing press ups, regardless of you telling yourself not to.

Trying NOT to do something is often easier than trying to do it. It's easier for you to think of a cow doing press ups if I tell you not to do it than if I tell you to do it. This is because in order for the brain '**not to think**' about something your brain has to think a thought and then suppress it. Stopping thoughts takes up more brain processing power than generating the thought in the first place.

The Subconscious Mind does not know the difference between what is real and what is imagined.

You met this lovely girl who was attractive, charming and intelligent. When you started talking to her you were surprised she showed you interest because you thought she was out of your league. Yet she gave you all the signs that indicated that tonight was going to be your lucky night. You were ready, your blood was pumping and your bodily juices were preparing themselves.

The party was over and it was time to go home. You escorted her home, as she lived around the corner from the club. She invited you upstairs, dimmed the lights and gave you the best night of your life. You were deep inside of her, deeper than any other time. After numerous thrusts, you reached your climax and booooooommmmm, you ejaculated.

All of a sudden you woke up in a wet puddle of seminal fluid.

You ejaculated in your sleep. Your mind thought it was real.

Your subconscious mind does not know the difference between what is real and what is imagined.

Michael Jordan was known for sitting in silence picturing himself doing jump shots, slam dunks and making assists. He actually played a whole game in his head. Why? Because he was aware of the power of his mind.

The Subconscious Mind learns by repetition, over and over again.

Practice doesn't make perfect; practice makes permanent.

When you learn any new skill, you must practice it a lot. Saying powerful affirmations helps you get what you want. You can't just say them once and expect them to work. You have to say them repeatedly until your subconscious mind acts upon them. But as with all skills, the more you use your subconscious mind to get what you want, the easier it works. Wearing special colours, listening to music, getting tattoos, posters, reminders and praying/meditating all help focus your mind manifest your wants and desires.

Emotion is important when wanting to manifest something into your life.

When comparing a boring, monotone speech to a passionate, heart-warming testimony it's pretty obvious that the latter will get a more favourable response. So put emotion, personality and INTENTION into your affirmations.

Logic vs. Illogical

Your conscious mind is very logical, rational and organised. It finds it hard to accept something that makes no sense. If I were to tell you to jump off the building and fly, your conscious, logical mind will kick me to the curb.

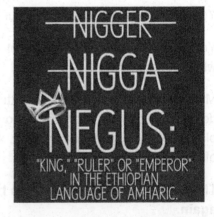

However, your subconscious mind is your illogical, or irrational mind. It will believe ANYTHING whether it makes logical sense or not. It never questions or analyses anything you tell it. So when using your subconscious mind to get what you want, set your sights as high as you can. Don't think what you're affirming isn't realistic as your subconscious mind will not think that.

Warning

If you do not treat your subconscious mind with care and attention other people will use it for their benefit. Media companies spend billions of pounds in advertising that tries to plant subliminal seeds into your subconscious mind. The colours that they use, the music, symbols and word sequences may have been missed by your conscious mind, but your subconscious mind will record everything. When you catch yourself having strange thoughts, cravings, or visions remember that someone could have planted them there. Your subconscious mind can be your best friend, or your worst enemy, act accordingly.

Essay Sixteen

23rd October 2011

I hate the Pigs

A conversation facilitated by Davis J Williams

"There are three sides to every story.
His version, her version and truth just like there are three sides to
every coin, the head, the tail and the edge."
5Star General

I decided to spread a message to people I came into contact with. I wanted to give back and inform those on my journey about what I've learned. I focused my attention on the youth, their essence, their goals and their environment and I used various programmes, youth and community focused initiatives, social enterprises, projects, events and meetings to broadcast this message. I joined many groups, organisations, facilitated presentations and forums to communicate the message of freedom to the youth. I have been around; you name it, I've done it.

In the early days, I was raw with knowledge. I would bombard my friends with teachings and lessons whether they were interested or not. I would annoy and judge them for their habits and for not adhering to the message that was rooted in facts. I used to constantly insult people about eating pork, yes people, the wicked swine. I loved telling people why it was evil and how eating it would shorten their life. Back then, I would blame the swine for everything, even though my family members who lived back home in Dominica love pork!

They eat it daily and lived to be 100 years plus, but that made no difference to me.

The people who read the same books as me, my new set of 'conscious' friends said it was evil and because I related to their teachings, I believed it. Dissing that animal and hurling insults at my friends was easy, but never got me the results I wanted, because people around me didn't stop eating it. Who likes to be TOLD what to do or what to eat? I was labelled egotistical, judgemental and uncompromising. During this period, I made more enemies than I did friends, all because I wanted people to accept my truth.

Why is there such hatred for pigs, so much so they call police, "pigs"? We all know that many, young and old, hate the police. Many people refuse to eat the pig even if they are not religious!

In the Caribbean, Dominica in particular, people have been eating the pig for generations and yet they have a healthy life. They say eating it has not affected them at all, but made it even better!

Here is a conversation that I had on Facebook one night (names have been initialized). I am DSB

DBS: *Why do you guys hate the pig, but if you went back home you would still eat it?*

GTI: *Bring come the jerk sauce!*

DSB: *Ha! GTI, you make me laugh....you love that hog don't you?*

EE: *Yeahhh maan. Ribs, ham, gammon, bacon, pepperoni all day! ...nah, not even!!! That's not the way forward.*

DSB: *Why not EE...?*

EE: *I used to eat it like 8 years ago though! But I lacked* knowledge then and felt wasted. Right about now though, I'm not a fan of worm accumulation in the gut bro! From when it was used to clean the cadavers of the caucus mountains and they have the genes of a rat, cat and dog and eat rubbish. I can't have that take residence within. My body is a temple and only the best can enter.

DSB: I don't think you read my status. If you live back home, and had elders, waxed wise in knowledge munching the hog, and telling you to do the same, would you? They are 100 years + and act 50 years old, still working and enjoying life. WOULD YOU TELL THEM ABOUT WORMS?!

Nat: Don't even let me start on this status here!! I blame you for a lot of sh*t!!! I miss my souse and it's all your doing!!!

(*souse is a Caribbean dish containing every part of the pig, EVERY PART, boiled down into a soup like texture).

EE: Yeah I read the status. And I understand that they are resilient creatures, but for me, if I was back home I still wouldn't eat that dirty bastard. Once I know that when you pour coke over pork, you see worms emerge. Just to eat pork because they said I should... nah. I won't eat it and I'd show em the worms...then I'd show em a colon cleanser, regardless of their age.

Micro: EE, I bet you haven't even tried that Coke experiment, stop watching YouTube. Guys, has anyone tried pouring coke on a pig?

DSB: Nat, I agree, I was bad, I told loads of people that pork was bad, evil etc., but I was young. I am grown now and my understanding is different. Sorry for your missed souse! I heard that it is still in fashion so go get yours lol!

DSB: *EE, do you know anyone who has issues with worms. I have read that stuff also, but I have never met anyone with the symptoms people are referring to.*

Nat: *DSB, I'm punching you through my phone!!!"*

DSB: *Nat, I know, I just banged my toe on the door, so I assume you was aiming there... Shortie.*

FJ: *If the animal is healthy and treated with kindness then I would try, yeah.*

EE: *Yeah? So are you a pork lover, DSB?*

WB: *DSB, so I take it after years of confusion and banging your head against a brick wall called inevitability... it's bacon sarnies all round with a splodge of ketchup? Ha-ha I never thought I'd see the day!*

NCBI: *I am sure there is plenty of fish. Are the people of this ancestral home known for their fighting spirit?*

PFE: *Yeah...they're living to 100 years + and still eating flesh...I have a feeling if they cut it out they may live even longer. There are many other things in Caribbean culture that contributes to their good health just as there are many other things than just pork eating contributes to our bad health here, so answer? Nah I wouldn't.*

Nat: *The bottom line is this people. Red meat in general is not very good for humans. The time it takes for red meat to break down in the body is a very long time. I'm sure if you did experiments with all meat and fish by putting alcohol on it and leaving it out; you would all see fascinating results. I haven't eaten pork in over ten years and won't eat it because of what I was taught all those years ago; but I don't think at this stage of my life I would warn others off it if they enjoy eating it. There are worse things out there that people can eat. One day I may crack and eat pork again because I enjoyed it immensely. I don't think it.*

RM: *Dominicans should bottle those PORKIES as the new will affect my life span whatsoever elixir to longevity... make it the new OINK-ment .Watch out Oil of Olay!*

DSB: *The people of Dominica are like many of the other islands. They are warm, affectionate, family orientated and proud! We all know the rumours about worms, about going blind and all that but let's face it, many people hate pork more than they hate the police. I use to think like this too, but now that I am well-travelled, I had to change my view. I can only speak for Dominica. Why do people hate it so much? It has to be something else besides worms. We have been told many things about pork, but they are not always right.*

DO: *Nope! I would not eat it!*

MK: *Hahaha! My sides are splitting maybe they've had the pork immunisation on the Caribbean NHS!*

DSB: *What has the swine ever done to you? People know the breakdown, but I have first-hand experience on pig eaters and their longevity. The breakdown is coming from a third party, do you trust their explanation? We all know that deception and lies are rampant!*

DSB: *But come on. I can understand someone deciding not to eat something because of the taste, but to say you hate it is a massive statement. Random question, does hate exist?*

FS: *Only if love exists.*

Ras: *It is possible it could be an illusion, but we cannot ignore its presence completely? It can be balanced with love.*

DSB: *I don't think hate is real. I think hate is an illusion. Love is the only reality. Someone can love life, or someone can love death, two extremes of the same energy. What you all think? I am still reasoning it out.*

FS: *If you love someone, you always want to be around them. What would you call it when you feel the opposite of that?*

KCPK: *Hate definitely exists, cos you wouldn't be able to express or know love otherwise.*

DSB: *Hate needs love to exist, but love does not need hate. A child knows love, but not hate, right? Hate is a learned behaviour.*

DSB: *The opposite of love can't be hate, I think, because hate depends on love, love doesn't need hate.*

DSB: *For example, I hate someone because I used to love them, but I love someone just because I do.*

Ras: *I hear what you're saying but can you consider the act of giving a hug and the act of stabbing to be in the same category of feeling? I think they are two sides of the same coin.*

FS: *Don't you think hate can exist because of a comparison? For example, I know what Jamaica is like so I hate England?*

DSB: *Same energy, different polarity. Just like water… at what point does hot become cold? Either way, it's still water right?*

KCPK: *They are both emotions so the same could be said about love. It can come as a result of socialising love could be infatuation or extreme fondness.*

Ras: *It's still water but the particles change form during the transition from hot to cold. Your reasoning is helping me see things from a different angle though.*

RLPRY: *HATE DOES NOT EXIST ONLY IF YOU MAKE IT EXIST BY GIVING IT LIFE. HATE IS JUST A WORD THAT HAS A POWER WHEN USED. THAT POWER IS ONLY MADE POWERFUL FROM YOUR POWER AND YOUR ENERGY.*

ES: *Hate is real, but it stems from a love of something or someone. E.g., if someone were to harm my child I can guarantee I would hate them. But only because I love my child so much. They are inextricably linked and while you are right in theory that love does need hate to exist, I would add however, no more than a parent needs their child to exist. They don't. Nevertheless they are closely connected but separate beings in their own right. So yes.*

DSB: *Hate exists.*

ES: *Meant to say love DOESN'T need hate to exist... duh.*

RH: *Actually, love and hate are opposites of the same emotion so Davis your analogy about water is as good as without one you wouldn't have the other. You don't have to be religious to realise the universe has one consistent theme, opposites. Day and night, hot and cold, life and death, beginning and ending, good and evil, man and woman, love and hate. So without one you couldn't measure the other, hence why the universe is in a constant struggle for balance.*

DSB: *All these labels are social constructs, used to help us better communicate. For example, my left is your right if we are facing each other, it's all about perception, so on one level everyone is right. But the reality is that love radiates and manifests differently. We call it hate and a lot of people made reference to hate being used to understand love. So I guess this is a case of social truth verses universal reality.*

DSB: *Having said that, what is the opposite of love? The polar opposite.*

MA: *Hate is often a reflection of what love once was.*

Geoff: *Of course hate exists!!*

DSB: *Geoff you're right. Hate is real, on a social level, but universally it isn't real blood.*

WIS: *When it is present, it is ALWAYS a symptom of self-hate, so, does self-hate exist?*

DSB: *Our minds can create whatever we want, so yes it does exist, but universally it does not. This matrix and its social constructs hurts my head.*

WIS: *That's right Dexter...known as perception!!*

5
Take a Break, Breathe, Inhale, Exhale, then come again.

As you can see by this conversation, people hate the pig and sometimes this hatred is unfounded and unsubstantiated.

Over the years, I developed my communication skills and in doing so realised that my approach had been all wrong. I could no longer bully people into submission, nor could I verbally attack them if they didn't see things as I did. I decided to change my approach and instead started listening to other people's opinions and accept their truths.

Being accepting of something you disagree with? Not agreeing with it, but accepting it as their personal truth? That was one of the hardest things I have ever done! I began to accept that everyone is unique in their own way. I accepted that everyone is a star and that they have their own path. I dropped a lot of baggage and any high expectations I had for others reduced dramatically. The only person that I was occupied with now was myself; not in a selfish away, but I realised that the more I pointed my finger, judging and criticising, the less I paid attention to myself, my personal patterns, my inner light and my own path.

As they say, when you point your finger at someone, there are three fingers pointing back at you...try it.

Truth is a funny thing. You think everyone will believe you if you tell the truth, but that is a lie. Truth is relative, not absolute. What is true to me can be untrue for others. We all have our own unique perspective and we all see things differently. My truth is certainly not the same as someone else's truth due to our different experiences, so I began to focus on people's personal truths and getting them to unpack it, dissect it and rebuild if necessary, in the name of self-development.

These days' people are duped into living a lie, being forced to wear social masks to conform whilst those who choose to remove their masks are labelled, isolated and treated unfairly simply because their views seem radical and politically incorrect.

These views encourage people to look within and reflect. To be honest some people don't like to be told the truth.

People tend not to stand up and say how they truly feel about a situation. They're not encouraged to challenge the status quo and are instead expected to accept negative labels and conform to something detrimental to their being.

Scores of revolutionary, iconic and celebrated heroes and she-roes have tried to speak up against their mental and, or physical oppressor. You can often hear their screams for help, exploding and imploding in the process, but nothing gets done.

In March 2007, the British government, the Church of England and the British monarchy were all present at Westminster Abbey to commemorate the British Abolition of the Slave Trade Act.

Millions of people watched the ceremony on television; the British establishment wanted to celebrate William Wilberforce who they believe freed millions of African people from chattel slavery. To this day, the British have still not apologised for the part they played in the slave trade. Their commemorations in 2007 touched a lot of Africans living in Britain and across the world in the wrong way because of a truth that has never been acknowledged.

During this highly publicised ceremony, one man stood up and demanded they apologised for what they did. Toyin Agbetu stood up in front of the Queen, the British Prime Minister, international dignitaries and the world media and spoke up for what he believed in.

How many of us would do the same?

The support he received was minimal from the African and Caribbean communities. I am sure that what he did, he did for himself and that connection he has with his ancestors. It was not a media stunt. People like Toyin are few.

Like Malcolm X said, "If you stand for nothing, you will fall for anything.

I guess some people will rather live on their knees than die standing on their feet.

A Poem by Daron the Baron:

Appetiser
I'm Varaha the Black Pig coming so sick with it,
consumed all the filth, now I'm so slick with it.

About to bore through your mind like Barbary Boars in the wilderness,
eating acorns and berries still I know you vegans won't be feeling this.

I'm dealing the truth, but religion got my people spooked,
rather than play your hand you run around thinking you're cute.

With your iPhone, a MORTgage and a salary below your means,
or a head wrap, an ankh chain but don't know what it really means.

So I'm coming through just like a Zulu when I write this down,
lyrical hoodoo is my voodoo your mind I light it NOW.

You find the apple in the pig's mouth because I've been here since the gardens,
tryna give you humans a heads up, soon you'll be begging for my pardon.

Watch! Black Pigs the movement don't need your "approvement",
watch us Black Nigs bring in the improvement.

Look, I bit the apple just to spit the truth,

Davis Williams

but if you can't feel this then it isn't for you.

Still I'm so sweet I got your granny hooked on my muscle,
and these farmers on a worldwide hustle, they love a truffle.

You'd bust a shuffle for a juicy chop,
now you turn around and talk about me like a piece of slop.

Now my pigsty has more foundations than you,
do pigs fly? Well I've elevated past you.

You've never known of a hog with more wog than a golly,
my trance to advance for your folly.

Starter
Now it's Varaha the Black Pig all in your atmosphere,
so listen up, pay attention, and read these words clear.

This ain't no EGO trip; I keep it realer fam,
but don't trip if you aren't ready for this mega plan.

You need to understand we're living in a hologram,
where my niggaz kill for kilograms and the government is a killer
clan.

And things will never be the same again you dummy,
look how a credit crunch has got you packing lunch and still you
can't munch money.

Funny how money isn't worth anything again!
Funny how petrol spilling and rising again!

Yeah... still I'm feeling so neat, and life is so sweet,

And Along Came a Lion

look how the systems looking so weak.

On its last legs because it's their last days,
so don't get caught up in their hype ways.

That keeps you plugged in this rat race full of stress
and keep your eye on the girl in the red dress.

Main

The truth will set you free and so I had to drop out of college,
to dealing with information that makes the average person vomit.

But still I'm on it getting sicker as I'm about to blow up,
out of this dimension, did I mention it will make you throw up?

Sipping psilocybin, with my click I'm riding...
We are all one ain't no dividing...

Like a fraction we ARE the law of attraction,
Out of body, walking on the moon with Michael Jackson.

Call me a psychonaut better yet the Black Pig,
a black hippy keep it trippy for my Black Nigs.

Now where my Thuggees at, where are all my Sambos,
and where would we be without all of you Mambos.

That's how the plan goes, get a crew of black witches,
they switch it from witches and now they call them black bitches.

Seriously she's a DOG star and I'm a HOG Yah!
And now it's time for you to step out of the fog ya'll.
So Oink Oink's the mantra, raise your kundalini like its tantra,

so your mind's eye can see my yantra.

Dessert

I give you game like your Daddy should, stretch your mind more than a caddy could,
so fresh, so clean, I flee the scene like a baddie would.

You shoulda, coulda, woulda while us Hogs make it happen,
tapping into these Psychedelics, but due to taboo you think we're slacking.

This ain't no crack ting. This right here is for the realist,
Those prepared to face their fears right through to the happiest of feelings.

Where these Gees lift you up and pull you right through the ceiling,
Into a Mario's World so, so appealing.

While revealing all your hidden side, but just relax and let the rhythm ride,
We're still inside your mind and about to turn it inside out.

No doubt, we're on a mission like Shinobi and roll with Nagas like Obi Wan Kenobi,
but you don't really know me.

I told you this right here's for the realers,
psychological navigators aka my banana peelers.

All my Black Pigs and Golliwogs, Pretty Witches and Mama Hogs...
And Anubis said to give a shout to all his gutter dogs.

Looking For A Lucrative Opportunity?

PRISONS for PROFIT

**U.S. Has The Highest Incarceration Rate In The World
More Than 2.3 Million People Already Locked Up
And Plenty More On The Way!**

Start Your Own Business!
**Three Strikes Incarceration
Immigration Detention
Debtors' Prison
Penitentiaries**

The greatness of a man is not in how much wealth he acquires, but in his integrity and his ability to affect those around him positively. Bob Marley

Davis Williams

Essay Eighteen

23rd August 1988

You're Not Allowed

Written by the alter ego known as 5ive (Davis J Williams)

*"That old law about 'an eye for an eye' leaves everybody blind.
The time is always right to do the right thing."*
Martin Luther King, Jr.

I am tired. Tired, tired, tired.

Tired of what? Tired of people telling me what to do, all I want to do is do what I want. Obviously, within reason. I am a good person; I do not lie, honestly I don't; and I don't steal. I don't mislead people and I have never physically abused anyone in my life, so why are these bastards bothering me?

Always bothering me, always asking me for money or making threats against me if I don't follow orders.

What the fuck...?

Why are these people always asking me to do something? Do I work for them? If so I quit!

I already pay tax every time I get paid and they tell me that my contribution helps them, the government to serve and protect me.

But wait.

Correction. They *take* tax because I don't ever remember giving anyone permission to tax a large sum of money from my account and what's worse, they then use my money to go to war on innocent people in Iraq and other places around the world.

You see, that's what it all boils down to, money and power; forget respect, they don't need it. Once you have the money everything else comes automatically. And if it doesn't come automatically, it will be taken by force.

That's what happened to me recently.

I felt their power first-hand and didn't like it; I received a parking Penalty Charge Notice on my car and the circumstances surrounding this angered me immensely. I remember the day clearly, like it was yesterday.

I remember because Arsenal were about to play Manchester United. I'd been preparing for this game all week. Everyone was going to watch this massive fixture and there was no way I going to miss it.

Power nap – check!

Half-time drinks – check!

Facebook and Twitter – logged in!

The game hadn't even started. but the pre-match banter had already begun. United fans were boasting as usual, but THE MIGHTY GUNNERS were out in full effect.

The wife and kids were away for the day - motherfucking checkmate!

Everything was accounted for. I worked all week to ensure this day was stress and distraction free. As I reached to put my phone on silent, I received a text message from my old lady reminding me to buy electricity.

Awww maaan, I knew I had forgotten something. For fuck sake! I was fuming, but couldn't dwell on this rage because time was against me. I couldn't be vexed at anyone but myself because I'd always wait till the last minute to top up the electricity. We had already gone into the £5 emergency allowance and having that expiring really wasn't an option.

With only 00.14p remaining on the electricity meter I had no choice but to speed off to the shop and top it up. The rage had to wait because if this electricity was cut off not only would I miss some of this match of the season, I wouldn't have any internet access either which would be fucked up because I was playing online poker and was about to win. Don't get it twisted; I am not a gambler, just a hustler!

With socks and house slippers on and car keys in hand, I dashed out the house in a frenzy.

One minute later, I arrived at the corner shop based on Camden High Road, in a very busy inner city area in North London. There was no free parking so I had to park in an allocated Pay & Display bay where one pound allowed me to park for forty-five minutes.

Yes, a pound was a lot to pay for what I needed, but I had no choice. All I needed was a minute to charge this foolish key. I reached for my wallet and realised I had no change for the parking meter so I went into the shop a few yards away to get some so I could pay. I left my car door open and my hazard lights flashing, making any sneaky traffic wardens aware that the driver must be close by.

Literally one minute later, I got back to my car and found a Penalty Charge Notice on the window.

"HEY MATE!"

I shouted loudly at the traffic warden.

"HOW CAN YOU GIVE ME A TICKET?! You can't give me a ticket just like that!"

"Did you know read the sign sir? Parking here is totally prohibited during these hours."

"Boss, I respect that but I went into the shop to get change, can't you reverse the ticket brother?" I asked him calmly.

"Absolutely not", he replied. "You aren't allowed to park here. Therefore, you have no grounds to appeal. I suggest you pay quickly sir, before the fine increases."

Aaaarrrrggghhhhhhhhh!

We argued for a couple of minutes and as each minute passed, I got more and more upset.

After five minutes I was mad. Fifteen minutes later I had turned into the Hulk. I threatened him, his family and knocked his hat off his head. I really wanted to knock him out but the CCTV cameras were active and I couldn't take that chance.

I was there for twenty long ass minutes trying to persuade him to reverse the parking ticket; he refused, telling me, a grown man, that I am not allowed to do this, and I am not allowed to do that. Twenty minutes of my life wasted!

I insulted him some more and went home defeated in a huff like a big baby.

My attitude shifted from excitement to being consumed with rage, negativity and weakness.

What made it worse is that the game was shit, my team lost, and the patience I had that gave me a great chance of winning some money on online poker, vanished!

All in, all in (for those who play).

I had to do something, as I had no intention of paying this fine. In the past my tactic was simple, if I get a Penalty Charge Notice I would ignore it, ignore it and ignore it. This was a good tactic at first until the fine increased and I was threatened with court action. Oh Lord, the stress. I felt so trapped! I didn't have the money to pay and was under enormous pressure.

I had to do something, so I referred to my bible, Google and typed in a question -

How do I avoid Paying Parking Tickets?

The response was instant; I was bombarded with theoretical advice from people's personal experiences. I read their accounts, watched various video clips and examined the letter templates people said they'd used; I was amazed at what I discovered.

After several hours of research, bloodshot eyes and conflicting emotions I drafted a letter.

Why were my emotions conflicted? Simply because I was undertaking something completely new to me and I didn't want the authorities to fine me further for trying to take them on, rather than pay up.

Yes I was shit scared, but I took the risk.

This letter was sent by recorded delivery to Camden Council.

Re. *Your letter dated 14 May*

Parking Charge Notice 500009/537095

To whom it may concern,

Thank you for sticking a bright Penalty Charge Notice on my vehicle. As a response to your Notice I am writing this Notice, to inform you that I am seeking a remedy to this solution and wish to avoid all forms of conflict and judicial intervention.

The Charge Notice that was received has been accepted, I repeat, it has been accepted, however in order to pay I must first act as Administrator and exercise due diligence in this matter.

You see, as it stands now, I do not understand the basis of your requests and therefore cannot lawfully fulfil them; I seek clarification of your Notice so that I may act according to the law and maintain my inalienable natural human rights.

In order for me to make sense out of nonsense I need your help in establishing what authority you are implementing and what gives you that right to ask me for payment.

Davis Williams

I am a human being, I am not perfect and so there might be something that I have missed; do not take this letter personally as I would really like to know.

I recently read the Human Rights Charter where it says everyone is innocent, until proven guilty; therefore please provide me with evidence supporting your judgment.

You must have read in the newspapers that there are some dodgy people sending people BOGUS PCNs and other requests for payment and I am sure that you wouldn't want me to be a victim of a fraudulent claim.

These same people are also claiming to have authority over innocent people by using certain Acts and Statutes as muscle, forcing people to pay by claiming they have broken the law.

Just to be clear, I would like to know, as I mentioned before, what authority you are using, because you can't use force to get me to do something that I do not want to, as slavery ended years ago. Am I your servant? If you are going to use the Traffic Management Act, or any other Act or Statute, I would like you to be aware that an ACT or Statute is defined as 'a legislative rule of a society, given the force of law with the <u>consent</u> of the governed.'

You do not have my consent to govern me.

But, in case I was drunk and signed some sort of form, or contract giving you consent, please present me with

And Along Came a Lion

evidence where I have given you my consent to be governed.

What you posted on my window was indeed a Penalty Charge Notice, and a Notice is not a Bill. I pay bills all day long and all the bills I pay are supported by a contract or something with my consent.

I've never liked paying fines; I hate them, but felt obligated to pay them. Your records would have shown that I have given you over £1500 in fines over the last 24 months. My attitude has now changed. Before I pay any fines, please provide me with a proper and lawful contract with my signature on it and a witness stating that I am liable to pay your fines. I will need a bill, the Bills of Exchange Act 1882 confirms this and this is an Act you guys should be following. How can I pay anything without a bill? And don't forget the two party contracts, with my signature, which necessarily must precede the issuance of lawful bills (just in case you missed me asking the first time).

Now, to be able to spot people committing fraud I have to arm myself with knowledge, because knowledge is power. According to the Office of Fair Trading's Debt Collection Guidance it clearly states that it is unfair to send demands for payment to an individual when it is uncertain that they are the debtors in question.

Please provide me with evidence that I was the driver at the time.

　　　　Davis Williams

I would also point out that the Office of Fair Trading's Debt Collection Guidance says that it is unfair to pursue third parties for payment when they are not liable. In not ceasing your pursuit of the alleged debt you are using deceptive/and or unfair methods. Furthermore, ignoring and/or disregarding claims that debts are disputed and continuing to make unjustified demands for payment amounts to physical and/or psychological harassment.

The only entity that was contractually bound was the driver of the vehicle at that time.

You see, I have been here many times before with you guys, demanding payment and stressing me out. NO MORE WILL I EVER PAY UNLESS YOU CAN PROVE THE ABOVE.

Finally, for my understanding and clarification, please explain to me why the Penalty Charge is so FUCKING expensive and disproportional to the actual cost of the ticket?

A car is parked in a Pay & Display meter and the terms are £1 for one hour. But for some reason, that one hour becomes two. On what basis can you charge the driver £80? The actual loss in this case would be just £1.

Would you like the driver to cover your cost of £1, as that would be a suitable resolution? If so you need to contact that person making a written request. Don't bother to ask me who was driving at the time, as I don't have to tell you.

Why do the costs you claimed to have suffered reduce from £80 to £40 if repaid quickly? This suggests that the money claimed is not even a genuine attempt to assess loss, therefore it is a penalty clause and is null and void.

You have 14 days to provide me with PROOF of your AUTHORITY, A CONTRACT, and A BILL OR INVOICE. This would be of great help as I am totally confused as to what makes you think I HAVE TO PAY YOU!

Please address every point in this letter.

If you cannot fulfil my request I would ask that no further contact be made concerning the above.

The Letter ends.

To date, they've never bothered me again.

Since then I have received six more Penalty Charge Notices and every appeal has been won. Although my letters varied, the fundamental request remained the same.

IF YOU ARE GOING TO FORCE ME TO ACT, SHOW ME EVIDENCE OF MY CONSENT. SLAVERY IS ILLEGAL.

Free yourself from this oppressive and corrupt government. Use of titles such as *Mr* and *Mrs* are dangerous for freedom fighters because such titles bind you, but I will save that story for another time. Challenge everything; you will be surprised what people get away with these days.

I dare you to take responsibility for your freedom.

RESPOND + ABILITY = **RESPONSIBILITY**

The first rule is to respond and the second is to ensure you have the ability to respond. If you don't, get your game up player!

Essay Nineteen

14th April 2011

Mind 2 Matter

Written by my mentor Mr. Harding

"The only thing that I see that is distinctly different about me is I'm not afraid to die on a treadmill. I will not be out-worked, period. You might have more talent than me, you might be smarter than me, you might be sexier than me and you might be all of those things you got on me in nine categories. But if we get on the treadmill together, there are two things: You're getting off first, or I'm going to die. It's really that simple, right?"

"You're not going to out-work me. It's such a simple, basic concept. The guy who is willing to hustle the most is going to be the guy that just gets that loose ball.

The majority of people who aren't getting the places they want or aren't achieving the things that they want in this business are strictly based on hustle. It's strictly based on being out-worked; it's strictly based on missing crucial opportunities. I say all the time if you stay ready, you ain't gotta get ready."

Will Smith

My name is Elick Harding and I run an organisation called

Mind2Matter. You may already be familiar with the name, as we have visited schools across London delivering programmes and workshops. One of my sayings is "*Every young person represents a piece of the puzzle that forms the picture called tomorrow.*"

This means that every one of you has a vision and a unique gift that if not manifested, will potentially alter the future for those people who you would have touched through your work. You see, we all have a purpose; this purpose is encoded in your very DNA.

I have known Davis Williams for a very long time and I know for certain that he too is dedicated to making a difference to the lives

of young people. If you ever have the opportunity to meet Davis, you will understand exactly what I mean. For me to be asked by him to write a few pages for this book is humbling and I welcome the opportunity to be part of this work.

My motivation in life is to help make a better tomorrow. I am not a dreamer when I say this. I have a vision and a gift to present to the world and more than ever, I realise that's why I'm here. The thing is, we all have our own unique vision and gift and depending on which of us flourishes, will determine who has a say in how we shape our communities and ultimately our world, our tomorrow.

Now, there are already many programmes and workshops out there and you might ask what the point of yet another programme is. It seems there are many organisations doing what you're doing. Yes and no. As far as the format of a programme is concerned, yes; but as far as content is concerned, no. I use the word 'programme' for various reasons relating to inclusion in the education sector. If you ask me what a better terminology for what we do is, we could say *'Mental Surgery'* – a term you will become more and more familiar with.

The next question might be what does that mean? Our reply would be that surgery is a last resort treatment. Surgery is used to transplant organs or correct structural damage or impairment in the body. If you understand that like the organs of the body, the mind is the great organiser of one's life, then it too can become damaged or impaired. Where there is damage or impairment is a result of misuse, neglect, lack of discipline, ignorance, poor education and so on, mental surgery is used as last resort treatment for example, when we conduct transplants, we are transplanting impaired, non-functioning minds with a new way of thinking.

If you ever get the opportunity to participate on the '9 Flaw Elevator Programme', you will remember a vast amount of information delivered in a very short amount of time. By this we mean the principles you will learn, if utilised will make you realise you have great potential and information stored inside you that has been locked through various KEY STAGES. By learning the principles we will pass on to you, you will, remember how to move an object without touching it by use of the energy you harness naturally.

What can I say that will make you listen young man and young woman? For hundreds of years in our community and others, elders have lost the ability to relate to young people. However there is a saying that my late, great and beautiful grandmother Leonora Hazely-Wilson always used to say -*"Pikin wey timap noh dey see pass mami wey sidom."* The translation from Krio (spoken in Sierra Leone and other parts of West Africa) is, *"a child standing up cannot see further than a mother who is sitting down"* – fathers too, whichever relates to you as the parent. In other words, no matter how tall you are, you could even be taller than your own father, they are years ahead of you on this journey called life. On that journey you might not take the exact same steps they did, but you'd be silly not to ask what to expect along the way on your journey through life. Each step-in life is a question and most of the time, your parents have the 'Ansaars'.

This brings me to my main point. We are all in serious need of a new way of thinking if we want to progress in this once-in-a-lifetime opportunity called living. The key to unlock an imprisoned mind is a change in perception. We are often prisoners of our own ignorance. Our ignorance is no different to a driver ignoring road signs and all their driving lessons and then attempting to drive from point A to B. We are all guilty of making our journey harder for ourselves when the journey is actually very straightforward. After you take your driving lessons and study the Highway Code, you pass your driving test and you free yourself from being limited to smelly night buses and underground trains. In this situation, you are not entirely in control. Your life is no different.

There are many locks/luck to be opened that will give us access to higher levels of energy. Video games work with the same principle; that is, by mastering one level of life, you unlock the gateway to higher levels of existence and then find you become better and better. Therefore, the master you're to become is already inside you - the 'you' that has already mastered that which you now dream to accomplish tomorrow. You just have to become that being you already are in the future. However, the spell must be lifted first.

THE SPELL

A little over twelve years ago, I was made aware of a spell that had been cast on me, a spell that had resulted in my low self-confidence and self-esteem. Although there were very successful black males and females I could turn to for inspiration, none stirred the sleeping giant I felt imprisoned in my chest quite like the man I affectionately call 'Baba'.

At the time, when I heard the word *'spell'* I immediately associated it with pixie dust and magic wands. However, today I am very much aware that those concepts were created for that very purpose, for me to think 'fairy-tale', to make me think the whole idea is crazy that there is such thing as a spell, like you perhaps do. It dawned on me later that for a period (a spell), while you still believe (charmed) the words (spellings) of people who lie (sleep/trance) you are indeed under a literal spell.

Spells and utterances like *'hubba bubba mish kaboosh'* or *'abracadabra'* are regarded as nonsense; on the contrary, spells are carefully selected words of power that have been placed in a sentence to cast (throw) a listener to a spell (period of time) in order to be captivated (imprisoned) by the effects of the speaker's words. In other words, to create an effect on the listener's mind, which in turn will affect the listener emotionally, which in turn will infect the listener's thinking and place the listener under a hypnotic spell-like trance, leaving them wondering (wandering) in a land of make-believe (special effects).

A word is a burst of sound energy and colour used by human beings to transfer messages from one mind to another. These energies (words) are transmitted (spoken) in various tones and frequencies. Interestingly, both colour and sound consist of different tones and frequencies. In other words, sound and colour are the same thing resonating on different frequencies.

Tones are also colours called pantones. These pantones are what paint vivid images in the mind and stimulate the imagination. Words are a powerful form of energy which, should determine how we affect the minds of those we come in contact with and ultimately their contribution to the world we live in.

The new mind that we must adopt is about reprogramming the misinformation we have been fed over many years that has left us in a terrible state. It breeds laziness which is the result of a spell that shuts down our motor (motivation). If we continue to believe what we are taught about ourselves from others, we will always be in a position of low achievement both at community and a personal level. To believe is to accept a potential lie (beLIEve). You will be lazy if you believe that you are no good and worthless. This lie makes you lay down (LIE down) and you become 'LAY ZEE' lazy. Understand and know for certain that you are UNIQUE and as such you're an asset to the world if and only IF, you decide to get up from the bed they've made for you to LIE in. Hopefully we will have the opportunity to discuss this subject in more depth but for now, WAKE UP!

Essay Twenty

Youth Crime

A conversation featuring Davis J Williams on Facebook

"Rebellion without truth is like spring in a bleak arid desert"
Kahlil Gibran

Violent crime amongst young people is on the increase and professionals, parents and carers all say it's getting worse. Having said that, is it even possible then, to build that village to raise our children? Despite the various projects, meetings and Facebook groups, why do things seem to be getting worse? Is the concept of the village raising a child outdated?

What do we do, apart from going back to Africa? Do you have any suggestions?

Excerpt from a Facebook conversation: I am DSB

DSB: *This is my revised question as the last one was too general!*

DSB: *And to the person who inboxed me already, don't be afraid of your views. Let people see your true feelings. Post it on my wall.*

NKNC: *Restructure comes to mind. There seems to be no proven structure in place that suits! Too much individualism ah gwan and without all the ingredients, the cake can't bake.*

DSB: *Thank you. You have set the standard.*

RKS: *To be honest with you, I knew that none of the youth groups would reduce violence (no offence to the successful ones); what we need to do is start all over again and actually think for a moment. What is the latest trend right now? Having said that, imagine a young person smiling at you on road instead of screwing. Well that would be my dream...the solution is that the gap (between so-called gangsters) needs to be broken and then the violence will reduce. The way young people are living nowadays as well once they're associated with a gang–I've seen them automatically disconnect from the whole community which all goes back to stereotyping. Then the young person ends up thinking the community don't give a f**k about them. Lastly, I haven't read about what Love is Just a Verb is, but from title what I would like to think it's a leader's group trying to build a village of their own from scratch.*

We need a new start. Thousands and thousands of pounds are going into shitty projects for young people that they don't even attend. WE NEED TO BUILD THAT NEW VILLAGE. LET'S TEACH OUR YOUNG PEOPLE OUR WAY OF THINKING. Plus it's all about the mind-sets of young people too. If you want me to elaborate some more let me know as this only brief. I could go on forever but I'll leave it there. I hope I am making sense because I'm just speaking my mind.

DBS: *It begins with the parents; they are crucial. There are too many stupid people having children. Sorry to have to put it that way but it's true. What morals can they teach? Raising a child is more than providing clothes and food and sending them to school. Then when they grow up and turn to madness these parents leave it to us to create projects, or ask what the government is doing to help. I know it doesn't happen in all cases and some people do change for the better; we can't change everyone as it takes time, patience and love. A person has to be willing, but I believe we can still make a difference. This is a spiritual matter I think and people mustn't forget that. And it's the education and various other systems that put disempowering, weird thoughts into the minds of young people. And it really isn't working. Ask the kids what they really want; in the majority of cases it's about family life, parents, childhood and how they feel about their current situation."*

SE: *@RMS thatz basically wat I was thinking! Hi guys, 2 say 'apart' 4rom going bk home. I don't think the solution is 'apart' I feel it's very much 2gether with. Firstly we must break down the gang culture by educating and publicly correcting all young people whether u know dem or not. I have notice sum big ppl are afraid 2 address issues they witness on road 4 fear of getting stabbed or shot, BUN DAT mentality straight away! If u address any child correctly and assertively they will listen." (negativity generally gets a negative response).*

Prepare da young people 4 repatriation. We are on foreign land we must stick 2geva, learn 2geva, live 2geva, & love 2geva until freedom comes. Tune positive thinking consciously n sub-consciously da same way 'dey' submerge our children in wickedness. We must revive by surroundin each other with love (love is HIGHLY contagious) and our youth will pick it up n follow suit. Treat all children lyk u treat ur children... Love NEVER fails. Peace n Love."

Amit Patel: *Could it be that if more young adults were given the opportunity to shine in a more natural, harmonious community, things would change for the better? I encourage youths to break the cycle of getting up late n living each day the same as the last. But without incentives like money attached, many show no interest. It's ok to go college to study topics of interest but once you get that qualification then what? Go work for some corporate company that doesn't truly respect or care about them or the communities they come from? Let's encourage and value those who do want to get up in da morning and break that cycle and give them the right knowledge and tools that will enable them to one day actually own their own business. This is 100% possible given the right support & guidance; it also gives them a sense of working towards something. Imagine them being in a position to support themselves and their families, no longer needing to watch over their shoulder for the feds who want to take away their possessions/freedom and best of all, having something positive to pass on to their children in later years. People are too quick to blame the young adults for the problems but how many older adults can say that they have set up a business with the intention of passing it on to them or showing them that a few years down the line they could go set up their own branch and run it effectively?*

Start small, think big! The size and type of business they seek to start first is unimportant, the fact that they start on the path of self-reliance is!!!

PS. I also see it as very important to support/get involved with a trusted black organisation that is closely linked to Africa; everything we have here in the West, first came out of Africa and as a collective in the diaspora we need to reconnect with our roots n traditions in order to really speed up the process of effective change. Bless up!

Sally Jessica: *The media play an integral role in how and what we think. For example, the EastEnders scene were Phil punches Ben... to me this is just promoting violence against children and it's UNACCEPTABLE! So many children suffer at the hands of bullying parents or peers and then we have a popular soap legitimising it and influencing already dysfunctional minds.*

I just don't understand how people can't see the danger and damage these storylines perpetuate. Alarm bells should be ringing but instead people seem to be completely desensitised. It's like people actually enjoy and get satisfaction from such storylines.

This type of script writing does nothing for the spiritual upliftment of our communities. TV producers have a responsibility to us as viewers and at the moment, EVERY soap is negative beyond belief and people just accept it as the norm! Please people don't be hoodwinked, fooled or tricked into thinking this is it and just accept it. These producers influence us through their programmes and the young pick up every single frame. Don't you realise that these same producers could write storylines that represent real true inspiration, not gun-wielding murderous characters! They could go a long way to help solve gun and knife crime but they don't... they just perpetuate it!

Personally, the only way out of this reality is to stop doing the things that are causing the problem, one of the things is employment, something that consumes most of our precious time. I know people are gonna say they have bills to pay; I would have to say our children need you more than paper money needs you right now. Next move! What should bills consist of? Fundamental requirements - food and shelter, water, electric, gas (phone is not a necessity).

Now watch how I delete them one by one; shelter - every creature has its shelter and they're not paying rent on it. They have their food which they don't pay for, they have water yes again they don't pay. Electric/gas needed for utilities, cooker, fridge, heating etc. but not life threatening, one can do without even for a while!

All this technology they invented to keep us occupied away from our ESSENCE, our TRUE self. IT'S THE BIGGEST SCAM ON HUMANITY AND WE BETTER WAKE UP. IF YOU WANT TO SEE CHANGE YOU HAVE TO BE THE CHANGE YOU WANT TO ACTUALISE. OTHERS CAN'T DO IT FOR YOU, BUT WITH YOU!

As DSB said, what do we do?

The only way I see this working is for the majority to make the first move and set the pace - abandon employment (let's be real here, there is not, has never been, and will never be enough jobs for the population and I'm not including those that can't work), so the illusion of educating oneself for employment's sake will be obsolete; so no more striving to reach the highest ranks because we are all equal in the eyes of our Creator. The days of getting a degree to pack shelves will be no more. The days of learning for the sake of learning will be here!

Next, demand that we get access to shelter, food and water for free...yes free and it is our entitlement, period! There is no way these life essentials should come at a price. It is so wrong for us to be charged financially for these and for corporations to be making billions in profit from utilities we literally can't live without.

The current economic system must go! It doesn't work for the masses and it can't sustain us so it should be abandoned! (I can hear you saying but... but...but...) no buts... do you really think we were created to be slaves to a system that doesn't care for us or our children? I think not! We don't need money; we don't need to be governed by a monetary system. We are the highest beings in this planet of creation. We have love, kindness, compassion, inspiration, understanding and intelligence. It is this intelligence that distinguishes and enables us to create machines and technology that can do all the manual work for us. This is why they undereducated us because once we know the truth about who we truly Are, our essence... they will no longer have the power over us. While we are attached to the illusion they have us where they want us. They have the power to do what the hell they want!

THIS IS THE REAL CHANGE WE NEED, WANT AND HAVE BEEN WAITING FOR AND IF WE DONT ACT NOW, NOTHING WILL CHANGE... BUT WORSEN MOST DEFINITELY!

THERE IS NO MESSIAH COMING TO SAVE US. BE MESSIAH OF YOUR OWN SOUL... SO YOU BEST START BELIEVING IN YOURSELF.

MW: I agree with Amit Patel, money is the biggest motivator for a lot of negative activity. Many youngsters with talent don't actually think they have a choice about where their lives are heading. It takes discussions like this, followed by goal-setting and planning. You can definitely get the youths attention if you're showing them how to come up financially. That's how it's done on the streets, so do it in the business world. At the same time they need to understand the way the media is controlling their minds. From the posts that I have read, there are plenty teachers equipped to do the job. Let's do it.

JPH: I've been thinking about this for ages but who has the answer? I don't want to hear no more blaming the government as that's played out. We (people of all ages and races) are the only ones that can stop our youth killing each other ...where will it all end man, how many more dead this year? I'm always up for supporting the cause, get at me!

SSC: People need to stop chat. It takes action. Parents need to start at home, but it is also down to us to engage and plant seeds.

FN: I actually don't know! I don't know what will make a human being kill an innocent person so casually. Look at the amount of stabbings this weekend, just maddd! I really don't know! Like you said, so much has been done already. Whatever we've been doing and are doing has NOT worked (or at least I haven't seen the success of it). We need something very drastic because I'm hearing the same reasons/excuses, yes, that's what I will call some of them. Don't they see that they have blood on their hands?? Like what the hell, it's innocent people as well. They must think it's a war zone or something. And it's days like this I totally agree with the joint enterprise law. I was talking to someone and they even mentioned capital punishment. I'm not saying that's the solution but all I know is that we need something drastic that's never been done before.

DSB: I'm hosting a meeting next week and your thoughts will form the basis of the direction it goes. Thank you!

SS: It all starts with the parents...this is not to blame the great work that the great parents do...those that DO GREAT THINGS MUST OF COURSE BE COMMENDED. Yet many don't even know what their children get up to. This can be for many socio-economic reasons. Yet the KEY always goes back to the parent.

The development of a child begins with a subtle thought. Parents need to be more conscious whilst raising children are RESPONSIBLE FOR THE EARLY DEVELOPMENTAL YEARS OF A CHILD.

That means they must prepare the way.

Love, support, education, being there, showing they care, knowing what they are up to, etc.

WHAT WE NEED IS MORE INTERACTION FROM EXPERIENCED PARENTS AND THE GROUPS THAT ARE PRO-ACTIVE OUT THERE.THERE IS NOTHING WRONG WITH BEING IN DIFFERENT GROUPS, OR HAVING DIFFERING BELIEFS SO LONG AS COLLABORATION FOR THE BETTERMENT OF OUR CHILDREN IS THE PRIORITY.TEACH A CHILD IN THE RIGHT WAY AND IT WILL MAINTAIN THOSE WAYS

DG: I believe the reason we are in this situation is because of a lack of understanding of our young people as well the division that we as elders of the community have put in place by being influenced by the media. We no longer look after each other's children like we use to and have left the youths to their own devices and this is the result. We need to stop comparing and looking at other countries and show our young people how to make legit money, i.e. helping them to set up companies and educate themselves. If this was put in place we could save many lives.

5
Take a Break, Breathe, Inhale, Exhale, then come again

A schoolgirl was raped by a gang who poured caustic soda over her body to destroy DNA evidence. The gang, said to have been five black youths, beat the teenager before taking turns to rape her in an empty house. Doctors feared the girl might die, but she pulled through and is now stable in a burns unit... A police source said, "She has appalling injuries from which she will never fully recover..."

Why is this happening?

I have been to hundreds of meetings, conferences, debates and consultations where people discuss the effects of gangs on the community. I have become increasingly frustrated when professional box ticking 'know-it-all's always conclude the meeting by highlighting the fact that it is only a small percentage of young people doing these terrible violent acts so better to focus on most young people who do not. Let's continue doing DJ workshops, helping them write CVs and totally ignore the minority. They are not important. Let's just focus on the good kids, the bad ones are few and far between. If we ignore them long enough, they will just disappear.

This minority should not be looked upon and treated as the problem, but rather as people who have issues they need help with.

This way of thinking separates the person from the behaviour.

War and disorder generates revenue and opportunities for the businesses that thrive on it.

The government can actively challenge gangs, drugs and anti-social behaviour, but if this happens and gangs disappear, then thousands of people will lose their jobs. The war on gangs, like the war on drugs, is a war that needs to be sustained for decades and those in higher positions get paid to offer solutions that do not work. The war on terror, 'terra' being Latin for earth.

We need to listen and engage with the minority and respond to their needs and requests!

In truth, it is the minority that is ruling over the majority.

We need to recognise that the minority has created a social trend and lifestyle that is sending shockwaves throughout inner city communities.

Various sources suggest that, 90% of the world's wealth is controlled by just 10% of the population; this 10% is made up of fewer than five families. The most famous is the Rothschild family (known as The House of Rothschild, or simply the Rothschild's), a European family of German Jewish descent that established European banking and finance houses in the late eighteenth century.

Minorities rule the world; they rule the way we behave, the way we think and the way we perceive our reality. Governments are based on the principle that a minority of elected members create rules to govern the majority.

The Board of Directors at Manchester United Football Club is made up of individuals who decide the salaries for both players and staff and influence every aspect of the club's management. Again, the minority here governs the majority – the pyramid model.

This method of influence is nothing new. Often, the minority will lie, steal, deceive, kill, defame and cheat to ensure the majority follow them, often blindly. It clearly works, as there are NO MORALS IN BUSINESS. Anything goes. Ask Sony. They release music that has a detrimental effect on the innocent and fertile minds of the youth. They have the power to flood the market with positive images and role models, but they do not.

Speak to the oil tycoons who make billions in profit, at the expense of the Amazon rain forest and the indigenous population whose way of life is being destroyed. The film *Avatar* is a great example of this where humans wanted to ruin the Na'vi culture of Pandora, a distant planet. Earthlings needed a rare mineral found there to solve their energy crisis so their aim was to acquire this mineral from Pandora at any costs.

There is another type of minority. Those who tell the truth, never lie, don't cheat, preserve life and have values and morals aligned with Mother Nature. Their voices are silenced due to their power and influence. Their uncut truth, raw stories and undiluted expressions can create a new orbit for the black stars currently caught up in someone else's orbit.

Always strive to be that minority. Don't be afraid to stand out; that is where true power and wealth dwells.

Essay Twenty-One

23rd July 2012

London is burning HD (High Definition)
Written by Abby Sonko

"Knowledge makes a man unfit to be a slave."
Frederick Douglass

On Thursday 4th August 2011 in Tottenham, North London, 29-year-old father of four Mark Duggan was shot dead by police.

By Saturday 6th August 2011, the need to find facts and gain intelligence from police regarding the death of Mark had become a priority for his family and the local community. Mark's family and friends organised a peaceful protest to be held outside Tottenham police station with the primary objective being to seek answers to their many questions. On stating their purpose of protest to the police, the crowd waited in vain with no information being communicated to the crowd. By 8pm, the peaceful atmosphere amongst the protestors was replaced with tension, hostility, frustration and anger as their requests for information continued to be ignored. A 16-year-old girl approached the police, in all fairness, openly displaying her hostility towards them. Witnesses said the police turned on her using unreasonable force. They also suggested this riled the protestors and the spiral of events that subsequently took place was a result to this initial catalyst - police insensitivity.

By the end of that night and the three days that followed, England witnessed a shocking array of criminal acts, looting, arson and violence. Groups of people stormed the streets of multiple cities across the country including London, Birmingham, Liverpool, Manchester and Bristol, leaving a path of destruction in their wake; smashing shop windows and looting goods; setting cars and buses alight; hurling bricks, cans and bottles at police; buildings were burnt to the ground. As millions at home watched live news reports in disbelief, it became increasingly obvious that things were about to get worse before getting better.

Were they a care-free (less) generation or a disadvantaged generation of lost citizens?

Live coverage of the riots was shown on all mainstream news channels. The copycat behaviour that spread from city to city was the talk of the nation. Lives, jobs and homes were destroyed. Why was it that those committing these acts of violence, theft and arson were doing so? And happily, at that, it seemed, according to the footage shown on 'news' channels. These were the questions running through the minds of many. The initial protest on the Saturday over the circumstances of Mark Duggan's (following his death two days prior) seemed to fall down the media's 'ladder of priority'. The main priority quickly shifted to 'the riots' or 'the looters'. At the time of the riots, I was engaged in countless debates, mostly via Facebook. I have included the different arguments of some that were put forward on my page. Per some, the behaviour of rioters/looters was explained in the following context:

"The looters and those causing mayhem on our streets do so simply for the gratification of destruction and the perceived notion that they can get away with it. They are not rioting as a statement or to force a change to any system, be it judicial or educational. They are not the disaffected youth protesting for any cause. They

are simply opportunists. The protesters in Tottenham and the subsequent rioting were making a strong and worthwhile statement. There is no denying there is a two-tier education system that needs addressing. There is also no denying inner city schools need more investment. However, those who value education in disadvantaged areas, attend it, and benefit from it. The teachers in inner city schools do a fantastic job and have the skills and determination to provide their pupils with a good education. Children from a good family, with the right attitude will obtain an education. It is the parenting skills of these teenagers on our streets that need addressing to prevent mindless destruction. To suggest that the rioting we see on our streets now is as a result of anything other than feral youths taking advantage of an opportunity to cause destruction is incorrect." (Facebook friend)

Those were generally the same people who were consumed with disappointment, anger and contempt for the ludicrous behaviour of 'thugs' destroying the streets that hard-working people's taxes contribute towards.

However, others argued that while the behaviour demonstrated by rioters could not be condoned and was highly disappointing, it had to be considered separately to the physical acts of destruction. In other words, one cannot simply consider the act without addressing the root causes of the act, the implications of these acts and the wider social context. Why is it that a generation of people clearly have such little regard for 'their' streets and clearly do not feel any sense of belonging to 'their' society, so much so that they will readily trash, steal and burn their own local supermarkets? Why are some people so angry and frustrated that they would see this as an opportunity to vent that anger through destruction? Those seeking answers to this type of question were mostly those arguing that the youth are a product of their environment, that 'the system' has nurtured such careless irresponsible people through its class system which fuels division and subjects many to social deprivation. As reported by, those who believe this philosophy the behaviour of rioters could be explained in the following context:

"There have been a lot of people making comments that simply indicate their lack of understanding of the complexity of social issues. I have said countless times that I do not support the actions of rioters and I still stand by that. What I am saying is that it cannot be disputed that there are social issues that have not been addressed since they were documented in the Scarman Report following riots in the 1980s and the McPherson Report following the murder of Stephen Lawrence in 1993.Most the people who lived in the areas where the riots occurred did not approve of the looting and violence. Right now, we have a section of our population who feel no regard or responsibility to the state. Yes, the riots were conducted by opportunists and I've said all along I don't condone that, BUT I also don't condone a system that fails to scratch beneath the surface, dig a little deeper and take some responsibility for facilitating the growth of this type of mind-set.

Support for community organisations and projects has deteriorated over the years leaving many people feeling that as far as the government is concerned, they are simply not worth investing in. Fact is, equality was never a part of the official agenda. It is true that the teachers in inner city schools do a fantastic job and have the skills and determination to provide their pupils with a good education. I am one of them! I also agree a lot of time should be invested in teaching adequate parenting skills. However, to suggest that these children all come from broken homes with poor parenting skills does not take into account the social 'norms' amongst today's youth. This includes the expectations from peers, the disconnection from education, employment and attainable aspirations. It's clear that some of these core issues were PARTLY nurtured by a system that does not value equality! I want people to consider this disgusting rioting in a wider context; the idiots have overshadowed what this was initially all about!

The major institutions that have a direct impact on the riots in my opinion are the police and education institutions.

I believe there is a lack of confidence in the police force combined with a lack of faith in the education system, particularly amongst those from African-Caribbean descent. This distrust has manifested over the years, after countless cases of institutional racism. Because of this distrust and broken relationships have caused the integrity of educators and the police to be questioned. Many people are feeling disconnected and disenfranchised from the major institutions that are designed to support them (in theory).

The contempt felt by some towards the police but also towards the education system, cannot be studied and interpreted without an understanding of the sociological and psychological contributing factors. The 'fuck the police' mentality has been nurtured by a systemic society that is defined by its social division under Conservative rule and has manifested itself in the form of dysfunctional, disengaged, poorly educated people. The same people that the government did not want to invest in are the same who we see have the least regard for the government and law enforcers. Is it a coincidence that those who lack education, employment, opportunity and attainable aspirations were those that made up the largest proportion of looters?

Some more Coverage...

Abby Sonko "*To the ppl on my Facebook making ludicrous statements suggesting that the education system treats ALL pupils equally and that we all have the same life chances I won't even grace such nonsense with an argument, clearly such views are derived from an extremely shallow, one dimensional level of understanding of our society! I'm not supporting the 'looters' just stating fact*"

"The war is not meant to be won, it is meant to be continuous. Hierarchical society is only possible on the basis of poverty and ignorance...
The war is waged by the ruling group against its own subjects and its object is not the victory over either Eurasia or East Asia, but to keep the very structure of society intact."
-George Orwell, 1949, from "1984"

CondemnedHistorian.blogspot.com

Facebook friend: *Well said Vince, a protest is a way of having your voice heard and as Vince said this was making a worthwhile statement. To call people such as myself shallow and one-dimensional is absolutely ludicrous. You cannot sit there and justify the mayhem that has run through the country. There are ways and means of getting your point across, this is not it. I don't care about people's ethnic origin, a human is a human to me. Gangsters, drug dealers, murders are all the same regardless of their background. One less on the streets only makes it a better place for our families and children. The educational system may be lacking in some areas but this is not the way to go about it, those who want to learn will learn. It's those that don't want it and want livelihoods handed on plate are the ones running riot. The ones that need the help are at home saying why are you doing this and making it worse? If you are going to support anyone, support the innocent people.*

Conclusion:

Not all of those that took to the streets during the riots were black, FACT! However, in my opinion, the riots were fuelled by the fact that the family of a black man were outraged that he was shot and killed by the police. This essay has been written with that in mind. That fact, as well as an institutionally racist police force and an education system that excludes black Caribbean boys three times more than any other group. One cannot begin to understand the causes of the riots without looking at the bigger picture.

The actions of looters cannot be condoned in any way, BUT it cannot be looked at in isolation either. In 1981 Lord Scarman documented his research findings after studying the events that had led to the riots that had erupted in Brixton earlier that year. On that occasion the riots were sparked by the police shooting of a woman called Cherry Groce, when they raided her home looking for her son. She was paralysed from the waist down. The report concluded that police were unjust and discriminatory towards black men (see PACE Act).

The Macpherson Report, released in 1999, six years after the murder of Stephen Lawrence, re-iterated such findings, highlighting the institutional racism in the Metropolitan Police.

In 2001, the Department of Education produced 'Get it Right Get it

Right' and funded the Black Pupils Achievement Programme (BPAP) to be delivered in mainstream schools to target the disproportionate high exclusion rate and low achievement of black pupils.

I have made brief reference to these publications for anyone who argues that a corrupt, racist system has not contributed to the social disorder that we are currently witnessing.

Essay Twenty-Two

5th June 2012

My Truth is Not Your Truth
Written by Jenavi

"The best way to defeat your enemy is to make him your friend."
Unknown

I'm writing this to share my truth, my ideology, my solution and my passions. I'd like to think it is raw, uncut and undiluted —making it valid, sincere and insightful. I was thinking of using an alias (pen-name) but that would only taint the 'real' nature of this, so fuck it, I'm using my real name and real names of friends and colleagues.

My truth is that we're all prostitutes and life is our pimp that constantly bitch slaps us when we fail to pay our dues. Like the sex industry, in life we rarely get out what we invest, making the idea that life works on a meritocratic system a joke and a poor joke at that.

Growing up behind the Sommer Layton estate on the frontline in Brixton - the road that links Brixton to Herne Hill - me and my family have been through more than our fair share of trials and tribulations.

As a twin, my sister and I grew up the youngest of seven siblings with a proud mother and absent father; well physically he was around, but functionally in terms of his role as a father,he was missing like an object goes 'vamoose' in a Houdini magic act.

Thinking back, it amazes me how five of us would share one bedroom, mum, dad and my older brothers had a room each. Despite the lack of privacy, constant arguments, bickering and fighting, which was inevitable in such a confined space, it fostered a deeper sense of love for my siblings. We're all grown up now and have our own respective commitments, the love I have for my family is unconditional and will never wane.

Not to brag, but I have great brothers and sisters; none of us smoke or drink excessively and nobody has been on the wrong side of the law either. That doesn't mean we're a dry and 'square' bunch, but it's rather indicative of the morals and values instilled in us by our hard-working mother who always taught us to "treat others how you would expect to be treated."

But the fucked-up nature of life did not play by the rules espoused by my dear mother and life had not treated me or my family in a way we would treat others. There's been the attempted mugging of my mother on her way home from an Urobho (our tribe in Nigeria) party. She was punched and kicked to the ground; just thinking about it gets me angry and I fucking swear that whoever did that will get more than their comeuppance. It was only divine intervention that a Rasta walking his children home from a relative's house saw this and gave chase but didn't catch the fucker.

Like the rope-a-dope tactic Muhammad Ali used in the 'Rumble in the Jungle' fight, life will take all the blows you can muster, then when you've worn yourself out will hit you with a knockout punch – out of the blue. Well that's what it felt like when I experienced the next tragedy that has been indelibly impressed into the archives of my mind.

Coming home from school on a Friday afternoon and seeing an ambulance parked outside my house seemed innocuous enough, until I noticed the front door open. When I came up the stairs and saw my twin sister in floods of tears and the duvet in our spare room covering the 6'1' frame of my brother, my world came crashing down around my ears. Crushed windpipes were what the ambulance man said, crushed windpipes, nothing could bring back my brother, nothing!!!

The coroner deemed it misadventure and possible suicide but my brother had the world at his feet. He was head prefect at school, a ladies' man, debonair, with swagger in abundance. So why would a 16-year-old want to extinguish the flame that was his life? Although I was only 13 at the time I started thinking about how fucked up life is and how certain people who were 'bad breed' went through their entire life doing 'bad things' and never once lost a loved one. Whereas my family who had never done any wrong, lost a beloved brother and son. Sorry but that's not right in the slightest.

The idea of a God seemed like a piss take, because I was thinking, "well if there is a God why would he put me and my family through this?"

My fledgling resentment, anger and confusion towards God was temporarily tempered by the secondary school dedicating a day to my brother and holding a church service in his name. Even though some pupils saw this as a day off, those who were supportive attended and showed love.

Last year, this all changed when my dad passed away from diabetes. In my humble opinion, Kings College Hospital is the most wot-less, fucked up hospital and I'd love to sue them for every penny they have. They said my dad was checked in for swelling of his leg and testicles, which should have been a routine overnight procedure to make sure things didn't get too bad. Overnight turned into a day, days became weeks, then before long my dad was in that stinking, horrible and unsanitised ward for the better part of a month.

His untimely death came about when a procedure they passionately stated would pose no significant risk to him ('pleural aspiration'), caused internal bleeding and led to a heart attack, which killed him. At the inquest into his death, the doctors used various medical terminologies to provide a rationale for their blatant ignorance and neglect this meant we had no basis to form a claim for neglect for his death.

Being the Christian she is, my mother shook hands with the doctor who undertook the operation that led to my dad's death, but fuck that, I was not about to put on a front and act like everything was hunky dory; I'll see those doctors burn in hell before I'd ever shake their hand.

Things like this make a mockery of the idea that hard work pays dividends and being able to reap the benefits later in life. My dad worked his whole life and 'lived his life to work' as opposed to 'working so he could live his life'. And what did he have to show for it? Nothing, apart from negligent doctors offering a pathetic apology for his death; right now, words will never convey the disdain I hold for those doctors.

Every time I look at my pay slip I get so vexed, knowing that my hard-earned money is going to support a National Health Service that is shit to say the least. Another example was a different visit to the hospital to see my dad. I saw some chips someone dropped on the staircase leading to his ward, a week later the chips were still there. Hygiene was obviously not a priority on Kings College Hospital's list; no wonder the MRSA bug is going around. It defies belief that the government will try and pass this off as some new hybrid fatal airborne disease going around. It's a fucking dirty environment which is bound to cause germs spreading you morons, there's nothing scientific about that is there? Clean sterile environment equals lack of germs equals no MRSA.

Some of you might be thinking that the examples I've provided thus far are quite extreme. I mean two deaths are bound to make anyone feel disillusioned about life. Ok so let's talk about my career and this should also highlight and provide further rationale as to why I think life is cruel.

No matter how many laws passed through parliament to support equal opportunities, discrimination is still rife. As a young Black man, I get irate that I have to work twice as hard as my White counterparts just to receive some form of recognition whilst they have the luxury of doing jack shit and still receive praise.

My last job as a young people's substance misuse practitioner summed this up perfectly; whilst I had no problems with my ex-boss using my talents to further her own goals, I remained in the same lowly position in terms of salary and status at Addaction. Even though I had single-handily written dossiers and funding bids which had secured significant amounts of money, it was my manager who received all the praise, not me.

Now my White colleagues Jenna & Darin were not as proactive as me. It was revealed that the three of us were on the lowest salary, even though I had the most experience working with young people and had done things beyond my remit for the betterment of the organization that I worked for.

Some might call me green, but I'd generally thought my work was valued, appreciated and reflected in my salary but clearly it wasn't; my colleagues were earning far more than I was whilst doing far less work. What a JOKE!!!!

Small things I noticed like my manager allowing Jenna & Darrin to take cigarette breaks up to 20 minutes a time whilst I toiled away, if you add up each of the cigarette breaks over the course of a week I'm certain it added up to an entire day.

My advice to any Black person who knows they are good at what they do is to package yourself as a commodity, realise your value and never settle for less. I learned the hard way that people will feign friendship when it suits them but feel no shame in getting you to do their work whilst taking all the credit for it.

My truth also centres upon the concept of friends. I think people are too quick to refer to people as friends only to be let down by them shortly after. I am perfectly secure with the fact that I can count all my friends on one hand. Don't get me wrong; I'm a very sociable guy and have many associates that I use for certain things such as raving or making money for example.

I am sceptical about having too many friends for a couple of reasons; one, maintaining multiple friendships can be draining and taxing and entails that adage of 'a problem shared is a problem halved'. Some friends take this to the extreme and shower you with all their problems, offering nothing in return.

I had one friend who was like a leech; he'd suck all the energy out of me by telling me about his domestic issues with his missus; how work was depressing and how he was always broke. After speaking to him I always felt deflated and positivity was void. When we went out, he always seemed to forget his wallet or his card was 'not working,' so I found myself acting like his dad and paying for him. When dropping him home, he would never offer petrol money and it was all take, take, and take.

There was another friend who would only call me to complain about something; one time he complained for two whole hours. He didn't even ask me how I was doing or allow me talk. He just spoke and spoke and spoke. And when he finished he said 'thanks for listening!'

Eventually I locked off our friendship, as having no friends seemed better than having a drain on my resources. Not to sound pompous, but with most of my friends I always felt like I was leading and they were chasing the pack. Sometimes, I'd wonder what I was getting out of maintaining a friendship with them.

I normally like to acquaint myself with people who I consider more advanced than me who I can learn from and inspire me to climb to greater heights and not friends that I must slow down for so they can catch up with me.

My solution to us being pimped by life is to adhere to my motto 'aspiration being the key to emancipation'. Without any goals to work towards you will continue getting pimped, used and left behind whilst others excel at your expense. Life will continue to beat you up whilst you simply take it like a damn fool.

Break the mould, don't follow the crowd, have your own autonomy, be your own person, think for yourself. I always strive to get information from various sources rather than taking information from one source as gospel. Failure to do this sets you up to be indoctrinated and easily led like a sheep.

Life is like a road; your goals and aspirations are your satnav and the pot-holes are the challenges life constantly throws in your path. Be prepared, don't drive with blinkers on and give your mind the sustenance it needs.

One thing I am trying to address is my laziness. I always put off things I can do today; don't let this be you as before you know it, you'll be in the same position you were in decades ago wondering where the time has gone and hopelessly wishing that you could turn back the hands of time.

I don't know about you, but personally I am tired of being pimped by life. It's time I started making life work for me, life is a bitch; that's why with my aspirations and goals I intend to dress life up in high heels and a short mini-skirt and send her out on the street corner to make that bread for me, not vice versa. After all life is supposed to be what you make it, right?

Essay Twenty-Three

14th December 2012

Promote the things you love
Written by Snaps (14-years-old)

"If you were your father, what would you say to yourself?"

A 14-year-old student was asked to produce homework on the above topic, this is what he said:

Yo homie, tell me something... what's your passion? What do you dream about? What are you willing to stand for G? Some cats say they dream bout running the blocks, being known on the streets. Please! Not you as well... please don't tell me that you want to run your postcode as well. That hard concrete you call the roads, which belongs to the Queen! And if you say you rep your family, does that mean you will try your damnedest to make them proud by setting the example? Or does it mean putting them through hell because you done dirt resulting in your home getting raided at 3 in the morning? Are you a rebel with a cause or without? I pray it' the latter. What would you like to change in the world? Your world, the world you see through your eyes? If you want to change it, why have you not done it yet? And what are you waiting for?

Are you too afraid? Afraid of being judged? Afraid of being different? Afraid of standing out and being noticed? Afraid of showing people how powerful you really are? Don't be!!! FEAR is big business you know, just ask newspapers whose sales reflect how fearful their stories are. Check out the churches whose congregations are filled by fearful Christians hoping to avoid the fire and brimstone. Stop half-stepping, stop walking sideways, stop doubting yourself and listen to that inner voice. Can you hear it? That squeaky voice telling you that nobody is ever going to give you permission to be great.

You must give yourself that permission, homie! All you got to do is look in the mirror to find out that it is you who is preventing you from making that change you yearn for! Stop waiting for someone else to give you something you already have!

Yeah, I see you running, making excuses...the ifs and the buts! Stop running away. Stop being afraid of change, be fearless. Nothing is more contagious than fear. Chances are, you have been running away from that which makes you vulnerable for so long, you probably forgot that you were running.

Embrace that fear, that pain. Stop running and face it. Once you look at it, own it, and reframe it, no longer can it hurt you again.

Do not be afraid of failing. There is no such thing as failure, just feedback, or something you know how to do better. The many failures taught you valuable lessons, look back to see them for yourself!

Life is so simple when you live your life, and not the life others want you to live.

Realise this: you are powerful and valuable beyond measure. POWERFUL and VALUABLE! So, powerful and valuable that they would rather lock you up instead of educating you. The more prisoners in jail the more money they make, durrrrrr...When you play dumb, ignorant and foolish you only do what others want you to do. Like a muppet! You acting this way makes them feel comfortable. How can you fly like a hawk, when you choose to peck all day with the chickens? What you see depends on what you are looking for! Life is beautiful when you focus on what you want. Life then becomes awesome when you learn how to utilise the people in your life. Understand this: you might not be able to stop people bum rushing your life like a bull in a china shop, or prevent inevitable events from occurring because some things are simply out of your control. Fair enough. But there is something you can control, and that is your mindset. When you upgrade your attitude, your perception and focus, what was once a problem or burden now becomes an opportunity. Go forth, open your mind to the possibility that you can achieve anything your mind can perceive.

Pay attention to what you want, why you want it and how you are going to get it, and do not let anything distract you.

5
Take a Break, Breathe, Inhale, Exhale, then come again

Essay Twenty-Four

5th November 2013

WHY DOES MY HAIR GROW UP?

Written by Coco Bean

"The man who has no imagination has no wings."
Muhammad Ali

There is no party like Mrs Hall's dinner party. I repeat there is no party like Mrs. Halls dinner party. I say this twice whilst clicking my heels like Dorothy, hoping the harder I try the more likely I will end up at my sister's kitchen table taking in the heavenly scents of 5* Michelin cooking. Let me set the scene for you. You walk into a house filled with the scent of the food simmering on the hob, cocktails in sugar-rimmed glasses with strawberries floating in the bottom of the glass, soca music playing in the background courtesy of the West Indian baby fathers. The sweet laughter of children as they run riot through the house. And a hot debate brewing amongst the adults whilst feasting on homemade bread, dips and the piece de resistance, canapés. They ain't no party like Mrs. Hall's dinner party. Now back to the HOT debate, which is always as steaming hot as the simmering pots - dark skin versus light skin... inhale...for real? Exhale...

I thought we had killed this topic! Looking around me as the debate heats up, I take in the perfect picture that makes up my family, a perfect advert for United Colours of Benetton.

Beautiful shades of brown, from pure sumptuous coco to

variations of delicious caramel.

We rock!

With extremely divided opinions, I am left in a bit of a baffled state. What do these people mean dark skin girls were never overshadowed by their fairer skinned counterparts...WHAT? Where are these people living, under a rock? Or, are they trying to hide the truth under the same rock? Is it purely a case of different experiences? My voice gets higher pitched and I have to stand to be heard. Coming from a big family, you have to have a larger than life personality to be heard. The first person I call to the witness stand is my 14-year-old baby boy. Now my son is a beautiful, handsome, pretty, chocolate brown boy. The sun kisses his skin at every opportunity and leaves him with scorching, rich, red undertones.

I know every mother thinks their child is a beauty, but I tell you no lie... this is far from a biased opinion.

A few months back I took my son to Westfield. I had to prove to him that no way on God's planet, did those boys at school purchase their Louis Vuitton goods from these heavily guarded designer shops! However, I was willing to give him a tenner to pop round Wembley market and purchase a bootleg one. Of course, he kindly declined my offer, horrified at such an act. As we talked over and addressed his ever-growing list of teenage issues he came up with a blow to the gut. "Girls like the light skin boys better than the dark skin boys.... nobody wants a dark skin boy" inhale...inhale...I couldn't breathe! My heart started pounding furiously and I got an instant headache. For real? Are we back here again? I honestly thought that we as a community had come to terms with each other and could live in harmony like the flavours in a tub of a Neapolitan ice cream. Complementing each other.

The reasons I call my son to the panel is to prove that old wounds still run deep. The damage has run deep and is still affecting a generation we thought it never would. My reality has become my son's reality. The debates continue with this new-found evidence. I begin to sense that because the women and men in my family are proud, cultured and highly educated people it seems to be a high possibility that we now want to sweep the skeletons back in the darkest part of the closet and pretend that we didn't fall victim to light skin, long hair, straight hair, mixed heritage, white girl syndrome.

Truth is truth.

Now I'm going to be honest with you, I have fallen victim to most of the above.

Guilty!

And I cringe when I say this because, I'm letting you into a past I'd also like to pretend doesn't exist. I'd love to tell you I've always been proud to be a brown girl. I'd love to tell you that I'd never wished my ponytail swung left to right like a white girl, or curled in a wild exotic way like a mixed heritage girl. Please god, anything but the afro! I don't ever remember wishing I was light skin or is that memory so disturbing I wish not to remember? Hmmmm... However, I do remember having an eye for the light skin/mixed heritage boys. Not that I never found brown boys attractive, light skin boys just stood out.

It seemed that when you were darker in complexion, you had to be twice as good looking as the light skin boy to justify the back-breaking double take for that second glance. I would love to say I have always known and embraced my beauty and have never felt less attractive than the flowing hair mixed heritage girl standing next to me. I would love to say that black men always appreciated a natural looking sister over the more exotic looking sister, with her easy to digest blackness. Most of all, I would love to say I didn't do what I could to try and fit in or compensate for what I felt was lacking. So, I did my best to look the part. I burnt my scalp in the process, tore out my hair line, tonged, flattened, pressed, glued, tagged, pulled and wished and wished on a shooting star to make my hair 'flickable'. You know, just like the white girl described in the fiction books that I spent long hours engrossed in or and those other chicks in the movies.

This is my story. Let me take you on a personal journey. I have an African name, one name...no middle name to fall back on, nor an English name to help my CV out either. Just one African name. When I moved to this country, the first friend I made was a Ghanaian girl named Olivia...I yearned for a pretty name like Olivia. She was an African girl with long permed thick hair. I on the other hand (Johnny just come), had my hair twisted with black thread in that my mum thought was a 'bang on trend' hairstyle. I went on a journey of the 'straight hair syndrome', perming it to an inch of its life. Perming my hair had never been a topic of discussion in my household. Putting braids in was an issue with my clinically clean father who despised the sight of synthetic hair often sighted for around two weeks after the job had been done. We got banned! The joys of an African upbringing.

In Africa, everyone kinda looked like variations of me, so having thread in my hair was cool. I never grew up with a doll but, was taught to braid on long grass and combed the hair of a dried mango seed. We were a middle-class family and had well-travelled parents. I played in the sun for hours on end, until finally watching the sunset. I was never stuck in front of a TV for hours on end. I didn't have access to magazines either. I grew up in a free world. Free from paedophiles lurking in the dark to take you away. Free from gang-bangers and bandanas, free from slavery, free from the confinements of London's high rise flats, free from fear of the unknown...free spirited. A free mind, uncontaminated.

My world and my culture taught me the endless possibilities of being anything and everything I wanted to be. A lawyer, a doctor, a president, an entrepreneur, a surgeon, an actress, you name it, I could be it. Where I come from, people in my image and my likeness held these titles. I loved my life.

In London, I remember my very first doll, Gem. I think she was a rock star with long flowing hair. I lived in a shared house, tiny back garden, TV on tap, magazines on the ready and more and more people that looked and spoke differently from me. I was too shy to put up my hand in class because God knows I knew all the answers and mentally, I was light years ahead of my peers. Then I found out being smart wasn't cool. I didn't need to call any more attention to myself. I already stood out like a sore thumb, so my hand stayed stuck to my side and I spoke only when necessary. Prior to my silence, I was a nine-year-old who spoke three languages fluently, including English.

Self-esteem, love for self and confidence soon vanished. At the age of 18, I went through a transformation. Mind, body and soul. I woke up, smelt the coffee, ditched Father Christmas, questioned Adam and Eve and erased white Jesus from my memory bank.

And that's cutting a very long story short.

I required more; needed more.

First step was self-discovery, or re-discovery. Somewhere down the line I had forgotten how to be free. I had allowed myself to become mentally enslaved. It was now the mission to de-programme and re-programme.

First thing to go, the perm! Just because it didn't make sense!

Cheap poisons that can be purchased on pocket money. I now value my life more than the stringy hair look.

Next on the to-do list, my name... bearing in mind I came from a large family. Out of twelve siblings, I am the 9th. All my siblings above me have pathetically British names. When I say pathetic, I mean names that even the British have archived... no longer in circulation. Me, number 9, gets one name, one African name. So out of curiosity I ask, why me? Why out of 9 children did my parents get all cultural on my name? The answer is powerfully simple. I was born after Zambia had got its independence from the United Kingdom. At this point, people started to claim their culture back, this included traditions, language and names; my story gets better.

I find out that my father's tribe links back to the Zulu warriors of South Africa; hell yeah, I'm amazing! Two minutes of research has me down as a warrior... I want more, I need more.

I searched for more.

After 11 years of my journeying to find myself, I came up with my biggest challenge ever... my 5-year-old baby girl, my Nubian princess. I have met my match plus some. She recently started full time school after finishing a year in nursery. This is supposed to be a time for me to celebrate, freedom! And yes...an "education" and a social life for my baby.

However, this small shift in my daughter's life has bought about a glitch in the matrix. I am dealing with white girl syndrome, long hair syndrome, why do you speak funny syndrome, leave my hair out syndrome, why does my hair grow up and not down syndrome? This has got to be punishment for me!

As a culturally conscious, proud African woman, I have ensured that my children have been surrounded by everything that represents their genetic makeup. Trips to Trinidad and Mama Africa, books bought over the internet full of little brown boys and girls, dolls brought from across waters that show a reflection of my daughter's beauty. My home, surrounded with wall hangings from my travels, all African. I gave my children black Jesus...ohhhh controversial, black prophets! Nubian Goddesses adorn the bedroom walls, Egyptian Pharaohs to name a few...I went in! Leaving nothing to the imagination. I have gone to town ensuring that my children have had an early education about who they are and who they can be, based on their rich heritage. I look back and question what and where I have gone wrong in my approach on instilling natural beauty into my baby girl. I come to realise the larger forces i.e. the mass media are occupying most of young people's free time and pulling the wool over their eyes and providing them with images that will never reflect their true greatness.

Today's youth lack confidence and are not motivated largely due to the non-conducive environment we live in. There is a lack of adults willing to take responsibility for creating the role models and images we want and need to see. My first female role model was my mother. She was a naturally beautiful woman. Wore no makeup and rocked a natural Afro. I spent a lot of time as a child combing my mother's hair and greasing her scalp. Sticking to good old trusted products, my mother had a head full of thick, fluffy, cotton wool hair that you wanted to bury your head in. She was a successful businesswoman, as well as a captain in the army. She was strong, talented, classy, professional, disciplined and well-educated. She was a goddess who thought anything was possible. My superwoman, my hero. She exceeded that by being a pillar of strength, a perfect wife and a wonderfully stern mother. My mother... God on earth, the all-seeing, all-knowing nurturer. If this woman said the sky was red, I would argue to the end of the earth that she was right.

Today's role models are your Beyoncés, Rihanna's, Lady Gaga's and your supermodels, etc. These individuals are idolised by our daughters often offering nothing more than superficial qualities. The admiration for women like my mother has decreased immensely and become less appealing to many young females. With the help of good old mass media, the physical characteristics of a Nubian woman are not considered a thing of beauty. Nose too thick, hair too coarse, hips too wide, skin too dark, structure too strong, forehead too flat, proportions just aren't right...wrong, wrong and wrong. Every image that has been put out by mass media has peeled another layer of confidence from the Nubian woman. With their precious self-esteem knocked back by a forced perception of what is acceptable beauty. Nubian beauty has just not been palatable to the masses.

However, does that qualify for us Nubian women to modify our appearance to be desired or accepted? Has it been worth the often-desperate measures we have taken to fit in? Creamy crack (perm kits) destroying us by leaking into our bloodstreams, meanwhile the white woman's perm makes her hair appear thick and curly, just like yours. Yet we continue to contaminate our temples. We bleach our skin whilst white women risk cancer to tan her skin to gain 'your' naturally healthy glow, what's going on? Weaves too tight, hiding and destroying the beauty underneath. I must admit, weaves and ponytails have come a long way since my childhood. They looked so ridiculously fake back then, yet we all pretended they grow from the scalp. Nowadays they are sewn in like a Persian rug and around the cost of one too; the Nubian woman has evolved and is the living transformer.

Weave now actually looks like it's growing from the scalp. We have lost the shame once felt, handing over business cards of the

Guinness hairdresser, who is often nothing short of a miracle worker. We proudly complement each other on how much the hair blends in and looks like our own. We discuss the Indian shop we purchased the ridiculously priced Indian hair from... oh sorry...my bad... we've upgraded to Brazilian hair now... then I wonder. With the rise of the conscious mind, how long will it be before we start asking when the Afro hair is coming in? The Nubian woman has forgotten that the combination of the things that make her different is her unique selling point. These things distinguish her from any other woman on this planet; failing to see that every being desires her, wants to be just like her...a rare delicacy.

A divine being, mother of all humanity. A Goddess, born from greatness... royalty!

Does the Nubian female get educated on who she really is? On the richness of her culture, her people, her story? You have been refused your rightful place as the queen bee of humanity, with your queenly kinks, melanised rich skin and royal attires. She has been lied to and deceived, whilst others fight for your rightful spot like leeches, weak imitations of the original. Through all the struggles of the Nubian Goddess you have been pushed to the extreme of your being. Broken down and trampled on, made to feel less than yourself, under sold, dressed down, stripped bare, but still standing stronger than ever. There is no other like you. A little twist on the old saying, their greatest fear is that you are powerful beyond any measure in your natural state.

I started my business in ethnic inspired fashion out of frustration of not being able to attain anything fashionable to wear that didn't look like it belonged to my mother. I wanted natural, I wanted Africa, I wanted tribal. I needed high fashion, I needed sassy and I needed freedom from the norm. I needed for my traditional cloth to be recognised as clothes and not as a "costume." I needed to surround myself in an environment that had images that supported and reflected my cultural background, fearlessly! So, I made it happen for self.

I began to create and sew clothes that reflected me, the modern-day Nubian Goddess. I took responsibility for me and my children's re-education on being Nubian royalty. I refuse to become a victim of the ideologies of a corrupted society. Let me share my favourite quote with you. "The coat of the buffalo never pinches under the arm, never puckers at the shoulders; it is always the same, yet never old fashioned nor out of date."

First rule in life, be comfortable in your own skin because it's the perfect fit. Don't wait until it's fashionable to be you. Tribal trend, ethnic inspired print, boohoo chic, safari, resort etc., it goes under many names.

The media controls the perception of beauty, take that control back and refuse to be a slave to a group of people's often-racist ideologies. Waiting for them to sell your culture back to you at a broad daylight robbery price. Being in a process of re-educating myself I realise, you don't have to give up the weave if that's your thing. Just think about the reasons you wear your weave. Is it because it's playful to switch things up a bit? Is it to give your hair a break from the weather conditions? Or is it because you can't face your true identity and would rather die than be seen without your weave, lashes, nails, contacts and the push up bra?

Empower, embrace, uplift and educate yourself. One small change causes a ripple effect in the big ocean that is our community. It's time to rebuild the village and take full responsibility for the changes we need to see. When are we going to realise that nobody else cares? The helping hand is at the end of your own arm, let's do this! When my daughter asks me, *"Why does my hair grow up and not down?"* I tell her it's because everything that is alive grows up and all things dying grows to the ground. I then put colourful beads in her hair, take a picture and daddy seals the deal by telling her she is the most beautiful little girl in the universe.

Davis Williams

Essay Twenty-Five

23rd July 2013

Fear of a Black Planet

Author: Xtra

*"If the hand that pushes him into the ghetto must eternally feed
the Negro in the ghetto, he will never become strong enough to
get out of the ghetto."*
Carter G. Woodson

There is a lot confusion about what our power is when it relates to
dealing with the police and all services this government body
provides. What I am about to detail is fact, the truth, and law! Any
exception is illegal, unjust, unlawful and a dereliction of duty on
behalf of the po-lice and or whoever is trying to force you to
believe, think or feel otherwise, or oppress the information herein.
This is not only directed at the police, but traffic wardens, bailiffs,
lawyers/solicitors, judges, teachers, lecturers, carers and all civil,
public servants.

We, the people are the power!!!

The Po-Lice do not have more power than you, mankind and until
we start to act appropriately, then these power-hungry bullies with
their over excessive forceful tactics shall continue to treat us as
beneath them and keep treading us into the ground until we stand
up to be counted and hold ourselves and them accountable and
responsible for their actions and our own!

For now, I shall keep it is as simple as learning to ride a bike and with a little practice every day, you'll soon be away with the wind.

All the legislation that is passed as law through parliament is not law. It is not for us to be governed with, and threatened, by those acting under a binding oath to serve the Queen and protect the same laws, customs and people, the Queen herself has sworn, under binding Oath, to protect and secure.

Sobek, a student of power and authority had this to say:

"In a THEOCRACY, GOD rules.

In a DEMOCRACY, people rule.

In a BUREACRACY, officials rule, it's all a matter of seniority or, in other words, superiority and authority.

At Level One: <u>GOD is over Man</u>: -GOD created Man. GOD is superior to Man.

At Level Two: <u>Man over Parliament</u>: -Man created Parliament. Man, is superior to Parliament and everything that Parliament births.

At Level Three: <u>Parliament over Corporations</u>: -Parliament creates Corporations, Companies, Acts, Legislations and Policies. Parliament is superior to Corporations.

At Level Four: <u>Corporations over nothing</u>:-Corporations create nothing. Corporations are superior to nothing and inferior to everything. Corporations can never have ownership over human beings unless permission and consent is surrendered."

Many still end up giving consent in some way or another, either verbally or written, because we have not been taught our basic universal human.

We are indigenous to this earth not just a country!

Humans have rights, universally given at conception, by the Most High Creator. These rights are not transferable so unless you consent to giving them away, they are with you forever. It is what you do with your rights that define your life; from the streets home work place and your relationships. The law exists everywhere; nature is law, natural law, the law of attraction, gravity and so on and it is your 'God given right' to do as you like by law, if the law is not broken!

Learning this and more made me realise that natural law is the best thing for us to study as a people and nation. This would also include studying oneself because we are natural beings that also exist under natural law, regardless of how religion and science would like to reign supreme over our existence. We exist as natural human beings regardless of race, religion, class, age, creed or geographic location.

When you are legally classed as a person (police custody/court/jail/school) you have fewer rights than that of a man; when being referred to in this manner you are being dealt with as a corporate entity known as *legal fiction*. According to the Black's Law Dictionary (used by the Law Society) a person is defined as the following: - *1. A human being also termed natural person. 2. The living body of a human being. 3. An entity (such as a corporation) that is recognized by law as having most of the rights and duties of a human being.* Pay attention to definition number 3, an entity such as a **corporation**.

The question is, when they are calling you a person, are they referring to you, the human being? Or referring to the birth certificate with your name on it, your legal fiction? Remember, you are not your name, your name is a tag that has been fixed on you. You are a human being, you were given a name, one which you can change legally whenever you like. When the Law Society refers to your name and NOT you, the human being; that is known as **legal fiction**. It is called legal fiction because legal is the framework from which they, the police, MP, and other government agencies operate from, and fiction just means that it is not real!

This legal fiction is just another number to keep tabs on you and your progress through life so they can track your monetary flow and how much you are worth to them. You are seen as cattle to their system and to see if the cattle is no longer of no use.

When you feel incorrectly feel like a decision was unjust, this has a lot to do with it. Never ever accept being called a **<u>Person</u>**; only ever accept that you are a Man (male or female) a sole independent within a world of sole independents collectively known as mankind.

This next piece of information will empower you with enough information to deal effectively with this system especially its corporate enforcers (po-lice, bailiffs, ticket inspectors etc.).

Firstly, you need to know that you have the right to defend yourself if you are being assaulted or feel threatened by anyone! As you well know.

Now the same goes even if it is a Po-lice constable you must protect yourself from! They have a duty to protect and a right to defend, but this duty does not mean that they can stop and search you every day at will. Nor does it give them the right to harass the point that people are scared shitless of them when they are supposed to be out here protecting our best interests. Not only have there been numerous assaults by officers on the public, there has been an untold number of civilian deaths in police custody and to date, not one officer has been charged for murder.

You should never feel intimidated, harassed, in fear of your personal safety, uneasy in anyway or have your personal space violated, when dealing with a Public Serving Peace Constable of the Law. As this is what they are, public servants and each serving member swears an oath (Attestation/Affirmation) in the Office of Constable to serve the Queen (this means anything she says, for them is law), giving equal respect to all people, whilst upholding fundamental human rights and preserving the peace at all times...

Peace Constable!

Police Constables Oath/Affirmation:

*I, ... of ... do solemnly and sincerely declare and affirm that I will well and truly serve the Queen in the office of constable, with fairness, integrity, diligence and impartiality, upholding fundamental human rights and according equal respect to all people; and that I will, to the best of my power, cause the **peace** to be kept and **preserved** and **prevent all offences against people and property;** and that while I continue to hold said office I will to the best of my skill and knowledge discharge all of the duties thereof faithfully according to law.*

En.wikipedia.org/wiki/Police oath

This is a duty-bound oath, sworn in and on record as just and true, binding and accountable, just as you would be held accountable for swearing under oath for your verbal statement (Affidavit/Affirmation) or physical action...the charge would be, perjury or treason.

This equally stands and should be made to stand for someone who swears to preserve the peace as their everyday duty!

The government relies on the use of FORCE to get you to act, hence them being referred to as a 'police force', rather than 'police service'.

When you are going about your daily business, there is no reason for any Po-lice Constable or PCSO *(Police Community Support Officer)* to harass, humiliate or cause distress whilst interacting with you. This is already a breach of the peace, your peace and borders on a dereliction of duty. This constitutes a number of charges that can be filed against the po-lice constable/s in question; from the moment, they stray from their duty (dereliction), anything they do or say, can, will and should be held against them.

We only have government through the consent of what they claim is the majority vote; this is where people voting for various political party leaders to make changes to society and make it a better place for us to live. They then give us wage rises, tax increases and there is never enough money for the poor and too much money for the rich. No matter whom you vote for nothing seems to change.

What happens if you don't vote?

What happens if you don't give consent to be governed by a government who doesn't benefit you (if the government system does not benefit mankind it is not keeping its part of the contract).

I tell you what does happen, you are free.

Free to do what you like if you are not causing harm, loss or injury to another man or his property (His property) not a government building, then you have committed no crime because all corporations operate at risk and are insured for being limited liability companies. You, the natural man is operating at full liability yet can hardly ever claim for any wrong doings done against you.

This information at first can be difficult to grasp, simply because it is something that the schools never teach. They do not want people to know this information because they understand this gives you the keys to freedom. If this essay went over your head I would like you to remember these simply points.

1. Crime is to cause harm, loss or injury.

2. Only a natural living man can make a claim against another living man.

3. If someone is making a claim upon you, ask them if they have proof of claim?

4. When someone wants you to do something against your will ask them if they have proof of authority?

5. Not sure what to say? Say nothing!

6. You are not your name! You were born nameless, until your mum or dad decided to name you days or weeks later.

7. Never give consent or permission for someone to be above you.

Stop and SEARCH

If the police stop you:

Ask for ID.

Ask them to recite their oath.

Get your recorder out and record every single word.

Stay in control of your emotions and words. Do not physically resist.

Keep your hands visible.

Remain silent. That is your right. They have weapons, pepper spray and Tasers; your strongest weapon is your mind!

The less you say, the better. There is no law that says you must speak! Think about that. If you are unsure, ask the police officer what law requires you tell them your name.

Ask if you are free to go? If they keep you, you are being detained.

Ask, why are they detaining you? To detain you, the police must have a concrete reason to suspect you are involved in a specific crime.

Davis Williams

The Lioness's Roar

On 18 February 1994, the government of Sweden publicly announced the final timetable for the ban on the use of mercury/silver amalgam as a dental filling material. The use of amalgam will be totally banned for children and adolescents up to the age of 19 by 1 July 1995 at the latest and for adults by 1997. It is scientifically proven that mercury is the most poisonous naturally occurring, non-radioactive, substance on our planet. Mercury is far more toxic than any of the other heavy metals, including arsenic, lead and cadmium.   According to the World Health Organization (WHO), there is NO HARMLESS level of mercury! Nor is there any such thing as 'good or safe' mercury. The elemental mercury used in amalgam fillings is just as toxic as the elemental mercury that was used in paints - until it was recently banned. Nor is it any different from the elemental mercury used in thermometers and other medical instruments and equipment - until it too was banned.

Essay Twenty-Six

1712 AD

Big Willie

Author: Willie Lynch

Powerful people cannot afford to educate the people that they oppress, because once you are truly educated, you will not ask for power. You will take it.
John Henrik Clarke

Just a quick bit of background for you. Since 1995, there has been much attention given to a speech claimed to be delivered by a 'William Lynch' in 1712. So much attention has been given to this speech that films, documentaries and debates have centered on it. This speech has been promoted widely throughout African and Caribbean circles, mostly via emails and social media. Many scholars have examined the details of this Willie Lynch speech and it's clear that it's another modern myth. There are simple clues, such as Willie Lynch not being mentioned by *any* 18th or 19th century slave masters or anti-slavery activists.

To be honest, I don't really care; what is important is the contents of this speech.

This speech was said to have been delivered by Willie Lynch on the bank of the James River in the colony of Virginia in 1712.

Lynch was a British slave owner in the West Indies and was invited to the colony to teach his methods to slave owners there.

[Beginning of the Willie Lynch Letter]

Greetings, gentlemen.

I greet you here on the bank of the James River in the year of our Lord one thousand seven hundred and twelve. First, I shall thank you, the gentlemen of the Colony of Virginia, for bringing me here. I am here to help you solve some of your problems with slaves. Your invitation reached me on my modest plantation in the West Indies, where I have experimented with some of the newest and still the oldest methods for control of slaves. Ancient Rome would envy us if my program were implemented. As our boat sailed south on the James River, named for our illustrious King, whose version of the Bible we cherish, I saw enough to know that your problem is not unique. While Rome used cords of wood as crosses for standing human bodies along its highways in great numbers, you are here using the tree and the rope on occasion. I caught the whiff of a dead slave hanging from a tree, a couple miles back.

You are not only losing valuable stock by hangings, you are having uprisings, slaves are running away, your crops are sometimes left in the fields too long for maximum profit, you suffer occasional fires, and your animals are killed. Gentlemen, you know what your problems are; I do not need to elaborate. I am not here to enumerate your problems; I am here to introduce you to a method of solving them. In my bag here, **I HAVE A FULL PROOF METHOD FOR CONTROLLING YOUR BLACK SLAVES. I** guarantee every one of you that, if installed correctly, **IT WILL CONTROL THE SLAVES FOR AT LEAST 300 HUNDRED YEARS**. My method is simple. Any member of your family or your overseer can use it.

I HAVE OUTLINED A NUMBER OF DIFFERENCES AMONG THE SLAVES; I TAKE THESE DIFFERENCES AND MAKE THEM BIGGER. I USE FEAR, DISTRUST AND ENVY FOR CONTROL PURPOSES. These methods have worked on my modest plantation in the West Indies and it will work throughout the South. Take this simple little list of differences and think about them. On top of my list is "AGE," but it's there only because it starts with an "a." The second is "COLOR" or shade. There is INTELLIGENCE, SIZE, SEX, SIZES OF PLANTATIONS, STATUS on plantations, ATTITUDE of owners, whether the slaves live in the valley, on a hill, east, west, north, south, have fine hair, course hair, or is tall or short. Now that you have a list of differences, I shall give you an outline of action, but before that, I shall assure you that DISTRUST IS STRONGER THAN TRUST AND ENVY STRONGER THAN ADULATION, RESPECT OR ADMIRATION. The Black slaves after receiving this indoctrination shall carry on and will become self-refuelling and self-generating for HUNDREDS of years, maybe THOUSANDS. Don't forget, you must pitch the OLD black male vs. the YOUNG black male, and the YOUNG black male against the OLD black male. You must use the DARK skin slaves vs. the LIGHT skin slaves, and the LIGHT skin slaves vs. the DARK skin slaves. You must use the FEMALE vs. the MALE, and the MALE vs. the FEMALE. You must also have white servants and overseers [who] distrust all Blacks. But it is NECESSARY THAT YOUR SLAVES TRUST AND DEPEND ON US. THEY MUST LOVE, RESPECT AND TRUST ONLY US. Gentlemen, these kits are your keys to control. Use them. Have your wives and children use them, never miss an opportunity. IF USED INTENSELY FOR ONE YEAR, THE SLAVES THEMSELVES WILL REMAIN PERPETUALLY DISTRUSTFUL. Thank you, gentlemen."

LET'S MAKE A SLAVE

I encourage everyone reading this book to look in the mirror and ask yourself this fundamental question - are you a slave to the programming of Willie Lynch?

Now that you have finished this book, I suggest you do your own research into some of the topics discussed here. What you have just read are varied essays and expressions designed to stimulate thought and motivate action.

Knowledge is power, but with power comes movement.

Share the ideas within this book with others, because the time for sitting at the back of the bus is over. We need to stand up, unify (like minds) and work on ourselves first. We must strive for perfection, we must reach our dreams.

For true change to occur we be honest with ourselves and stop externalising our problems, pointing the finger at other people for not doing what you are supposed to be doing.

You are NEO – One is the magic number.

If there is anything in this book that you want to implement, but don't know how to, or don't know the right people, get in touch.

If you want to interview any of the speakers or book them for public appearances, please get in touch.

If you want to hear more from a particular contributor, please, get in touch.

If you have your own essay to submit, please...get in touch.

Recommended Reading

Book Title	Author
Straight from the Heart	Dr Jewel Pookrum
The Vodou Quantum Leap	Reginald Crosley MD
The Kybalion	The Three Initiates
The White Book	Ramtha
Kemetic Diet Ancient African Wisdom for Health	Muata Ashby
Metu Neter complete volumes	Dr Ra Un Nefer Amen
The Healing Wisdom of Africa	Malidoma Some
The Spirit of Intimacy	Sobonfu Some
Of Water and Spirit	Malidoma Some
The Alchemist	Paolo Coelho
Heal Thyself	Queen Afua
Sacred womb/woman	
S'Otito-Be Truth: 18 Lessons in West African Spirituality	YeYe OlaOmi
Ona Agbani: The Ancient Path: Understanding and Implementing the Ways of Our Ancestors	Oshinyemi Iyaloja OlaOmi Akalatumde
The Secret	Rhonda Byrne
The Philosophies & Opinions of Marcus Garvey: Volumes1&2	Marcus Mosiah Garvey
The Science of Mind	Ernest Holmes
Two Thousand Seasons	Ayi Kwei Armah
The Emerald Tablets of Thoth the Atlantean	Dr. M.Doreal
Handbook of Yoruba Religious Concepts	Baba Ifa Karade
The Four Agreements	Don Miguel Ruiz

Tapping the Power Within	Iyanla Vanzant
Ifa Will Mend Our Broken World	Wande Abimbola
Conversations with God	Neale Donald Walsh
Ancient Egypt: The Light of the World	Gerald Massey
The Prophet	Kahlil Gibran
Indaba My Children	Credo Mutwa
Zulu Shaman	Credo Mutwa
The Seat of the Soul	Gary Zukav
Even the Stars Look Lonesome	Maya Angelou
Mami Wata vols 1 and 2	Mama Zogbe
Women Who Run with Wolves	Clarissa Pinkola Estes
Nature Know No Colour	J.A Rogers
Stolen Legacy	G.James
The Pale Fox	M. Griaule and G. Dieterlen
The Awakener	Sandy Stevenson
Anatomy of the Spirit	Caroline Myss
The Goddess Sekhmet	Robert Masters
12 Laws of Spirit	Dan Millman
Human Race Get Up Off Your Knees	David Icke
A Return to Love	Marianne Williamson
Son of the Ghetto: An Authentic Ghetto Story	Mr Magik
The Message from Water vol.1	Dr. Masaru Emoto
Isis Papers	Frances Cress Welsing
1984	George Orwell
Brave New World	Aldos Huxley
WE	Yevengy Zamayatin
Blindness	Jose Saramago
100 Years of Solitude	Gabriel Garcia Marquez
They Came Before Columbus	Ivan Van Sertima

The African Origin of Civilisation Myth or Reality?	Cheikh Anta Diop
The Secret Life of Plants	Peter Tompkins
The Fountainhead	Ayn Rand
The Black Jacobins	C.L.R James
1491-Charles C Mann The Shock Doctrine	Naomi Klein
The Awakening of Intelligence	J.Krishnamurti
Self Reliance	Ralph Waldo Emerson
The Glass Bead Game	Herman Hesse
The Urban Heritage of West Africa	Clements
The First Emperor of China	
Post Traumatic Slavery Syndrome	Joy Leary
The Ruins of Empires	C.F Volney
Song of Solomon	Toni Morrison

Davis Williams

Lightning Source UK Ltd.
Milton Keynes UK
UKOW01f1120191017

311269UK00001B/11/P